NARCISSISTIC NARRATIVE
THE METAFICTIONAL PARADOX

LINDA HUTCHEON

Narcissistic Narrative
The Metafictional Paradox

METHUEN

New York and London

First published in 1980 by
Wilfrid Laurier University Press
Waterloo, Ontario, Canada N2L 3L5

First published as a University Paperback in 1984 by
Methuen, Inc.
29 West 35th Street, New York, NY 10001
Reprinted 1985

Published in Great Britain by
Methuen & Co. Ltd
11 New Fetter Lane, London EC4P 4EE

Printed in Great Britain by
J. W. Arrowsmith Ltd, Bristol

Library of Congress Cataloging in Publication Data
Hutcheon, Linda, 1947–
 Narcissistic narrative.
Reprint. Originally published: Waterloo, Ont.:
Wilfrid Laurier University Press, 1980. (Bibliothèque de
la Revue Canadienne de littérature comparée = Library of
the Canadian review of comparative literature; v. 5)
Includes bibliographical references and indexes.
 1. Fiction—20th century—History and criticism.
2. Fiction—Technique. I. Title.
PN3503.H8 1984 809.3′04 83-25152
ISBN 0–416–37140–X (pbk.)

British Library Cataloguing in Publication Data
Hutcheon, Linda
 Narcissistic narrative.—(University paperback 857).
 1. Literature, Modern—19th century—History
 and criticism 2. Literature, Modern—20th
 century—History and criticism
 3. Literature and society
 I. Title
 809′.034 PN761

ISBN 0–416–37140–X

Contents

Acknowledgments vii

Preface to the Paperback Edition xi

Introduction 1

CHAPTER ONE
Modes and Forms of Narrative Narcissism: Introduction of a
Typology 17

CHAPTER TWO
Process and Product: The Implications of Metafiction for the Theory
of the Novel as a Mimetic Genre 36

CHAPTER THREE
Thematizing Narrative Artifice: Parody, Allegory, and the *Mise En
Abyme* 48

CHAPTER FOUR
Freedom Through Artifice: *The French Lieutenant's Woman* 57

CHAPTER FIVE
Actualizing Narrative Structures: Detective Plot, Fantasy, Games, and
the Erotic 71

CHAPTER SIX
The Language of Fiction: Creating the Heterocosm of Fictive
Referents 87

CHAPTER SEVEN
The Theme of Linguistic Identity: *La Macchina Mondiale* 104

CHAPTER EIGHT
Generative Word Play: The Outer Limits of the Novel Genre 118

CHAPTER NINE
Composite Identity: The Reader, the Writer, the Critic 138

Conclusion and Speculations 153

Index of Subjects and Names 163

Acknowledgments

Since the original impetus for this book came from ideas generated by my doctoral dissertation, my thanks are obviously due to those whose guidance and expertise helped shape my thinking over the years: Brian T. Fitch, Gian-Paolo Biasin, Mario J. Valdés, S. B. Chandler, Robert A. Greene, Cyrus Hamlin, S. P. Rosenbaum and other teachers too numerous to mention. I should further like to express my thanks to Tzvetan Todorov and Wolfgang Iser for their advice and encouragement. Thanks are also extended to my friend, Janet Paterson, for those many hours of "auto-referential" discussion and to my husband, Michael, for his *aequanimitas*. For help with the manuscript, my gratitude is due to A. Alexander, S. Harper, and L. Rabkin.

Parts of this work have previously appeared in print and are published here with the permission of the editors of the respective journals. Chapter One was first printed in French as "Modes et formes du narcissisme littéraire" in *Poétique* 29 (février 1977). Part of Chapter Four appeared as "The 'Real World(s)' of Fiction: *The French Lieutenant's Woman*" in *English Studies in Canada* 4, 1 (Spring 1978), and part of Chapter Eight also appeared as "The Outer Limits of the Novel: Italy and France" in *Contemporary Literature* 18, 2 (1977) and appears with the permission of the Board of Regents of the University of Wisconsin. An expanded version of Chapter Seven was published by *Forum Italicum* (1980) as "Paolo Volponi's *Automa-autore*."

This book has been published with the help of a grant from the Canadian Federation for the Humanities, using funds provided by the Social Sciences and Humanities Research Council of Canada.

Toronto
1975, 1980

All great fiction, to a large extent, is a reflection
on itself rather than a reflection of reality.
 Raymond Federman

Les grands récits se reconnaissent à ce signe que
la fiction qu'ils proposent n'est rien d'autre que la
dramatisation de leur propre fonctionnement.
 Jean Ricardou

Preface to the Paperback Edition

In the wake of the recent and radical post-structuralist challenge to the basic categories of the entire intellectual enterprise, it is hard for a literary critic not to be self-conscious today, no matter what her critical persuasion might be. This is all the more true if she is writing about a form of fiction which is itself acutely self-reflexive. Although we are in the process of witnessing a concerted attempt to break down the barriers between disciplines in the name of a more general category of discourse or textuality, *Narcissistic Narrative* retains the separation of theory, criticism, and literature. The reason for doing this is not to pretend to contribute to the current debate on the relative merits of interpretive criticism versus literary theory. Rather, my focus is a different one: that of describing, or at least of beginning to describe, the "poetics" of what we seem determined to call postmodernism. Since, by poetics, I mean that ever developing theoretical structure by which we order both our aesthetic knowledge and our critical procedures, then it is clear that any poetics of the contemporary must take into account both the literature and the criticism or theory being produced at this time. The particular focus of this book is on the interaction of the literary and the theoretical, and more specifically, on the implications of the former for the latter.

Textually self-conscious metafiction today is a most didactic form. As such, it can teach us much about both the ontological status of fiction

(all fiction) and also the complex nature of reading (all reading). Its central paradox for readers is that, while being made aware of the linguistic and fictive nature of what is being read, and thereby distanced from any unself-conscious identification on the level of character or plot, readers of metafiction are at the same time made mindful of their active role in reading, in participating in making the text mean. They are the distanced, yet involved, co-producers of the novel. This non-passivity is true of all reading, as psycholinguists, speech-act theorists, and phenomenologists have argued for years. What is interesting here is that it is the fiction itself that is attempting to bring to readers' attention their central and enabling role.

The fiction that is discussed in *Narcissistic Narrative* is, in some dominant and constitutive way, self-referring or autorepresentational: it provides, within itself, a commentary on its own status as fiction and as language, and also on its own processes of production and reception. I have often wondered if this might be one of the reasons why its didactic lessons have been so little heeded. Might metafiction, in its self-analytic overtness, be perceived as pre-empting the critic's role as commentator? After all, its frequent parodic intertextuality even saves us the bother of situating it in literary history. Whatever the reason, critics and theorists today have seemed much more willing to read and assimilate the latest theory, hot off the press, than to trust to the insights revealed by the self-reflexivity of the equally recent fiction. I suppose that this is nothing new: we have always tended to prefer to leave to time and the anonymity of communal consensus the responsibility of deciding from which literary works we are willing to learn. But I would want to argue that the formal and thematic self-consciousness of meta-fiction today is paradigmatic of most of the cultural forms of what Jean-François Lyotard calls our "postmodern" world[1] —from television commercials to movies, from comic books to video art. We seem fascinated lately by the ability of our human systems to refer to themselves in an endless mirroring process. In focusing on the literary manifestations of this current obsession, I intend no judgment as to its value as a cultural phenomenon;[2] I merely want to signal that it does exist and that its ubiquity alone should demand that more attention be paid to it. The polemical edge of this book no doubt derives from my feeling, in the mid-seventies, that critics were all too quick to dismiss metafiction as a fad that would be outgrown. Ten years later, we have lived to see more, not fewer, of such novels: the genre has not died after all, not unless we still feel the temptation to write off such writers as Italo Calvino, Salman Rushdie, Timothy Findley, Gabriel García Márquez, and many others.

In the Introduction, it will be clear that several years ago I explicitly rejected the term "postmodernism" and opted instead for the more descriptive one of metafiction. Although I would still stand behind my

objections to the label, it seems to have stuck, and it would be foolish to deny that metafiction is today recognized as a manifestation of postmodernism.[3] My discovery of the use of the same term to characterize contemporary architecture that is doubly-coded (modern plus something else) has helped reconcile me to the inevitable, however. Architecture since 1960 reveals striking ideological and structural similarities with the fiction of the same years. Architects such as Portoghesi, Venturi, Moore, Stern, and Graves, to mention only a few, have self-consciously restored the idea of architecture conveying meaning through a language and a rhetoric. Eschewing the hermeticism and denial of function and relevance characteristic of high Modernism, Post-Modern architects reveal "an interest in popular and local codes of communication . . . , in historical memory, urban context . . . , participation, the public realm, pluralism and eclecticism."[4]

Like this architecture, postmodernist metafiction has worked to make readers aware of both its production and reception as cultural products. If, at the obvious risk of overgeneralizing, we could say that the poetics of Romanticism involved a concentration on the author and his biography, that realism then brought social and historical reference to the fore, that modernism proceeded to orient critics and readers formally and formalistically toward the closed text and its difficulties, then it would seem that the poetics of postmodernism has been responsible for continuing the work, begun by modernists like T. S. Eliot, in welcoming the "hypocrite lecteur" into both the literary and the critical fold. But the heritage of the modernist text's formal complexity was not just an awareness of the activity needed on the part of the reader to make texts mean: there was also an intense self-awareness regarding the process of artistic production itself.

While modernist texts may have worked to combat the imposition of single, authoritative meaning, postmodernist metafiction tends more to play with the possibilities of meaning (from degree zero to plurisignification) and of form (from minimalist narrative to galloping diegesis). Some have argued that postmodernist art does not aim, as did modernist, at exploring the difficulty, so much as the impossibility, of imposing that single determinate meaning on a text. Yet it is also true that it does so, not so much by means of textual difficulties alone, but—paradoxically—by overt, self-conscious control by an inscribed narrator/author figure that appears to demand, by its manipulation, the imposition of a single, closed perspective. At the same time, of course, it works to subvert all chances of attaining such closure. Many feel that these almost Brechtian techniques of defamiliarization and distanciation have allowed for the possibility of a greater degree of ideological self-awareness in literature today, as I too suggest at the end of this book.

It is part of the interest of postmodernist novels that, though readers are drawn inward to the language and fictionality of the textual product

(no longer the representation of a seemingly unmediated reality), they are simultaneously urged into that active participation in its process of meaning production. But, the strategy of such fiction is to focus not on the reader and author as individual historical agents, but on the processes of the reception and production of language. Since *Narcissistic Narrative* was written, a particular variety of metafiction has proved especially popular: what we could call an historiographic mode. What is most significant about this relatively new form is that the hard-won textual autonomy of fiction is challenged, paradoxically, by self-referentiality itself. If language, as these texts suggest, constitutes reality (rather than merely reflecting it), readers become the actualizing link between history and fiction. But this does not occur on the model of traditional historical fiction, where history is meant to authenticate fiction on a product, or representation, level, but in a new (or at least newly articulated) mode. It is not just a matter of life and art both being socially constructed fictions. Historiography, argues Hayden White[5] is really a poetic construct; novels, suggest Robert Coover in *The Public Burning* or Salman Rushdie in *Midnight's Children*, are historically mediated forms. Historiographic metafiction, therefore, works to situate itself in history and in discourse, as well as to insist on its autonomous fictional and linguistic nature.

This return to history is neither naïve nor unproblematic. In his novel, *Doctor Copernicus*, John Banville's questioning of history makes us acutely aware of the post-Heisenberg reality not only of history, but of fiction and of science itself. Here we are in the realm of discourse, of perception and interpretation of reality through language. His Copernicus echoes Wittgenstein: "We only think those thoughts that we have the words to express."[6] Language structures and orders our perceptions. *Doctor Copernicus* is a self-conscious meditation on the relationship between names and things, and therefore between theory and the universe: it is both science and history as metafiction. Copernicus realizes that his great work, "instead of approaching the word, the crucial Word . . . was careering headlong into a loquacious silence. He had believed it possible to say the truth; now he saw that all that could be said was the saying. His book was not about the world, but about itself."[7] But to speak of itself is paradoxically to speak of the world. All reality becomes a "form of saying."[8] History—both private and public—is discourse; so too is fiction.

In *Doctor Copernicus*, a powerful and ambitious military leader refers to himself and to the scientist as the makers of history, that is, the "makers of supreme fictions." The deliberate echo of Wallace Stevens makes the connection here between art, science, history, on the one hand, and power, on the other. In all three cultural forms, discourse constitutes more than a repository of meaning; it involves both the potential for manipulation—through rhetoric or through the power of

language and the vision that it creates—and also the possibility (if not the permissibility) of evasion of responsibility through silence. It is this relation of discursive power to history and fiction that is explored in novels like Ian Watson's *The Embedding* and Timothy Findley's *Famous Last Words.*

What the apparent paradox of historiographic metafiction brings to the fore is, once again, just a characteristic of all fiction. It is the degree of self-consciousness *within* the fiction that is different here. We are taught that fiction is never only autonomous, but rather is always mediated by contextual forces, including its historical, social, and ideological determination. Fiction and non-fiction genres interpenetrate in this internally conflictual new form through the realization of their equally essential discursive identity. Metafiction teaches, as does contemporary theory, that discourse is language as *énonciation*, involving, that is, the contextualized production and reception of meaning.

Since Jakobson's[9] formulation of his model of communication, if not before, both literature and literary theory have been increasingly self-conscious about the context-dependent nature of linguistic meaning, about the importance to signification of the circumstances surrounding any utterance. And, the discursive situation always includes an enunciating addresser as well as a receiver of the utterance. However, in the collective name of scientific universality and objectivity, of novelistic realism, and even of our own formalist anti-Romanticism, we have tended today to suppress the role of the textual producer.[10] Metafiction, however, would contest this suppression. The Romantic "author," as originating and original source of meaning may well be dead, as Roland Barthes argued years ago,[11] but his position—one of discursive authority—remains, and increasingly is the focus of much contemporary literature and also much theoretical debate. In the midst of a general dethroning of authority by the decentering of everything from the transcendental *cogito* to the economy and the instincts, we are also witness to a new literary and theoretical emphasis on the interactive powers involved in the production and reception of texts. The position of authority remains to subvert the notions of objectivity and naturalness in art and theory, as it also does in science today.[12] If, in *Narcissistic Narrative*, I have tended to stress above all the power and freedom of the reader, it is a reflection of the impact in the seventies of all the varieties of reader-response criticism. Today, however, it is equally difficult not to feel that the balance of power has to be restored.

What Québécois novelist, Hubert Aquin, suggested in the sixties (as I argue in my Conclusion), feminist and marxist theorists have also been proposing for a while now: there exists a set of social relations between producer and audience that could perhaps be revolutionized by a change in the forces of production that would turn the reader into a collaborator instead of a consumer.[13] In today's metafiction, the artist

reappears, not as a God-like Romantic creator, but as the inscribed maker of a social product that has the potential to participate in social change through its reader. Such an acknowledgement of the power of language is also an acknowledgement of the potential for ideological manipulation by the wielder of that language. The best way to demystify power, metafiction suggests, is to reveal it in all its arbitrariness, to allow Calvino's narrator at the start of *If on a Winter's Night a Traveller* to order the reader around, for instance. Alternatively, metafiction may choose to show power in terms of an almost erotic manipulation, to be enjoyed as Barthesian bliss.[14] In other words, a text can call attention to authority structures in such a way as to subvert the Romantic ideology of the myth of originality that once subtended them. No longer to believe in the manipulating "author" as a person is to restore the wholeness of the act of the *énonciation*: the "author" becomes a position to be filled, a role to be inferred, by the reader reading the text. When we speak of producers and receivers of literary language, then, we speak less of individual subjects than of what have been called "subject positions"[15] that are essential constitutive features of the work. The Romantic myth dies and, as Edward Said points out in *The World, the Text, and the Critic*, the "writer thinks less of writing originally, and more of rewriting. The image for writing changes from original *inscription* to parallel script,"[16] as attested to by metafiction's parodic intertextuality. The position of the textual producer has certainly not disappeared, no matter how dismissive of it contemporary theory may be.

In some metafiction there are direct addresses to the reader—insulting, commanding, provoking addresses that overtly point to two subject positions in the text, that of both reader and producer. Sometimes, however, these positions are more subtly established: in novels such as Nabokov's *Pale Fire*, D. M. Thomas's *The White Hotel*, or Chris Scott's *Antichthon*, the play of various narrative perspectives and devices (narratorial directives, complex structural analogies, intertextual allusions) manoeuvres the reader into a position from which an anamorphosis (here, the text's meaning ascribed by the reader to an inferred producer) can be reconstructed. I use the image of the baroque anamorphosis to stress both the complexity of the production of the formal construction and also the manipulation of the receiver, who is manoeuvred by the work into a "proper" position from which to perceive the paradoxically hidden, but perceptible, structure of meaning. This meaning has been generated (usually with great effort) in the process of the reception and production of the work, a process often thematized in the text itself.

In opposition to much contemporary theory, the general critical works that have recently tried to deal specifically with this kind of self-reflexive art have often fallen back into a modernist or even Romantic concentration on the mental processes of the historical artist.[17] Such a strategy

tends to lead to a view of postmodernism as the new aestheticism[18] or to the interpretation of our literature's ironic self-awareness as only the product of today's particularly linguistically-conscious critical climate.[19] I wonder, however, what would then explain *Tristram Shandy*, not to mention *Finnegans Wake*. No poetics has yet, it would seem, been articulated that fully deals with the demands of postmodernist fiction for a reinstating of the act and responsibility of the entire *énonciation*, that is, of the socially and historically mediated production and reception of texts, their interdependencies and interactive powers.

Paralleling these teachings of contemporary metafiction is our own (narcissistic?) need to make ourselves more self-aware as critics, a need manifested in the rise of a new metatheoretical critical genre today.[20] There would seem to be a desire to de-marginalize theory and criticism, to move them away from both humanist vagueness and formalist finality. This is clear in Edward Said's aim for criticism: "to read and write with a sense of the greater stake in historical and political effectiveness that literary as well as other texts have had."[21] Much metafiction today, from that of Salman Rushdie to that of Umberto Eco, while calling attention to its linguistic and fictional nature, shares this aim. To understand Said's position—"that texts are worldly, to some degree that they are events, and, *even when they appear to deny it*, they are nevertheless a part of the social world, human life, and of course, the historical moments in which they are located and interpreted"[22]—is to understand the paradox of textually self-reflexive fiction's relation to the world. I would still see metafiction's "vital" link between art and life (by which we define the novel as mimetic) as existing, as I argue throughout this book, on the level of imaginative process. But today I would wish to situate that process and its products much more firmly within a consideration of discourse. And it is contemporary fiction, as much as recent theory, that has taught me this.

These, however, are the kind of unavoidable afterthoughts and inevitable modifications brought about by new reading. As it stands, in the blend of formalist and hermeneutic perspectives demanded by its corpus, *Narcissistic Narrative* offers an introduction to an important form of literature that, I feel, should not and indeed cannot be ignored today. It also provides an examination of the formal types of self-reflexivity found in contemporary metafiction and of the implications of its teachings for theories of the act of reading and of the novel as a mimetic genre. The one thing, however, that we must never forget is that metafiction is not new; nor is it in any way more "evolved" or aesthetically better than other forms of fiction. Rather, it is part of a long novelistic tradition, and it is only its degree of internalized self-consciousness about what are, in fact, realities of reading *all* literature that makes it both different and perhaps especially worth studying today. At most, we might be witnessing in postmodernism what John

Banville has called a new synthesis. "What will it be?" he asks. "I do not know. But I hope it will be an art which is honest enough to despair and yet go on; rigorous and controlled, cool yet passionate, without delusions, aware of its own possibilities and its own limits; an art which knows that truth is arbitrary, that reality is multifarious, that language is not a clear lens."[23] It is significant that he then adds: "Did I say *new*? What I have defined is as old as Homer."

<div align="center">Toronto 1983</div>

NOTES

1. *La Condition postmoderne* (Paris: Minuit, 1979).
2. Though I do realize that a positive value judgment is, in a sense, implied in my very act of choosing to write of this form.
3. This is not to say that this is the only change I would make in form or substance, were I now to rewrite this book. I would certainly try to eliminate the awkwardness created by the impersonal academic anonymity of the third-person style, and, perhaps more importantly, I would today be more aware of my use of the male pronoun for the general and would make changes to include the obvious female presence (including my own).
4. Charles A. Jencks, *Late-Modern Architecture and Other Essays* (London: Academy, 1980), p. 13.
5. *Metahistory* (Baltimore: Johns Hopkins University Press, 1973).
6. John Banville, *Doctor Copernicus* (New York: Norton, 1976), p. 207.
7. ibid., p. 116
8. John Banville, *The Newton Letter* (London: Secker and Warburg, 1982), p. 51.
9. "Closing Statement: Linguistics and Poetics," in T. Sebeok (ed.), *Style in Language* (Cambridge: MIT Press, 1960), pp. 350–77.
10. See Timothy J. Reiss, *The Discourse of Modernism* (Ithaca: Cornell University Press, 1982).
11. "The Death of the Author," in S. Sears and G. W. Lord (eds.), *The Discontinuous Universe* (New York: Basic Books, 1972), pp. 7–8.
12. See Stephen Toulmin, "The Construal of Reality: Criticism in Modern and Postmodern Science," *Critical Inquiry* 9 (1982), 93–111.
13. See Catherine Belsey, *Critical Practice* (London and New York: Methuen, 1980) and Terry Eagleton, *Marxism and Literary Criticism* (Berkeley: University of California Press, 1976).
14. See Severo Sarduy, "Interview," *Diacritics* 2, no. 2 (1972), 44.
15. Terry Eagleton, *Literary Theory: An Introduction* (Oxford: Basil Blackwell, 1983), p. 119.
16. (Cambridge: Harvard University Press, 1983), p. 135.
17. There have, of course, been other approaches, but most have been in the restricted form of short articles, rather than books. The journals that have especially opened their pages to the postmodernist debate include *Boundary 2, Tri-Quarterly, New Literary History, Amerikastudien*, and *Texte*. See too Harry R. Garvin (ed.), *Romanticism, Modernism, Postmodernism* (Lewisburg: Bucknell University Press, 1980).
18. See, especially, Christopher Butler, *After the Wake: An Essay on the Contemporary Avant-garde* (Oxford: Clarendon Press, 1980). Other works focusing on the author are André Belleau, *Le Romancier fictif* (Québec: Les Presses de l'Université du Québec, 1980) and Inger Christensen, *The Meaning of Metafiction* (Bergen: Universitetsforlaget, 1981).

[19] Alan Wilde, *Horizons of Assent: Modernism, Postmodernism, and the Ironic Imagination* (Baltimore: Johns Hopkins University Press, 1981), p. 157. Margaret Rose reduces metafiction to only its parodic modes in *Parody and Metafiction* (London: Croom Helm, 1979).

[20] Besides the books by Said and Eagleton already mentioned, there are those by Frank Lentricchia (*After the New Criticism* [Chicago: University of Chicago Press, 1980]) and especially Jonathan Culler, whose most recent work is *On Deconstruction: Theory and Criticism after Structuralism* (Ithaca: Cornell University Press, 1982).

[21] Edward Said, *The World, the Text and the Critic* (Cambridge: Harvard University Press, 1983), p. 225.

[22] ibid., p. 4, my italics.

[23] "A Talk," *Irish University Review* 11, 1 (Spring 1981), 17.

Introduction

1

Narcissistic Narrative: The Metafictional Paradox was originally conceived as a defence of a kind of fiction which began to run rampant in the 1960s. "Metafiction," as it has now been named, is fiction about fiction—that is, fiction that includes within itself a commentary on its own narrative and/or linguistic identity. "Narcissistic"—the figurative adjective chosen here to designate this textual self-awareness—is not intended as derogatory but rather as descriptive and suggestive, as the ironic allegorical reading of the Narcissus myth which follows these introductory remarks should make clear. Nor are the inevitable psychoanalytic connotations to be taken negatively, as many who have not read Freud himself on the subject might tend to do. In fact, it was Freud who conferred on narcissism the status of the "universal original condition" of man, making it the basis of more than just pathological behaviour.[1] These psychological associations, while likely inevitable, are here, however, irrelevant in that it is the narrative text, and not the author, that is being described as narcissistic. Other potentially pejorative terms, such as introspective, introverted, and self-conscious, are likewise meant to be critically neutral. Many other adjectives will be used to describe the modes of narcissism in the pages to follow—self-reflective, self-informing, self-reflexive, auto-referential, auto-

1 Freud's paper, "On Narcissism: An Introduction" in *The Standard Edition of the Complete Psychological Works of Sigmund Freud*, general trans. James Strachey (London: Hogarth Press, 1953–1974), 14:67–104, marked an important turning point in Freud's thinking: the inauguration of the second of his three theories of instinct, that of the sexual libido.

representational—and while these are not exactly synonymous, their minor tonal and formal distinctions should be evident in context.

These admittedly rather defensive sounding comments reflect the fact that many reviews of new metafiction, especially in the early 1970s, were negative: cries of lamentation over the death of the novel genre abounded. Since then we have perhaps erred in the other direction: we now accept metafiction—that is, we have institutionalized it—and presume it to require no further defence. I would suggest that this change has come about largely because we now have a name for such works. Labels are always comforting, but often also castrating. In the criticism of the seventies, the term "postmodernism" began to appear to refer to contemporary self-conscious texts. John Barth conferred upon this label the status of fact in his recent address to the Modern Language Association in December, 1979 and in his subsequent article in the January, 1980 issue of the *Atlantic*, entitled "The Literature of Replenishment: Postmodernist Fiction." In this study, however, I have deliberately not used this label, no matter how tempting its institutionalized convenience proved to be. The reasons for this choice are many, and not the least important is that the term "postmodernism" seems to me to be a very limiting label for such a broad contemporary phenomenon as metafiction. This is not to suggest, then, that the name hangs loose about the fiction "like a giant's robe upon a dwarfish thief." Quite the contrary—for if it is a temporal, historical designation, as some critics have implied, it is much too inclusive. Barth himself quite obviously does *not* mean to include the work of equally contemporary but more "traditional" novelists within this category. So the term must denote a technically definable literary entity. The "post" of "postmodernism" would therefore suggest not "after," so much as an extension of modernism and a reaction to it.

However, could one not then argue that "modernism" is here a *culturally* limited and limiting label as well? That is to say, what we (in our European and North American context) see as the root of "*postmodernism*" can be—and has been—perceived in totally different terms within, for instance, the Latin-American frame of reference. But this is an area of fiction that Barth most definitely wants to absorb into his own "modernist" tradition. Cuban expatriate novelist and critic Severo Sarduy would not agree; he has clearly shown[2] that the origins of the techniques of what Barth calls the "postmodernism" of García Márquez, for example, lie instead in the Spanish tradition of the *baroque*. What Sarduy calls contemporary neo-baroque still uses the technical devices of the baroque—that is, linguistic artifice, inter- and intratextuality, and narrative mirroring. The change in the present usage of these techniques is in intention: the baroque search for consonance is

2 "El barroco y el neobarroco," in César Fernández Moreno (ed.), *America Latina en su Literatura*, 2nd ed. (Buenos Aires: Siglo XXI, 1974), pp. 167–84.

replaced by a willed neo-baroque lack of harmony and homogeneity which is literally and figuratively revolutionary in its transgressions of contemporary literary and linguistic norms.

Barth admits the difficulties in defining modernism; he probably could not define it as precisely as Sarduy defines the baroque. And yet it is not hard to agree with Barth—and with Gerald Graff and Robert Alter[3]—that there is a certain continuity of concern between contemporary self-reflective texts and those of the earlier modernist period. However, when Graff defines "postmodernism" in terms of a calling into question of the "claims of literature and art to truth and human value," does one not feel the need to point out the continuity as well between "postmodernism" and *Don Quijote*? In other words, that "post" is here too *ex*clusive, too limiting, not to say too awkward and anticlimactic, as Barth himself has noted. This is another reason why I have chosen to restrict myself to the more purely descriptive term of contemporary "metafiction." This choice allows as well for the suggestion that the kind of "postmodernist" fiction of which Barth speaks and writes is only one of *many* forms that metafictional self-consciousness can and does take today.

There is yet another reason for avoiding the "postmodernist" debate in this particular kind of study. Most discussions of "postmodernism" are concerned primarily with the psychological, philosophical, ideological or social causes of the flourishing self-consciousness of our culture. This book, however, makes no pretence to contributing to the interesting controversy that has engaged Robert Alter, James Sloan Allen, Gerald Graff and Ihab Hassan, among others.[4] Instead, it merely accepts that something has happened and that it has its roots deep in our culture, most strongly in the Romantic and modernist periods. The focus of a debate on the causes of the change must necessarily be on the perpetrator of the change—the author. The interest here is rather on the text, on the literary manifestation of this change, and on the resulting implications for the *reader*. Unlike Gerald Graff, I would not argue that in metafiction the life-art connection has been either severed completely or resolutely denied. Instead, I would say that this "vital" link is reforged, on a new level—on that of the imaginative process (of storytelling), instead of on that of the product (the story told). And it is the new role of the reader that is the vehicle of this change.

3 See Graff's article, "The Myth of the Postmodernist Breakthrough," in *Tri-Quarterly* 26 (Winter 1973), 383–417, and Alter's "The Self-conscious Moment: Reflections on the Aftermath of Modernism," *Tri-Quarterly* 33 (Spring 1975), 209-30.
4 Alter, "The Self-conscious Moment"; Allen, "Self-consciousness and the Modernist Temper," *Georgia Review* 33, no. 3 (Fall 1979), 601–20; Graff, "Babbitt at the Abyss: The Social Context of Postmodern American Fiction," *Tri-Quarterly* 33 (Spring 1975), 305-37; Hassan, *The Dismemberment of Orpheus: Toward a Postmodern Literature* (New York: Oxford University Press, 1971).

For these reasons I have deliberately rejected the term "postmodernism" and chosen to limit my discussion to metafiction, that is, to restrict my analysis to the textual forms of self-consciousness, and only then to allow myself to consider their literary critical implications. The broader cultural issues that an inquiry into causes and sources reveals are assumed as givens and indeed are implied in the diachronic development of self-consciousness in the novel that forms the temporal backbone, if you like, of this book. But what appeared to be most needed in discussions of this contemporary form of narrative was rather more analytic and descriptive work on the texts themselves and on the effects they were having, or ought to have been having, on literary criticism.

This is not to say that extended critical studies of metafiction do not exist. They do, but they are few in number. The cultural impact of the *nouveau roman* in France in the 1950s and 1960s did stimulate the provocative works of Jean Ricardou[5] and, more recently, Lucien Dällenbach's[6] study of one of the major modes of textual narcissism, the *mise en abyme*. In North America Robert Scholes[7] began the examination of this new taste in fiction. But it was not until 1975 with the publication of Robert Alter's *Partial Magic: The Novel as a Self-Conscious Genre* that the critical implications of *narrative* narcissism began to be confronted. Alter begins with the premise that "in many important novelists from Renaissance Spain to contemporary France and America the realistic enterprise has been enormously complicated and qualified by the writer's awareness that fictions are never real things, that literary realism is a tantalizing contradiction in terms."[8] As this statement suggests, Alter proposes, as a critical framework, a dialectic between fiction and reality—essentially a metaphysical, ontological, experiential, and epistemological focus. This he combines with a diachronic progression of the novel form which begins with *Don Quijote* (as a study of the moral and ontological implications of the realization that fiction is only fiction) and continues through the eighteenth century to the modern period, with what he sees as an eclipse of novelistic self-consciousness in the realism of the nineteenth century.

While this study begins from this same initial assumption—that Cervantes' parodic text is indeed not only the first "realistic" novel but also the first self-reflective one—it diverges from Alter's in the consideration of nineteenth-century realism. The critical framework here is not to be one of the dualism of consciousness and world, as it is for him. Instead, the frame of reference will be one of a dialectical literary

5 See in particular *Le Nouveau Roman* ([Paris]: Seuil, 1973).
6 *Le Récit spéculaire* (Paris: Seuil, 1977).
7 *The Fabulators* (New York: Oxford University Press, 1967), and "Metafiction," *Iowa Review* 1 (Fall 1970), 100–115.
8 (Berkeley: University of California Press, 1975), p. x.

progression from one kind of novelistic mimesis to another. If the novel is by definition a representational genre, the Aristotelian concept of mimesis is worth reinvestigating. For Aristotle, diegesis was a part of mimesis. Cervantes too saw this, and neatly demonstrated that in the novel form the narrative act itself is, for the reader, part of the action. For this reason the term "diegetic" might be preferable to the simpler and more familiar term "narrative," as an adjective to signal this study's rejection of the split between process (the storytelling) and product (the story told). Given the diachronic implications of this framework, the realism of the nineteenth century, which is based almost entirely on what will be called a mimesis of product, will be seen more as a reductive limitation of novelistic mimesis than as the paradigm or the defining characteristic of the genre—as Auerbach, Watt, and many others have insisted. The novel genre does seem to change dialectically, as Alter asserts, but in literary as well as ontological terms. Modern metafiction is largely what shall be referred to here as a mimesis of process; but it grows out of that interest in consciousness *as well as* the objects of consciousness that constitutes the "psychological realism" of Woolf, Gide, Svevo, and Proust at the beginning of the century. Rather than positing a break in novelistic self-consciousness in the last century and then a modern revival of it, this literary dialectic would suggest a continuum, but a gradually evolving one that has logically culminated in metafiction. However, once again, the "postmodernist" historical debate will *not* be evoked.

Alter's dialectic effectively separates "art" and "life," suggesting that modern writers ask the reader to examine these distinctions and see how they interact. Within the critical context of what will here be called process mimesis, such a separation would prove impossible. Reading and writing belong to the processes of "life" as much as they do to those of "art." It is this realization that constitutes one side of the paradox of metafiction for the reader. On the one hand, he is forced to acknowledge the artifice, the "art," of what he is reading; on the other, explicit demands are made upon him, as a co-creator, for intellectual and affective responses comparable in scope and intensity to those of his life experience. In fact, these responses are shown to be *part of* his life experience. In this light metafiction is less a departure from the mimetic novelistic tradition than a reworking of it. It is simplistic to say, as reviewers did for years, that this kind of narrative is sterile, that it has nothing to do with "life." The implied reduction of "life" to a mere *product* level that ignores *process* is what this book aims to counteract.

While Alter's work sets the ontological and literary historical stage for a study of modern metafiction, it does not venture into an analysis of its various forms and modes. This present study, however, seeks to investigate both the implications of these literary phenomena for novel theory, and the possibility of categorizing the many types of modern

textual self-consciousness in the interest of clarity and precision in discussion. Thus, the typology suggested in the next chapter is not to be seen as a rigid, externally imposed organization, but rather it is the result of an inductive approach to individual texts and a subsequent generalization from them. As such this critical structure neither is superfluous nor can it be said to have generated its subject, any more than any other methodology can be said to have done so.

No attempt has been made to propose a comprehensive theory of metafiction. In the first place, any such theory would be reductive, much more reductive than any other theory of the novel in general. This is because the point of *meta*fiction is that it constitutes its own first critical commentary, and in so doing, it will be argued, sets up the theoretical frame of reference in which it must be considered. Therefore some of the chapters which follow are "theoretical" only in the sense that they investigate various existing novelistic theories in the light of the challenge afforded by narcissistic texts.

This limitation of the "theoretical" part of the argument also explains, at least in part, the fact that the critical terminology employed here is by necessity eclectic. If self-conscious narrative by definition includes within itself its own first contextual reading, no single theory will be able to deal with it without considerable distortion. However, two particular methodologies have been drawn on more than the others — Saussurian structuralism and Iserian hermeneutics. This choice is dictated largely by the fact that metafiction has two major focuses: the first is on its linguistic and narrative structures, and the second is on the role of the reader. In the first case, the basic structuralist terminology of the "code," of the "sign"'s "signifier" and "signified," and of the "referent" of language proves useful, indeed necessary. The work in reader aesthetics by hermeneutic critics such as Wolfgang Iser and Roman Ingarden provides a vocabulary in which to discuss the functions of the reader who "concretizes" the text and whose role is also "thematized" and often "actualized" within the text itself.

Narcissistic narrative, then, is process made visible. In this sense, metafiction is "production" but not in the current French ideological use of the word. The generic terms of reference in metafiction are still novelistic; auto-representation is still representation. These narratives are only *about* "production," perhaps. Therefore this book is not part of the modern critique of representation; it does not partake of the Derridian post-structuralist discourse.

As the sections to follow which examine theoretical issues will probably suggest, however, metafiction does have very serious implications for the theory of the novel as a mimetic genre. Some redefinition of novelistic mimesis would seem to be in order if critical theory is to deal adequately with the new forms of the genre that have developed. This

redefinition would necessarily entail a reconsideration of the nature of novelistic language; in all fiction, language is representational, but of a fictional "other" world, a complete and coherent "heterocosm" created by the fictive referents of the signs. In metafiction, however, this fact is made explicit and, while he reads, the reader lives in a world which he is forced to acknowledge as fictional. However, paradoxically the text also demands that he participate, that he engage himself intellectually, imaginatively, and affectively in its co-creation. This two-way pull is the paradox of the reader. The text's own paradox is that it is both narcissistically self-reflexive and yet focused outward, oriented toward the reader.

The typology developed in Chapter One is based on the observation that some of these texts are diegetically self-conscious while others demonstrate primarily an awareness of their linguistic constitution. In the first case, the text presents itself as narrative; in the second, as language. But there seem to be two possible varieties of each of these modes, and these will simply be referred to as the overt and the covert forms. Overtly narcissistic texts reveal their self-awareness in explicit thematizations or allegorizations of their diegetic or linguistic identity within the texts themselves. In the covert form, this process is internalized, actualized; such a text is self-reflective but not necessarily self-conscious.

These four types of metafiction are discussed in terms of many specific texts which represent a selection of those from which the typology was originally derived. The choice of many texts discussed as examples rather than only a few analyzed in fuller terms was made in order to show the broad range of this metafictional phenomenon—and thereby to account for the view that the implications it holds for novel theory cannot be ignored. For reasons of authorial linguistic competence, only texts written in English, French, and Italian are dealt with in the original languages; translations are used for Spanish-American and German texts. The wider range of reference allowed by translations was deemed necessary to subvert the convenient parochial generalization that metafiction is a uniquely American phenomenon or that the *nouveau roman* or even the *nouveau nouveau roman* is the last word in novelistic auto-representation. If the novel is indeed not dead in our Western culture, but rather is very much alive, it is thriving in Europe, in North America, and in South America too.

Perhaps, in actual fact, it is narrative as a whole, and not just literary narrative that has progressed to a process-oriented mode. Jean-Luc Godard is one film-maker whose work might be cited in support of this notion of a developing narrative self-reflexiveness. Peter Wollen claims that in Godard's earliest work "the narrative and dramatic structure is taken for granted, but the characters in the films question each other about the codes they use, about the sources of misunderstanding and

incomprehension. Then, as his career continued, he began more and more to question, not the inter-personal communication of the characters, but the communication represented by the film itself. Finally he began to conceive of making a film, not as communicating at all, but as producing a text in which the problems of film-making were themselves raised."[9]

Perhaps it is even reductive to limit this formal narcissism to narrative genres alone, for the visual arts and music both have also shown signs of self-reflectiveness. It might even be tempting to posit a general cultural phenomenon: not "postmodernism," neatly labelled, no longer to be questioned or examined, but rather merely an increasing interest in *how* art is created, not just in *what* is created. The process may be becoming as intriguing as the product. But there is no doubt that the novel today has become the focus of critical interest in modes of auto-representation, and as such confirms Northrop Frye's[10] hypothesis that in literary history a recurrent opposition can be detected between the Aristotelian and Longinian impulses, between the view of literature as product and the view of literature as process. Frye even suggests that prose fiction today has much in common with that of the late eighteenth century, when Sterne in particular helped bring to "a peculiarly exquisite perfection" the sense of literature as process. In fact, in the discussion to follow here, *Tristram Shandy* will indeed sit alongside *Don Quijote* as the major forerunner of modern metafiction.

2

At the start of these remarks, an allegorical reading of the Narcissus myth in terms of narrative was proposed. The interpretation to follow is not intended as a digression. Instead it hopes to fulfill two functions: the first is to make the point—as Freud did in a psychoanalytic context—that narcissism can be argued to be, not an aberration, but the "original condition" of the novel as a genre. This is done by representing, by means of the myth, the diachronic development of self-consciousness in fiction in the briefest form possible. In the second place, this reading of the myth is in part definitely an ironic one. While it is clear that from Ovid's perspective, Narcissus is indeed self-obsessed to the point of self-destruction, even Ovid himself notes that Narcissus lives on—in *two* forms, one (his own) in the underworld, and one (as a flower) that, while different in form, does bear his name. Both Ovid and the naiads and dryads who lament Narcissus' change are seen ironically here as representative of those critics who lament the death of the novel—refusing to accept that the form of fiction might just have changed.

9 In the 1972 "Conclusion" to *Signs and Meaning in the Cinema* (London: Secker and Warburg, 1969, 1972), pp. 164–65.
10 "Towards Defining an Age of Sensibility" in his *Fables of Identity: Studies in Poetic Mythology* (New York: Harcourt, Brace and World, 1963), pp. 130–31.

The first one to test the truth of [Tiresias'] utterances is Liriope, the nymph whom Cephisus, the river-god, once clasped in his winding stream and ravished, as he held her in his waves. This beautiful nymph conceived and bore a child . . . and named him Narcissus. When asked whether this child would live to a mature old age, the far-seeing prophet answers: "If he does not know himself." For a long time, the words of the seer seem but empty ones. But they were to prove justified by the fact and by the manner of his death, and by his strange infatuation. For indeed the son of Cephisus had turned sixteen and could pass for either child or man. Many young men and women both desired him; but beneath that gentle form was a pride so hard that no boy, no girl could touch him.[11]

The novel too can be seen to be the child of rape, the parodic offspring of Cervantes, self-centred and self-beloved from its very birth. This self-consciousness is perhaps more evident in modern metafiction but it is not at all limited to it. Alongside the eighteenth-century realistic tradition of Richardson and Defoe, one finds once again Sterne's narrative play in *Tristram Shandy*. Diderot's self-reflexive fiction precedes Balzac's realism. This self-mirroring which, by its very nature, challenges the traditional narrow concept of nineteenth-century novelistic mimesis is seen most obviously in the *mise en abyme*, a technique so dear to Gide (who loved those small convex mirrors in the paintings of Memling and Quentin Metsys, mirrors which reflected the scene being painted).

At another level of self-reflectiveness, however, as in "The Betrothal of the Arnolfini," for instance, one notices not only a mirror, as above, but also a "Jóhannes de eyck fuit hic" as part of the composition of the painting itself, signalling the artist's presence as witness and virtuoso. Often the novel itself also consciously manifests a concern for the aesthetic presence of the writing novelist, drawing the reader's attention to the storytelling process, destroying what Ian Watt once called the defining characteristic of the novel—formal realism. As early as *Tristram Shandy* and *Jacques le fataliste*, then, not to mention *Don Quijote* again, the reader has been asked to participate in the artistic process by bearing witness to the novel's self-analyzing development. The narrator-novelist has, from the start, unrealistically entered his own novel, drawing his reader into his fictional universe.

Several explanations have been put forth to account for the novel's early self-consciousness. If, on the one hand, one accepts Barthes'[12] thesis that it is only with the rise of the bourgeois consciousness that literature begins to be self-regarding, then the novel's self-reflexiveness is not surprising, since, as critics as diverse as Watt, Auerbach, Levin, and Lukács have attested, the novel is a bourgeois

11 The translation here of Ovid's *Metamorphoses* (Book 3, 11. 341–55) is that of the author, and is based on Rudolfus Ehwald's edition of the Latin text (Berlin: Weidmann, 1903), following the example of the Loeb Classical Library. Line references will be noted in parentheses in the text, since only selections have been used, and not the entire story.

12 "Littérature et méta-language," in *Essais critiques* (Paris: Seuil, 1964), p. 106.

capitalistic narrative genre. On the other hand, remaining more within the strictly literary realm, one might choose to see the origins of this phenomenon in the parodic intent of the novel, in the unmasking of dead conventions by a mirroring of them — minus the "proper" motivation.[13]

Whatever the reason, the novel from its beginnings has always nurtured a self-love, a tendency toward self-obsession. Unlike its oral forbears, it is both the storytelling and the story told. Tiresias' warning about Narcissus' self-awareness is perhaps well directed *from the start*: he will live long, "si se non noverit," if he does not know himself.

One day as [Narcissus] is chasing the frightened deer into his nets, he is seen by resounding Echo, a strange-speaking nymph who could neither be silent when others spoke, nor speak herself unless first addressed. . . . Now she saw Narcissus as he was wandering through the fields, and, burning with desire, she stealthily followed him. . . . But he flees her and, fleeing, says: "Withdraw your hands, do not embrace me. I'll die before I give you power over me." She only replies: "I give you power over me." Scorned, she hides in the forest, covers her shamed face with leaves, and from then on, lives in caves, alone. But still her love remains and grows on the sorrow of having been spurned; and the cares that keep her sleepless waste away her wretched body; she becomes thin and wrinkled, and all the life force leaves her body, evaporated into the air. Nothing more than her voice and her bones remain; her voice lives on; they say that her bones turned to stone [11. 356-58; 370-71; 390-99].

In the myth, Narcissus' fate is interestingly prefigured — with significant variations — by that of "resonabilis Echo" who cannot remain silent, cannot be ignored, and yet cannot be a creative, autonomous force on her own. Her destiny is not unlike that of novelistic language.[14] It too cannot be silenced, for it exists independently of its artistic function. Yet it cannot operate completely autonomously, for it is also referential as well as being a vehicle for connotations outside of its willed control. However, yet another dimension must be considered, for, being novelistic, its referents are to a fictive verbal universe and not necessarily to the real world. Maurice Blanchot[15] once deplored the traditional realistic novel's scorn for its language, its inability to realize that it is through literary language that the novel captures something

13 See the work of Chklovski on *Tristram Shandy*, or more briefly, in Tzvetan Todorov (ed.), *Théorie de la littérature: textes des formalistes russes* (Paris: Seuil, 1965), Tomachevski's "Thématique," pp. 263–307, and Eikhenbaum's "La Théorie de la 'méthode formelle'," pp. 31–75.

14 The connection between language and narrative (similar to that between Echo and Narcissus) can also be seen as quasi-synechdocal. See Roland Barthes, "Introduction à l'analyse structurale des récits," *Communications* no. 8 (1966), 4. One could elaborate: narrative agents are like proper nouns in sentences (subjects and objects); their actions are parallel in function to verbs in sentences; the qualities attained are adjectival. See Tzvetan Todorov, "Structural Analysis of Narrative," *Novel* 3 (Fall 1969), 74–76.

15 In "Mallarmé et l'art du roman," in *Faux pas* ([Paris]: Gallimard, 1943), p. 203.

beyond the inauthentic and the everyday. It does not see, he lamented, that its language must be singular in the sense that it depends uniquely on the work in which it appears, as one of its means and one of its ends. Valéry also listed as the causes of *his* distaste of the novel, its disorder, its arbitrariness, and its scorn for language, the very matter that is its essence.

Therefore, at a certain time, when formal realism was seen as the accepted goal of fiction, the novel, like Narcissus, seemed to refuse to give independent power to (or even pay any attention to) its medium, language. Character, action, morality, representation of reality—not words—were its conscious concerns. Language was merely a means, never an end. As a result, the value of deliberate and careful linguistic choice in the writing and evaluating of the novel seemed to diminish until, like Echo's bones which turned to stone, all that appeared to remain were skeletal structures and petrified conventional terms to be adopted uncritically by the conforming novelist.

As Narcissus had mocked [Echo], so had he mocked other nymphs of the waves or mountains, and before that, the company of men; after that, one of these latter despised youths, raising his hands to heaven, said: "May he himself love in this way, and not possess the thing he loves!" The goddess, Nemesis, agreed to his rightful entreaties. There was a limpid pool with shining silvery water, which neither shepherds, nor goats feeding on the mountainside, nor any other cattle had touched, which neither bird nor beast nor fallen tree branch had ever disturbed. . . . The boy, worn out by the exertion of the hunt and the heat, lay down here, charmed by both the appearance of the place and by the spring; and while he seeks to quench his thirst, another thirst sprang up. And while he drinks, struck by the image of the form he sees, he falls in love with an illusion that has no body, and thinks that to be substance which is only shadow. He is astonished by himself and is fixed, motionless, with the same expression, like a statue carved from Parian marble. . . . Inadvertently he desires himself; he approves and is himself what he approves; and while he seeks, is sought; and equally he inflames and burns with love. . . . What he sees, he does not know, but he burns for that which he does see, and the same delusion that deceives his eyes excites them. Credulous boy, why do you vainly try to seize fleeting images? What you seek is nowhere; what you love, if you but turn away, you will lose. That which you perceive is the shadow of a reflected form: it has no substance of its own. It both comes with you and stays with you; it will depart with you—if you can depart [11. 402-10; 413-19; 425-26; 430-36].

Unaware of both the value in, and the impossibility of ignoring, the verbal component of its form (which, like Echo's voice, might be said to have retired in shame), the novel continued to prosper, seemingly self-important and unself-critical, until it became Romantically intrigued with its own reflection. Now even more self-conscious, the novel increasingly took this image as a thing in itself worthy of literary treatment: the novelist and his novel itself became legitimate subject matter. The process of narration began to invade the fiction's content.

Out of the *Bildungsroman* or *Entwicklungsroman*, then, came the *Künstlerroman* with its preoccupation with the growth of the artist. As in

the psychological novel in general, unity of action was replaced by unity of personality—here, the artistic personality. Interpretation became interiorized, immanent to the work itself, as the narrator or point of view character reflected on the meaning of his creative experience. This phenomenon of the nineteenth century may well, as Foucault has suggested, be a result of a change in the conception of the relationship between words and things, idea and object. (In *Les Mots et les choses* [Paris: Gallimard, 1966], Foucault shows how, after the eighteenth century, objects gradually became self-centred as if searching for the principle of their intelligibility in their own development and abandoning more and more the conventional space of representation.) But this wider debate is outside the limits of this study.

Nevertheless, such a change, whatever its cause, would allow, in literary terms, for the transformation of form into content: the subject matter would change again from the novelist to his writing. Novels then begin to reflect and to reflect upon their own genesis and growth. The mirroring involved begins to undermine traditional realism in favour of a more introverted literary level of mimesis: *Point Counter Point, The Alexandria Quartet, Portrait d'un inconnu*. The realistic story trappings are finally reduced to an allegory of the functioning of the narration. As Jean Verrier explains: "On est passé de l'oeuvre *dans* l'oeuvre à l'oeuvre *sur* l'oeuvre, puis à l'oeuvre *par* l'oeuvre."[16] It is here that a first principle of structuralist criticism—literary works are about language—would seem most obviously relevant. Perhaps the origins of this concern for writing and reading *within* the structure of the novel itself, lie in the early journal and epistolary novels. The writer calls his reader's attention to the activity of writing as an event within the novel, as an event of equally great significance to that of the events of the story which he is supposed to be telling. As Tzvetan Todorov explains:

Toute oeuvre, tout roman raconte, à travers la trame événementielle, l'histoire de sa propre création, sa propre histoire. Des oeuvres comme celles de Laclos ou de Proust ne font que rendre explicite une vérité sous-jacente à toute création littéraire. Ainsi apparaît la vanité des recherches du sens dernier de tel roman, de tel drame; le sens d'une oeuvre consiste à se dire, à nous parler de sa propre existence. Ainsi le roman tend à nous amener à lui-même; et nous pouvons dire qu'il commence en fait là où il se termine; car l'existence même du roman est le dernier chaînon de son intrigue, et là où finit l'histoire racontée, l'histoire de la vie, là exactement commence l'histoire racontante, l'histoire littéraire.[17]

Although perhaps an extreme formalistic view which could be countered by accusations of reductiveness in making a new "sens dernier"—a merely literary, formal one—this stance shows clearly the line of succession from the early self-consciousness of Cervantes and

16 "Le Récit réfléchi," *Littérature* 5 (février 1972), 59.
17 Tzvetan Todorov, *Littérature et signification* (Paris: Larousse, 1967), p. 49.

Sterne, to the *Künstlerroman*, to the novel about novels. The "narcissistic" change is one of degree, not kind. Narcissus had *always* been self-aware; he merely became more physically conscious of his own existence and charm, as seen in the still water-mirror — "the shadow of a reflected form."

No concern for food or rest can draw him from the spot; but stretched out on the shaded grass, he gazes at the deceitful form with unsated eyes and by his own eyes he perishes; and, having raised himself up a little, and stretching his arms to the woods around him, he says: "Oh woods, is there anyone who has loved more cruelly? . . . And, to make me grieve the more, no great sea separates us, no long road, no mountains, no ramparts with closed gates; we are hindered by a little water! He himself desires to be embraced. . . . [addressing the image] I have often noted your tears too, as I cry; and you return my signals with a nod; and, as I suspect from the motion of your beautiful mouth, you utter words which do not reach my ears. I am he; I have sensed it, my image deceives me no more; I am consumed with love for myself. . . . Death is not disagreeable to me, as sorrows are left behind in death; I wish that he who is loved might live longer. Now, united, we two shall die in one breath." . . . But as golden wax is accustomed to melting away before a slight fire or morning frost before the warm sun, so, weakened by love, he wastes away, and is gradually devoured by the secret fire. And no longer is his complexion that ruddy hue mixed with white; no longer is there the vigour and energy and all that lately was so pleasing to behold; nor does the body, which Echo had once loved, remain [11. 437–42; 448–50; 459–64; 471–73; 487–93].

Unable to stop at an acceptance of this mirroring vision of itself, the novel proceeded, at least in some critics' eyes, to pine away until the form barely remained. These critics share Ovid's viewpoint on Narcissus' fate. They argue that, like Narcissus, the novel began to lose those attractive features — of action, of personality — which had made it so beloved (in the last century) to become absorbed in a deeper self-reflective state which — and herein lay the fear — threatened to deny the novel's existence as a realistic narrative of something outside itself. Literature at this stage, writes Foucault:

n'a plus alors qu'à se recourber dans un perpétuel retour sur soi, comme si son discours ne pouvait avoir pour contenu que de dire sa propre forme: elle s'adresse à soi comme subjectivité écrivante, ou elle cherche à ressaisir, dans le mouvement qui la fait naître, l'essence de toute littérature; et ainsi tous ses fils convergent vers la pointe la plus fine — singulière, instantanée, et pourtant absolument universelle — , vers le simple acte d'écrire. Au moment où le langage, comme parole répandue, devient objet de connaissance, voilà qu'il réapparaît sous une modalité strictement opposée: silencieuse, précautionneuse déposition du mot sur la blancheur d'un papier, où il ne peut avoir ni sonorité ni interlocuteur, où il n'a rien à dire que soi, rien d'autre à faire que scintiller dans l'éclat de son être.[18]

One might consider this change either, as most "Ovidian" critics have, a negative one (as the decline of the novel as a realistic genre), or

18 *Les Mots et les choses* (Paris: Gallimard, 1966), p. 313.

it might also be seen as a positive one (as a renewed sense of language, formal craft, and aesthetic design). But either way it is hard to ignore this new development in the genre. More and more the reader is made aware of the fact that the existence of verbal and structural materials conditions the formation of images, that the human imagination is exercised in working with these materials — perhaps still at the service of some human meaning and value outside themselves, however. The thin paper is the reflecting pool; the text is its own mirror.

However when [Echo] saw [Narcissus' wasted form], she grieved, although angry and remembering still, and as often as the wretched boy said, "Alas," with echoing words, she repeated, "Alas," and when he beat his arms with his hands, she returned the same beating sound. This was his last utterance as he gazed into the familiar water: "Alas, vainly beloved boy!" and the place echoed back just as many words; and when he said farewell, Echo also said "Farewell." He lay down his weary head on the green grass; death sealed his eyes that were admiring their master's beauty. After he was received into the infernal abode, then too did he keep on gazing upon himself in the Stygian water. The naiads, his sisters, beat their breasts and consecrated to their brother their shorn locks; the dryads, too, lamented; Echo responded to their laments [11. 494-507].

If the novel has, to some "Ovidian" or "naiadic" critics, died Narcissus' death it seems, nevertheless, like him, quite able to live on in another less traditionally realistic world, ceaselessly regarding at least its formal beauties. Echo — or verbal process — can come out of hiding. While accepting the inevitably constant presence (even if hidden in the caves of nineteenth-century realism) of linguistic concern in the novel, one must still take note of the increasing obsession with the creative functioning of language in the novels of Roussel, Joyce, Beckett, Sanguineti, the writers of the "new new novel," and so many others. Jean Ricardou sees the works of the *Tel Quel* group as going yet further in this radicalization and so superseding the novel genre. If the *nouveau roman* is self-mirroring auto-representation, then *Tel Quel*'s works are anti-representation — "textes" which, like Echo, are similar in fate to, but not the same as, the Narcissistic narrative itself.

The very activity of the novelist seems to alter in direction when he becomes aware that he has been the unconscious producer of a synchronic model or sign-system; then perhaps he decides to do so consciously and self-consciously. Similarly, the activity of the reader is not one of being a consumer of stories, but rather one of learning and constructing a new sign-system, a new set of verbal relations. The novel becomes a new and strange kind of code written almost in hieroglyphs and analogous in process to primitive myth or fairy tales.[19]

Criticism, then, must concern itself with these privileged objects and their organization. Because of the primacy of the linguistic model, structuralist analysis concentrates most on the predominance of lin-

19 Fredric Jameson, "Metacommentary," *PMLA* 86 (1971), 13.

guistic structures in shaping meaningful experiences. But since many modern novels seem intent on identifying themselves with their own theorizing, perhaps descriptive research into these self-informing theories, such as what follows in this study, is the only possible form of novel criticism left.[20] The extreme of this view is Jameson's idea of "metacommentary" which would be a self-conscious commentary on the very conditions of existence of any given critical problem: it would be the *need* for interpretation, not the *nature* of it, that would be discussed. Each individual analysis, he feels, should include an analysis of its own existence, should show its own credentials, and justify itself.

With metafiction, then, the distinction between literary and critical texts begins to fade. Like Echo, verbal process comes out of hiding to accompany what some see as the novel's dying farewells, perhaps outliving it to echo the smug laments of the dryadic denizens of the critical deep. Literature itself has altered; this cannot be denied if one looks at the modern novel. But the change is logical and a less abrupt change than most "Ovidian" critics would have one believe. Even in Ovid's account, Narcissus is *received* into another world, not *cast* there. Self-conscious fiction is part of another trend or tradition within the novel, for this genre is as much a self-conscious bourgeois *aesthetic form* as it is a bourgeois social entity. The narcissism of Romanticism altered the degree but not the kind of self-absorption in the novel.

Barthes[21] once saw this process as beginning with Flaubert (and perhaps James, Manzoni?) and his "conscience artisanale de la fabrication littéraire." Mallarmé (and Gide, Huxley, Joyce, Svevo, and Mann?) brought to literature that mingling of literature and critical thought about it. Next came Proust's "espoir de parvenir à éluder la tautologie littéraire en remettant sans cesse, pour ainsi dire, la littérature au lendemain, en déclarant longuement qu'on *va* écrire, et en faisant de cette déclaration la littérature même." Stage four began, for Barthes, with the surrealists' (and the Italian hermeticists'?) multiplication of meaning of language, the refusal of the "signifié univoque," and ended in the "blancheur de l'écriture" that he perceived in the work of Robbe-Grillet. The radicalization has progressed even further since Barthes wrote this. Literature—and the novel in particular—seemed to many in the sixties and seventies, if not today, to have been playing with its own destruction. But has it not, rather, proved to be, as Barthes claimed, more like "cette héroïne racinienne qui meurt de se connaître mais vit de se chercher"?

And now they prepared a funeral pile and brandishing torches and a bier; but his body was nowhere to be found; instead of the body, they find a flower [11. 508–509).

20 See Umberto Eco, "The Analysis of Structure" in *The Critical Moment* (London: Faber and Faber, 1963), p. 138, and Edward W. Said's discussion of the self-reflectiveness of criticism since the idea of metalanguage, in "Eclecticism and Orthodoxy in Criticism," *Diacritics* 2 (Spring 1972), 5.

21 "Littérature et méta-langage," in *Essais critiques*, pp. 106–107.

Even if the novel today has, as the "Ovidians" claim, died as a traditional realistic narrative genre, there is still the fact that no proof can really be found. There is no corpse; the form has just slipped into another world, in a very similar shape and attitude. Something new, or rather something old and resurrected, has appeared in its old traditional place. Like the flower[22] which shares Narcissus' name, the "non-fictional *novel*" is a natural outgrowth of the old realistic tradition, a spontaneous rediscovery of those devices of formal realism[23] which Ian Watt once isolated in his study of the eighteenth-century novel.

Between the Echoing wail of the dryadic mourners of the novel's death and the stubborn concreteness of Truman Capote's reportage, the reader is left alone — to read metafiction, and to contemplate with some perspective Tiresias' warning, "si se non noverit."

22 Ovid did *not* make the associations that his later commentators did of the flower as sterile, poisonous, beautiful but isolated, and so on. See Louise Vinge, *The Narcissus Theme in Western European Literature up to the Early 19th Century*, trans. Robert Dewsnap (Lund: Gleerups, 1967), p. 18.

23 See Tom Wolfe, "Why they aren't writing the Great American Novel anymore: A Treatise on the Varieties of Realistic Experience," *Esquire*, December 1972, pp. 152-59 and 272-80.

Modes and Forms of Narrative Narcissism: Introduction of a Typology

Allow me a touch of McLuhanesque glibness: the product is the process. Language and literature must revive their true identity — as the cutting edge of perception. Creativity and the critical spirit must achieve a new harmony and interdependence.

David Caute

A few years ago, René Wellek wisely wrote:

Art is "illusion," "fiction," the world changed into language, paint or sound. It seems to me an oddity of our time that this simple insight into the aesthetic fact is construed as a denial of the relevance, the humanity and significance of art. The recognition of the difference between life and art, of the "ontological gap" between a product of the mind, a linguistic structure, and the events in "real" life which it reflects, does not and cannot mean that the work of art is a mere empty play of forms, cut off from reality. The relation of art to reality is not as simple as older naturalistic theories of copying or "imitation" or Marxist "mirroring" assume. "Realism" is not the only method of art. It excludes three-quarters of the world's literature. It minimizes the role of imagination, personality "making."[1]

Art has always been "illusion," and as one might surmise, it has often, if not always, been self-consciously aware of that ontological status. This formal narcissism is a broad cultural phenomenon, not limited by art form or even by period. The mirror studies of Velasquez and Picasso, and the perplexing self-reference in Escher's "Drawing Hands," find their musical counterparts as early as Cimarosa's eighteenth-century "Il maestro di musica" and as late as Richard Strauss's opera, *Capriccio*, or Ralph Vaughan Williams' "Serenade to Music." There are those who assert that similarly in fiction — and not just in modern radical texts — a work is apt to produce within itself a dramatized mirror of its own

1 René Wellek, "Some Principles of Criticism" (*Times Literary Supplement*, 1963), reprinted in *The Critical Moment* (London: Faber & Faber, 1963), pp. 41–42.

narrative or linguistic principles. The origins of the self-reflecting structure that governs many modern novels might well lie in that parodic intent basic to the genre as it began in *Don Quijote*, an intent to unmask dead conventions by challenging, by mirroring. The self-consciousness of Cervantes' text has been handed down, through the likes of Sterne and Diderot, to the Romantic artist-hero of the *Künstler-roman*, as has been discussed already in the Introduction.

From novels about the growth of the artist came novels about novels, apparently reflecting their own genesis and development, challenging, this time, the period-concept of nineteenth-century realism that threatened to become entrenched into the definition of the entire novel genre. If novels such as *At Swim-Two-Birds, Il fu Mattia Pascal, Les Faux-monnayeurs*, and the early *nouveaux romans* seemed "arty" when they appeared, it may be for any number of ideological or sociological reasons,[2] but art, as Wellek remarked, has not changed: literature has always been an ordered fictive construct in language. And is not the urge to create coherent worlds, or even just to pattern or to organize the chaos of experience, as natural an impulse as the desire to "imitate" Nature? Aristotle was certainly of this opinion: for him *mimesis* was balanced by *harmonia*.

Self-informing narrative does not signal a lack of sensitivity or of humanitarian (or human) concern on the part of the novelist. Nor is it a mark of crisis, of the asphyxiation of fiction by an overworked critical intellect, or by an excessive curiosity about writers, or by the novelist's loss of faith in his work, or by cubism, film or any of the other possibilities suggested by its detractors. If self-awareness is a sign of the genre's disintegration, then the novel began its decline at birth, as the ironic reading of the Ovid in the Introduction suggested.

An increasingly large international band of writers of novels and short fiction — Borges, Barth, Sanguineti, Fowles, Sollers — does indeed often transform the formal properties of fiction into its subject matter. Perhaps this is because they have discovered that these literary entities are as real, or unreal, as any external, empirical raw materials. Yet, this realization is part of the novel's origins and development as well, and its traces can be seen from *Tristram Shandy* through Pirandello's Serafino Gubbio (who allegorically and parodically resolves the novelist's formal difficulties with naturalism) and on to Maurice Blanchot's works, in which allegories of the writing consciousness replace realistic narratives.

What we today refer to as this kind of literary formalism has always existed; the more modern textual self-preoccupation differs mostly in its explicitness, its intensity, and its own critical self-awareness. This progression is likely connected to a change in the concept of language,

2 See Maurice Beebe, *Ivory Towers and Sacred Founts* (New York: New York University Press, 1964), pp. 312–13, for this perspective.

as Michel Foucault has suggested.[3] It is perhaps also a matter of finding an aesthetic mode of dealing with modern man's experience of life as being unordered by any communal or transcendent power—God or myth—and his new scepticism that art can unproblematically provide a consolatory order.

The classic realistic novel's well-made plot might give the reader the feeling of completeness that suggests, by analogy, *either* that human action is somehow whole and meaningful, *or* the opposite, in which case it is art alone that can impart any order or meaning to life. The modern, ambiguous, open-ended novel might suggest, on the other hand, less an obvious new insecurity or lack of coincidence between man's need for order and his actual experience of the chaos of the contingent world, than a certain curiosity about art's ability to produce "real" order, even by analogy, through the process of fictional construction. This latter possibility is particularly suggestive in partially accounting for the new need, first to create fictions, then to admit their fictiveness, and then to examine critically such impulses. This is as true of the short story today as it is of the novel. It is narrative in general that is narcissistic.

It is tempting to speculate on the possible relationship—that explicitly suggests itself in metafiction by John Barth and John Fowles, among others—between the subjectivity of perspective in modern existentialism and the concern of self-conscious fiction to assert some mimetic life-art connection in the face of its obviously introspective orientation. These novels and the existential perspective both deny illusion, falseness. Fiction is obviously fiction; as Borges has shown us, life is fictive, of our making, as well. Existential man is "free" so he too can bear no illusions about his mortality and about the limited nature of his perspective. For real "authenticity" there can be no absolute truths. Similarly narcissistic fiction can only be judged in terms of its own internal validity: "truth" has no significance in art.

On the other hand, in *Structuralism in Literature*, Robert Scholes sees the work of these modern writers, whom he calls "fabulators," as a rejection of existentialism and its ethic of freedom.[4] He interprets their stress on system as proof that metafiction is structurally inspired (in its assumption that man exists in a system "not necessarily arranged for his benefit"). However, the emphasis on system in these works is on an *intramural* textual level, whereas the freedom which is so constantly thematized and theorized about by texts ranging from Robbe-Grillet's to Nabokov's is the *extramural* freedom of the *reader*. These writers, then, have not so much moved from existentialism to structuralism as

3 *Les Mots et les choses* (Paris: Gallimard, 1966), p. 313.

4 *Structuralism in Literature* (New Haven: Yale University Press, 1974), pp. 193–95 and 162. This is a change from his earlier remarks especially on "Black Humor" in *The Fabulators* (New York: Oxford University Press, 1967), p. 43.

effected a sort of synthesis through that revealing of (not to say revelling in) system which itself demands of the reader new freedom—and new responsibility. Scholes himself admits indirectly that there is a problem in his metafiction-structuralism linkage and that it lies precisely in the rejection of the notion of subject in the latter and the stress on the role of the reader in the former. His further connecting of these two modern phenomena with cybernetics and with Norbert Wiener, in particular, brings at once to mind, however, an archetypal structuralist text which ironically attempts to *limit* the reader's freedom to operate within the tight system that is the novel—Thomas Pynchon's *The Crying of Lot 49*.

What narcissistic narrative does do in flaunting, in baring its fictional and linguistic systems to the reader's view, is to transform the process of making, of *poiesis*, into part of the shared pleasure of reading. Novelist John Gardner, despite his ambivalence toward self-conscious literature as a whole, sees this as one of the major attractions of the form. Its "gim-crackery," he fears, does suit "our for the most part childishly petulant contemporary mood—our self-congratulating self-doubt, our alienated, positivistic pessimism. . . . And it suits, also a nobler quality of contemporary life: our delight in discovering how things work, our pleasure in seeing objects for themselves, enjoying their colors and textures."[5]

John Barth has called this fiction a "literature of exhaustion"; similarly, Ortega y Gasset refers to the "dehumanization of art." Yet neither of these terms is as negative a description as its immediate associations might suggest. Both are linked to parody and to an attempt to exhaust literary possibilities—without succeeding. Borges more cautiously chooses the more neutral term of "baroque" to describe such art as his own.[6] In all three writers' views, however, it is the human imaginative *process* that is explicitly called into action, in both author and reader.

Despite both the hostile accusations of "preening narcissism" of many reviews, and the increasing number of self-reflective novels that appear, very little systematic study has been devoted thus far to determining the types, much less the causes of such literary introversion. Perhaps the negative connotations of the very language we have been forced to use here—narcissism, introverted, introspective, self-conscious—suggest a strong desire to keep criticism as a separate domain; fiction which constitutes its own literary analysis is, to the critic, naturally somewhat suspect. However, there have been a few auspicious beginnings such as the related work of Robert Alter and

5 Review of Larry Woidwode's *Beyond the Bedroom Wall* in the *New York Times Book Review*, September 28, 1975, p. 1.
6 Preface to the 1954 edition of *A Universal History of Infamy* (New York: Dutton, 1972), p. 11.

Lucien Dällenbach, already mentioned. Another important start is Robert Scholes's early enthusiastic work on *The Fabulators* (New York: Oxford University Press, 1967). In analyzing works by six modern English and American metafictionists, Scholes traces the revival of rhetoric, romance, the picaresque, satire, and allegory in fiction which he describes here simply as "more verbal," "more fictional," "less realistic," "more shapely," than earlier works. In a later article entitled "Metafiction,"[7] he separates these texts more precisely into four categories, in each of which emphasis is laid on one of the following: the formal, structural, behavioural or philosophical aspects of the text. This breakdown, however, relies totally on an acceptance of Scholes's four initially postulated, parallel categories of (fiction's) forms and ideas, and (being's) existence and essence. These become roughly paralleled again to four categories of fiction—romance, myth, novel, and allegory. Another problem with this system in its application is that Scholes limits himself to collections of short pieces, suggesting that the mode he investigates cannot be expanded successfully. His earlier book tends to belie this, however. Scholes concludes that Barth and Barthelme are merely chroniclers of our "despair over the exhausted forms of our thought and our existence." But Coover and Gass, on the other hand, "are reaching through form and behavior for some ultimate values, some true truth." Yet where is the *meta* in this metafiction? Is the fiction not also a form of art which works within a *literary* code—as well as a more generally existential or behavioural one?

On this more literary level, however, the only extensive theoretical or typological work is that done by Jean Ricardou, who conveniently provides us with a horizontal and vertical auto-representational cross[8] on which to crucify—systematically—metafictional modes. Ricardou's analysis is the more methodical, yet because of its appealingly neat, *a priori* structuring, presents problems for specific textual analysis, problems that Scholes's work tries carefully to evade. Ricardou presents a system which is structured on two types of self-reflectiveness, or, to use his term, auto-representation—vertical and horizontal. The vertical variety is *inter*dimensional, operating between the "fiction" (what is said) and the "narration" (how it is said). Horizontal auto-representation is *intra*dimensional. There are two sub-groups within these types, yielding four separate modes: (1) "auto-représentation verticale, descendante, expressive": here the "fiction" is in control of the "narration," as it is traditionally in realistic texts in which the referential dimension dominates; (2) "auto-représentation verticale, ascendante, productrice": this is in operation when it is the "narration" that controls, or at least influences, the "fiction." This is what Ricardou

7 *Iowa Review* 1 (Fall 1970), 100–115.
8 "La Population des miroirs," *Poétique* 22 (1975), 212.

earlier[9] had labelled as a "littérature du faire" or "scripturalisme," for the text points to itself allegorically or metaphorically as a written text, as an active production of writer and reader; (3) "auto-représentation horizontale, référentielle, productrice" operates on the level of the "fiction" only, in the form of structural event repetition, *mise en abyme*, or perhaps microcosmic sabotages of chronology and suspense; (4) "auto-représentation horizontale, littérale, productrice" functions on the "narration" level alone and indeed the "narration" becomes the "fiction."

There are at least three potential problems with Ricardou's structure here. In the first place, it is hard to see how his initial category qualifies as any kind of *auto*-representation except in his example of alliteration, a not particularly important technique in narrative. He does separate it from the others by its pejorative label of "expressive" (as opposed to the modern "productrice"), but one must still question its usefulness as a category of *auto*-representation. The second limitation of this system lies in Ricardou's lack of distinction between texts which are self-conscious about their *diegetic* or narrative processes and those which are *linguistically* self-reflective. This causes distinct problems in Ricardou's own analyses of, for example, Raymond Roussel, in which he confuses and combines the author's generative linguistic *procédé* with the different but equally self-reflective structural narrative mirrorings, a confusion he senses but does not clarify in his more recent writing on Roussel.[10] Both language and narrative structures are included in his category of "narration," but some texts—such as John Barth's *Chimera*—reveal their own diegetic operations, while others—Ricardou's own fiction—concentrate on their own linguistic functioning. It is true that, in the latter case, language often works to order diegetic modes, but as this is not necessarily so in the reverse instance (that narrative structures determine language), there would seem to be a need for a distinction between the two.

The third difficulty with Ricardou's cross of horizontal and vertical auto-representative categories lies in its very neatness, its *a priori* deductive nature. It has already been suggested that its fearful symmetry is rather questionable in allowing (or rather, requiring) the presence of what he calls the "auto-représentation verticale, descendante, expressive." However, one would still be left with a pleasantly structured triangle of types, were it not for the fact that there seem to be *more* kinds of metafictional self-consciousness than it can account for. There are texts which are, as has been mentioned, diegetically self-aware, that is,

9 *Problèmes du nouveau roman* (Paris: Seuil, 1967), pp. 12, 54; and *Pour une théorie du nouveau roman* (Paris: Seuil, 1971), pp. 105, 107, 156. See also "Penser la littérature aujourd'hui," *Marche Romane* 21 nos. 1–2 (1971), 7–17.
10 "Disparition élocutoire" in Leonardo Sciascia, *Actes relatifs à la mort de Raymond Roussel* (Paris: L'Herne, 1972), pp. 7–30.

conscious of their own narrative processes. Others are linguistically self-reflective, demonstrating their awareness of both the limits and the powers of their own language. In the first case, the text presents itself as diegesis, as narrative; in the second, it is unobfuscated text, language.

A further distinction must be made, however, within these two modes, for each can be present in at least two forms, what one might term an overt and a covert one. Overt forms of narcissism are present in texts in which the self-consciousness and self-reflection are clearly evident, usually explicitly thematized or even allegorized within the "fiction." In its covert form, however, this process would be structuralized, internalized, actualized. Such a text would, in fact, be self-reflective, but not necessarily self-conscious. One is left again with a four-part system, this time of overt diegetic and linguistic types of literary narcissism, and their covert counterparts, both diegetic and linguistic. In order to clarify and expand this system and to see its diachronic as well as synchronic implications, it is necessary to deal with each mode and form in turn.

In its most overt form the self-consciousness of a text often takes the shape of an explicit thematization—through plot allegory, narrative metaphor, or even narratorial commentary. This latter possibility opens up again the entire question of the modernity and origins of recent metafiction. It has already been suggested that these new manifestations are rooted in a tradition of literary self-awareness that dates back, through Romantic inner mirroring to the eighteenth-century garrulous, guiding narrator to *Don Quijote*'s Cid Hamete Benengeli. That is to say that there would appear to be a developing tradition of narcissism, rather than a definite rupture out of which sprang metafiction. Can one really make the distinction between older, more comfortable "textes de plaisir" and modern difficult "textes de jouissance," as Roland Barthes suggests in *Le Plaisir du texte* (Paris: Seuil, 1973)? Even if such a sharp differentiation could be made, could the "limit-text," of which Barthes speaks, perhaps not be more a result of gradual and earlier change in degree, rather than an abrupt change in kind? Is it, perhaps, another of the dialectic syntheses that mark the stages in the development of the novel genre? The reader's role changes with the demands made by Gide and Woolf before arriving at Sollers' recent concept of "travail." Perhaps it is even less complex than that: perhaps each novel has always had within itself the seeds of a "narcissistic" reading, of an interpretation which would make it an allegorical or metaphoric exploration of the process of articulating a literary world.

This admittedly appears more convincing a speculation if one does accept *Don Quijote* (rather than *Pamela*, the voyage tale, the *fabliaux*, etc.) as the first novel, since its parodic intent is essential to its formal identity. The Russian formalist concept of parody as an autonomous art, based on the discovery of "process" would therefore be of interest

to the study of the novel's dialectic growth. Parody, according to the formalist theoreticians, is the result of a conflict between realistic motivation and an aesthetic motivation which has become weak and has been made obvious. The consequence is the unmasking of the system or of the creative process whose function has given way to mechanical convention. It is as if a dialectic were established, as if this parodied material were backgrounded to the new forms and thus a formal synthesis effected. If a new parodic form does not develop when an old one becomes insufficiently motivated, the old form tends to degenerate into pure convention; witness the popular traditional novel, the bestseller.

Another operation is at work in metafictional parody, however, and this the formalists called "defamiliarization." The laying bare of literary devices in metafiction brings to the reader's attention those formal elements of which, through over-familiarization, he has become unaware. Through his recognition of the backgrounded material, new demands for attention and active involvement are brought to bear on the act of reading. This is true in other art forms as well. Standing before Segal's "Diner," one might postulate a parodic modern tie with the Dutch Masters' commonplace scenes; Augustus John's "Symphonie Espagnole" is a modern parody of El Greco. In music, the phenomenon is even more apparent: Vaughan Williams' reworking of "Greensleeves" and other English folk ballads, Mahler's funereal parody of "Frère Jacques" in his First Symphony, Prokofiev's entire "Classical Symphony."

Coming back to fiction, one finds John Fowles's narrator in *The French Lieutenant's Woman* parodying the conventions of the Victorian novel—but doing so as a means to a new and relevant, modern synthetic form. Yet this play could well be seen as the very essence of the novel genre: Quijote imitates *Amadis of Gaul*, Cervantes pretends to be Cid Hamete Benengeli, Alonzo Quijano pretends to be Don Quijote. Is, then, the modern concept of "intertextuality" or textual intersubjectivity[11] so very different from the parodic dialectic that appears to be central to the novel? One thinks of John Barth's backgrounded evocations in *The Sot-Weed Factor* of Rabelais, Cervantes, and the entire eighteenth-century novel tradition, or his parodies in *Giles Goat-Boy*, of the conventions of the Bible, the animal fable, Science Fiction, allegory, satire, and the epic, not to mention the novel. Is the "intertextuality" of Claude Mauriac's *La Marquise sortit à cinq heures* not perhaps of the same parodic mode?

Indeed, the techniques of the "littérature citationnelle" can be seen as both parodic and generative. Quotations from one text, when inserted in the context of another, are the same and yet new and differ-

11 See Julia Kristeva, *Semiotikè* (Paris: Seuil, 1969), p. 146, and Roland Barthes, *S/Z* (Paris: Seuil, 1970), pp. 16–17.

ent, a microcosmic version of T. S. Eliot's concept of "tradition" in literature. The parodic creation of new fiction through the rewriting of old is itself the narcissistic subject of metafictional parody in Borges' tale of Pierre Menard, author of the *Quijote*.

Parody is, therefore, an exploration of difference and similarity; in metafiction it invites a more literary reading, a recognition of literary codes. But it is wrong to see the end of this process as mockery, ridicule, or mere destruction.[12] Metafiction parodies and imitates as a way to a new form which is just as serious and valid, as a synthesis, as the form it dialectically attempts to surpass. It does not necessarily involve a movement away from *mimesis*, however, unless by that term is meant only a rigid object-imitation or behaviouristic-realistic motivation.

A text may self-consciously present its own creative processes, perhaps as a model of man's exercise of language and meaning production. And, it may do so, as Jonathan Culler suggests in *Structuralist Poetics*, with an eye to disarming attacks on its *vraisemblance* by admitting its artificiality. However, it might also be done in order to make a specific demand upon the reader, a demand for recognition of a new code, for a more open reading that entails a parodic synthesis of back- and fore-grounded elements.

There is yet another reason, of course, why modern self-informing fiction is not *anti*-mimetic. The "psychological realism" of early twentieth-century fiction, made possible by Romantic self-consciousness, expanded (again through a kind of dialectic movement) the meaning of novelistic mimesis to include process as well as product. For many social or philosophical reasons, Joyce, Proust, Virginia Woolf, Pirandello, Svevo, Gide, and many others began to question the increasingly narrow view of fictional realism that had grown out of the naturalism of the preceding century. Perhaps it is true that they began to doubt the claim of external reality to being real, and chose instead to substitute an inner world of subjectivity and imagination. What is important to the novel, however, is the aesthetic consequence of their doubt.

Their new "subjective realism" had two major effects on the reified novelistic tradition of the preceding century that are significant here, especially for overt forms of narcissism. The once important detailed presentation of external reality became somewhat atrophied or, at least, stylized as the focus of attention shifted to the character's inner *processes*—imaginative and psychological. Secondly, the role of the reader began to change. Reading was no longer easy, no longer a

12 Cf. Jonathan Culler, *Structuralist Poetics* (London: Routledge and Kegan Paul, 1975), p. 153, and Robert Scholes re romance modes in "Metafiction," *Iowa Review* 1 (Fall 1970), 103. See the author's "Parody Without Ridicule: Observations on Modern Literary Parody," *Canadian Review of Comparative Literature* 5 no. 2 (Spring 1978), 201–211.

comfortable controlled experience; the reader was now forced to control, to organize, to interpret. He was assaulted from all sides, often by a self-consciously literary text. In his *Journal des faux-monnayeurs*, Gide separates his novel's interest into two parts, into the plot events and the author's efforts to make a novel of them. Within Gide's novel itself, the reader is informed that the subject of Edouard's novel (also, of course, entitled *Les Faux-monnayeurs*) is the writer's attempt to impose order and meaning on events.[13] In trying to free the novel form from the constrictions of nineteenth-century realism, Gide had to give the reader a more active role.[14]

Indeed, much of the final ordering and sense-making labour of what we call modern "stream of consciousness" writing has fallen to the reader. Based in part upon the psychology and epistemology of, among others, William James and G. E. Moore, this fiction constitutes an attempt to render psychic processes rather than empirical products. If the novel is to be concerned with consciousness, it must deal with epistemological issues which in turn are likely to condition aesthetic realization.[15] The writers we are considering felt that the break with the static literary code of nineteenth-century realism had to be deliberate and often they chose to do it overtly, textually, self-consciously. The self-involved experimentation and parody of *Jacob's Room*, for example, seems paradigmatic of the form that fiction appears to take each time a change in the concept of novelistic realism develops. In it, Virginia Woolf concerns herself dialectically with both the processes of consciousness in their relativity and flux, and the empirical objects of that consciousness.

To move from these general psychic processes to the particular creative ones involved in the manufacture of a fictive universe was a natural step for writers such as Proust, Pirandello, O'Brien, and Gide. Their writing narrators added this dimension to the Romantic tradition of the *Künstlerroman*. Their diegetic or narrative self-consciousness was matched by the linguistic awareness of works produced by writers such as Italo Svevo.

What, then, is the difference between this type of auto-representation and what has here been named *modern* metafiction? It is not a matter of date, for William Saroyan's self-consciousness is in the

13 *Journal* (Paris: Gallimard, 1927), p. 45 and *Les Faux-monnayeurs* ([Paris]: Gallimard, 1925), p. 255.
14 See *Journal*, p. 74: "chaque nouveau chapitre doit poser un nouveau problème, être une ouverture, une direction, une impulsion, une jetée en avant→de l'esprit du lecteur."
15 See S. P. Rosenbaum, "The Philosophical Realism of Virginia Woolf," in S. P. Rosenbaum (ed.), *English Literature and British Philosophy* (Chicago: University of Chicago Press, 1971), pp. 316−56; and also Claudio Guillén, "On the Concept and Metaphor of Perspective," in *Literature as System* (Princeton: Princeton University Press, 1971), p. 310 on Cervantes.

service of traditional realism in stories such as "Seventy Thousand Assyrians" or "Myself Upon the Earth," and it is not quite what has here been called overt narcissism; nor is the even more recent Gidian parody of Milan Kundera's *Život je jinde (Life Is Elsewhere)*. One difference seems to lie in the role allotted to the reader. In its concern about writers and about novels, the "expressionistic" novel focuses on its own idea;[16] the main interest is in the *writing* process and its product. In both the covert and overt forms of metafictional narcissism, this focus does not *shift*, so much as *broaden*, to include a parallel process of equal importance to the text's actualization—that of *reading*. The reader is explicitly or implicitly forced to face his responsibility toward the text, that is, toward the novelistic world he is creating through the accumulated fictive referents of literary language. As the novelist actualizes the world of his imagination through words, so the reader—from those same words—manufactures in reverse a literary universe that is as much his creation as it is the novelist's. This near equation of the acts of reading and writing is one of the concerns that sets modern metafiction apart from previous novelistic self-consciousness.

It is certainly true that from its origins the novel has displayed an interest in *moulding* its reader, but few earlier texts will grant or demand of the reader, his *freedom*. Tristram Shandy constantly worries about his reader's qualifications and needs. In *Tom Jones*, it is almost as if the reader's primary relationship were meant to be with the guiding narrator-writer, rather than with the characters. Rovani and Manzoni chide their female readers; Diderot is quite amusingly rude to his presumed impatient readers. The epistolary novel form, in general, explicitly places the reader as letter reader within the structure of the novel, a convention neatly parodied by Gide in *Les Faux-monnayeurs*: everyone in that novel reads the letters and journals of others, forestalling and defamiliarizing many possible reader responses *en route*.

This earlier kind of thematizing and structuralizing of the reading role is close to that of overt narcissism, but without the necessary mirroring (the reflecting, as of mirrors, in reverse) of the reading process in that of writing. For instance, in *Uno, nessuno, e centomila*, Pirandello's narrator addresses the reader as if in a soliloquy, bringing him almost onto the stage, as if to invite (but fail at) dialogue. The crisis in human relations that is dramatized in the novel through the *characters*, is also presented, through the *reader*, in the form and structure, but the parallelism of the acts of writing and reading is not suggested by Pirandello. Often, as in Gide's *Symphonie pastorale*, the narrator can learn from the act of reading the text he himself has written, but in the Gidian case at least, there is not really a mirroring of the two processes, but rather a thematized recognition of the consequences of causal and

16 Murray Baumgarten, "From Realism to Expressionism: Toward a History of the Novel," *New Literary History* 6 (Winter 1975), 418.

temporal sequence. Metafiction, however, seems aware of the fact that it (like all fiction, of course) actually has *no* existence apart from that constituted by the inward act of reading which counterpoints the externalized act of writing.

In the overt form of narcissism, several techniques are employed which are compatible with Ricardou's "auto-représentation horizontale, référentielle, productrice" and also with the "auto-représentation verticale, ascendante, productrice" — that is to say, the use of *mise en abyme*, allegory, metaphor, microcosm to shift the focus from the "fiction" to the "narration" by either making the "narration" into the very substance of the novel's content, or by undermining the traditional coherence of the "fiction" itself, in the latter case.

The distinction between the two modes of narcissism within this overt form is necessary at this stage. In the diegetic mode, the reader is made aware of the fact that he too, in reading, is actively creating a fictional universe. Often a parodied, backgrounded narrative code will guide his awareness of this fact. In *The French Lieutenant's Woman*, for instance, Fowles's freedom-granting core plot involving Sarah and Charles is an allegory of the freedom granted the reader, the thematized reader, by another character, the narrator. John Barth's whole novel, *The Floating Opera*, is a macro-structure of his hero's use of "Adam's Original and Unparalleled 'Ocean-Going' Floating Opera" as a correlative for his own storytelling processes. Todd Andrews imagines too the viewers watching parts of a continuous play as this boat drifts along the river, and having to fill in the parts they miss with the aid of their own imaginations. This image of the experience of both living life and reading texts is further mirrored in the ironic *mise en abyme* of Todd's futile attempts at boat-building and also "Inquiry" writing. The original ending of the novel, restored in the 1967 reissue, added yet another fun-house mirror: the show aboard the "Opera" begins with Hamlet's soliloquy and ends with the "Great Steamboat Explosion." Meanwhile, Todd was to commit suicide ("To be, or not to be"), destroying the boat by an explosion in the process — and ending the reading of the novel, a no longer floating *Opera*.

Other overtly diegetic narcissistic texts, such as Coover's "The Magic Poker," are also explicitly aware of their status as literary artifacts, of their narrative and world-creating processes, and of the necessary presence of the reader: "perhaps tomorrow I will invent Chicago and Jesus Christ and the history of the moon. Just as I have invented you, dear reader, while lying here in the afternoon sun."[17] However, the second mode within this form, the linguistic, operates self-consciously at a somewhat more basic stage. In diegetic narcissism, the text displays itself as narrative, as the gradual building of a fictive universe complete with character and action. In the linguistic mode, however, the text

17 *Pricksongs and Descants* (New York: New American Library, 1969), p. 40.

would actually show its building blocks—the very language whose referents serve to construct that imaginative world. That these referents are fictive and not real is assured by the generic code instituted by the word "novel" on the cover. Mailer's *Armies of the Night* is deliberately schizoid for this reason: it is subtitled both "the novel as history" and "history as a novel." Some linguistic referents in the text will be functional in building up plot and character; others may seem gratuitous but will actually operate towards the creation of what Barthes has called an "effet de réel."[18] One need only regard a fragment of a text such as John Hawkes's "Charivari" to see what might happen if a shared mimetic contract were not explicitly established with the reader: "This was the day when the end of May joined the beginning of December. Sleigh runners cut through trembling grass, fires burned in the white streets and the Maypole dancers of early spring were carolers under lantern light."[19] But even here the reader works to unite the contradicting referents, to balance them neatly into oppositions, as if the dislocation of language brings out the meaning-maker in man.

In order to comprehend the language of fiction, the reader must share with the writer certain recognizable codes—social, literary, linguistic, etc. Many texts thematize, through the characters and plot, the inadequacy of language in conveying feeling, in communicating thought, or even fact. Often this theme is introduced as an allegory of the frustration of the writer when faced with the need to present, only through language, a world of his making that must be actualized through the act of reading: Hilary Burd is not the only "word child" of Iris Murdoch's novel of that name. Other texts, on the other hand, thematize the overwhelming power and potency of words, their ability to create a world more real than the empirical one of our experience. Paolo Volponi's *La macchina mondiale* is only one instance of this quite common variety of overt linguistic narcissism.

In both the linguistic and diegetic modes the focus is as much on the creative processes of the reader as it is on those of the writer: "Reader . . . we have roles to play, thou and I: you are the doctor (washing your hands between hours), and I, I am, I think, the nervous dreary patient. I am free associating, brilliantly, brilliantly, to put you into the problem. Or for fear of boring you: which?"[20] Overtly narcissistic novels place fictionality, structure, or language at their content's core. They play with different ways of ordering, and allow (or force) the reader to learn how he makes sense of this literary world (if not his own real one). Such texts are not outside the mimetic code. Twentieth-century realism allows for a mimesis of dynamic process, as well as static

18 "L'Effet de réel," *Communications*, no. 11 (1968), 84–89.
19 *Lunar Landscapes* (New York: New Directions, 1963), p. 96.
20 Donald Barthelme, "Florence Green Is 81," in *Come Back, Dr. Caligari* (1961; reprinted, Boston: Little, Brown and Co., 1964), p. 4.

product, or object. And it is not the rise of structuralism that has brought this about, as some feel,[21] but rather metafiction or fiction itself. Critical theory may influence art but in this case the literary tradition of novelistic development seems the more likely general force.

What has *always* been a truism of fiction, though rarely made conscious, is brought to the fore in modern texts: the making of fictive worlds and the constructive, creative functioning of language itself are now self-consciously shared by author and reader. The latter is no longer asked merely to recognize that fictional objects are "like life"; he is asked to participate in the creation of worlds and of meaning, through language. He cannot avoid this call to action for he is caught in that paradoxical position of being forced by the text to acknowledge the fictionality of the world he too is creating, yet his very participation involves him intellectually, creatively, and perhaps even affectively in a human act that is very real, that is, in fact, a kind of metaphor of his daily efforts to "make sense" of experience.

Morelli, the novelist figure of Cortazar's *Rayuela (Hopscotch)*, considers the possible new role of the reader (one that Sanguineti also presents in *Il giuoco dell'oca*): "that of making an accomplice of [him], a travelling companion. Simultaneanize him, provided that the reading will abolish reader's time and substitute author's time. Thus the reader would be able to become a coparticipant and cosufferer of the experience through which the novelist is passing, *at the same moment and in the same form*."[22] The reader and writer are engaged in acts which are parallel, if reversed in direction, for both make fictive worlds in and through the actual functioning of language. This is the responsibility, the almost existentialist freedom in responsibility, that metafiction offers and requires of the reader. This is a freedom which operates inside, of course, the bounds of that internalized grammar or code that genre expectations establish. In overtly narcissistic texts, the emphasis is upon bringing both this liberty and this duty to the reader's attention. In the covert form, however, it is assumed that he knows his duty and will respond accordingly. The stress alters subtly from the teaching of the thematized reader to the actualized act of reading in progress.

Texts which are considered overtly narcissistic are usually still admitted, even by the most negative of "Ovidian" critics, to be novels, although no doubt debilitating forms of a moribund genre. Perhaps this is because of their link with the tradition of novelistic self-consciousness dating back to Cervantes and Sterne. To most, however, covert narcissism presents graver doubts. Has Narcissus now died by the pool, lured

21 Jonathan Culler, *Structuralist Poetics*, p. 238.
22 *Hopscotch*, trans. Gregory Rabassa (New York: Random House, 1966), p. 397, his italics.

by his own reflection? Just as overt narcissism forces a consideration of the origin and "newness" of metafictional technique, so any discussion of this covert form of literary introversion raises the other important question, that of the outer limits of the novel as a narrative mimetic genre. How far can auto-representation go before it becomes non- or anti-representation? In order to answer this the two different modes of covert narcissism must be examined.

On this covert level, the self-reflection is implicit; that is to say, it is structuralized, internalized within the text. As a result, it is not necessarily self-conscious. This alters the form it takes and the form of the analysis. Since Ricardou does not separate the diegetic and the linguistic modes, he would probably have to group both of these under his category of "auto-représentation horizontale, littérale, productrice," for they both operate on the level of his "narration." Since the reader is not usually addressed directly here as he might be in the overt form, it is more difficult to generalize concerning the various shapes these two covert modes might adopt. However, one possible approach would be to take note of recurring structural models found internalized in this kind of metafiction.

On the diegetic level there are many models, or what might be termed paradigms, that are discernible. Among these are the following: 1) *The detective story* (the written plot and the plot to kill).[23] Based on the general pattern of the puzzle or the enigma, this literary form is itself a very self-conscious one: in fact, the reader of a murder mystery comes to *expect* the presence of a detective-story writer within the story itself, be it in Agatha Christie (*The Pale Horse* and many others) or Dorothy Sayers (the Harriet Vane stories). There is almost inevitably within the novel also a conversation about how such events as are then under discussion occur in detective stories but never in real life (that is, in that novel). John Fowles parodies this convention to metafictional ends in his recent story "The Enigma"—as Mike, the police detective, and Isobel discuss the case he is trying to solve and decide that it, unlike this story, has committed "the terrible literary crime of not sticking to the rules."[24] The murder mystery plot also has extremely strong and obvious structural conventions. There is a crime; it will be solved because of both the characters' psychological consistency and the detective's slightly superior powers. The incriminating evidence is within the text; some details might seem in the end irrelevant to the plot, but they are all functional, even if only in leading the reader astray. However, the cerebral intellectual triumphs of a Sherlock Holmes or a Nero Wolfe, who logically interpret the clues and discover the solution to the enig-

23 In Thomas Pynchon's *V.*, one of the characters, Herbert Stencil, has the function of plot-building, linking, connecting. But here, the plot-making instinct reveals itself as *paranoia*, perhaps another structural metaphor for diegetic narcissism.
24 *The Ebony Tower* (Boston: Little, Brown, 1974), p. 239.

mas, are in effect the reader's triumphs. Agatha Christie even parodies this as Miss Marple and the reader *both* spend the first third of her novel, *Nemesis*, trying to discover just what crime has indeed been committed and how Miss Marple is to right the subsequent wrong. The hermeneutic gaps of such fiction are explicitly made textually functional. Yet, is this not true of all reading, all attempts to discover meaning, unravel plots—be they of a novel or a murder, or both? The presence of what might be called "mystery modes" (generic self-consciousness, a deliberate hermeneutic model of reading) in the internalized parodic use of the detective-story structure of writers such as Borges and Robbe-Grillet qualifies them as writers of this particular covert kind of narcissism in which the reading orientation is so important. Other such authors will be discussed in Chapter Five. 2) *Fantasy.* Covert narcissistic texts share with all fantasy literature the ability to force the reader (not overtly *ask* him) to create a fictive imaginative world separate from the empirical one in which he lives. Tolkien's Middle Earth (like, of course, Homer's Troy, Milton's Eden, or Fowles's Victorian England) is as real to the reader as his own world, but it is different, other, a creation of his imagination. Whereas in overt narcissism the reader is explicitly told that what he is reading is imaginary, that the referents of the text's language are fictive, in fantasy (and the covert forms of narcissism for which it acts as model) the fictiveness of the referents is axiomatic. Fantasy literature must create new self-sufficient worlds, but has at its disposal only the language of this one. All writers of fiction create symbolic constructs or fictive worlds; but all writers of fantasy have to make their autonomous worlds sufficiently representational to be acceptable to the reader. As Tzvetan Todorov has explained, fantasy literature is a hesitation or compromise between the empirically real and the totally imaginary.[25] The fact that *all* writers must impose their fictive worlds on the reader's imagination by sheer presence through language, is an insight displayed openly in metafiction. In fact, it is a knowledge of the axiomatic imaginary character of the literary worlds of *both* fantasy *and* covertly narcissistic texts based on this model that is required during the productive act of reading García Márquez's *Cien Años de Soledad* or Giorgio Manganelli's "Un Re." 3) *Game Structure.* At the Cerisy conference of 1971, Robbe-Grillet claimed that all his work was an attempt to bring to light the structures of "jeu" and the ideology that its gratuity entails.[26] The *nouveaux romanciers* have certainly been the most outspoken in their use of the game model. In their fiction, the concept of codes, or of rules, known and followed in the acts of writing and reading (and which become ends unto themselves) can be found. The following of these rules,

25 *Introduction à la littérature fantastique* (Paris: Seuil, 1970), p. 29.
26 *Nouveau Roman: hier, aujourd'hui 1* (Paris: Union Générale d'Editions, 10/18, 1972), 127.

which places the emphasis on the process being enacted and not the product finally attained, can also be seen, however, as a demand made on the reader by the narcissistic use of the actualized game model in general. This is true in texts which differ radically in effect: from the baseball game structure of Robert Coover's *The Universal Baseball Association, Inc. J. Henry Waugh, Prop.* to Sollers' chess board in *Drame* to Sanguineti's more explicit dice shooting by the reader in order to arrange the 111 parts of *Il giuoco dell'oca*. In the latter instance, the reader's work and pleasure in combining and creating unities and making meaning through the gratuitous codes of the dice game are intended (according to Sanguineti's comments on the back cover of the 1967 Feltrinelli edition) to allow the reader to enjoy the same creative processes as those in which the writer had originally indulged. This shared parallel process is central to the interest of all texts that employ this model. 4) *The Erotic.* All fictional texts attempt to tantalize, to seduce the reader. As Roland Barthes has suggested in both *S/Z* and the more recent *Le Plaisir du texte*, they also seek to escape the desired possession. The essentially erotic relationship of text and reader or of writer and reader is one of the overtly thematized subjects of John Barth's *Chimera*. But the erotic model can be actualized covertly as well. The act of reading becomes both literally sensual and metaphorically sexual in its process of uniting "all the polarities" in Leonard Cohen's *Beautiful Losers*. The ironic resolution of image polarities and of narrative tensions in the reading of this novel mirrors inversely the deliberate lack of such solutions in the erotic structure of the fictional world of Edith, F., Catherine Tekakwitha, and the narrator, leaving the reader as the ultimate paradoxically beautiful loser. In *Willie Masters' Lonesome Wife*, William Gass compares the loneliness of writing to that of sexual encounter. His "heroine" also invents worlds (and parodies existing literary ones) during intercourse; she sees herself in Beckettian terms as "imagination imagining itself imagine." Hélène Cixous' *Tombe* presents the act of writing as an erotic activity—sperm as ink, phallus as pen, sheets as paper, bed (*lit*) as book (*livre*). (The actual basis, however, of this narrative structure turns out to be a linguistic play—*le lierre: l'hier, lit/erre, lit/hier*.)

These four diegetic models are not intended as exclusive and complete, but only as four already observed models or metaphoric patterns that are structurally internalized in self-reflective texts. A case, for example, could probably be made for just one general category—of a "system" model—to include also such works as Pynchon's *The Crying of Lot 49* and *V*. Similarly one might advance a paradigm of "parody": John Fowles structures *The Collector* on a double ironic parody of the fiction of the "angry young men" and of Shakespeare's *The Tempest*. However, as this structuring principle is also revealed thematically and explicitly (in the names of characters; in *their* realization of the literary

parallels), it would seem best to categorize the parodic model as a generally overt form of narcissism, self-conscious as much as self-reflecting.

The only type of narcissistic text left to be considered is the covertly linguistic variety. Here part of Ricardou's intradimensional (at the level of "narration") auto-representation category ("horizontale, littérale, productrice") comes into play. The models here are less easily discussed in generalized non-textual terms. One, however, would be the riddle or joke, a form which directs the reader's attention to language itself, to its potential for semantic duplicity. Language can both convey and conceal meaning. Other generative models are the pun and the anagram. Saussure felt that anagrammatic play existed in early Latin and Greek texts (for perhaps ritualistic or mnemonic reasons).[27] Such linguistic play can be found too in Hugo ("Gal, amant de la reine, alla, tour magnanime" yielding "Gallamant de l'arène à la Tour Magne, à Nîmes") and in Jules Verne's *La Jangada* or *Bourses de voyage* ("Rosam angelum letorum" yields "Rose a mangé l'omelette au rhum"). But rarely before the "textes de jeunesse" of Raymond Roussel did anagrammatic play function as the sole forming model of the "fiction." (In his later novels, however, this functioning is hidden to the reader and so becomes cryptogrammatic.) Metafictional texts such as Alejo Carpentier's "El Camino de Santiago" find their narrative structure in a punning or anagrammatic word play inherent in the linguistic logic of the text and title.

Joyce's foregrounding of language in *Finnegans Wake* is perhaps the real forbear of the *nouveau nouveau romancier*'s creation of "fiction" in the space between words. In the early Roussel, language begets language which begets a verisimilar narrative "fiction." In Joyce, as in Ricardou, language begets language which *is* the "fiction." The difficulty in reading these texts bears witness to the increased demands made on the reader. The creative dynamism and the delight in infinite interpretative possibilities that once were the property of the writer are now shared by the reader in the process of concretizing the text he is reading. In overt narcissism this new role is taught; it is thematized. In the covert form, it is actualized.

This mirroring in reverse of the creative process again raises the important issue regarding the limits of the novel genre. At what stage does auto-representation become anti-representation? Does Narcissus drown at this stage? Is the novel dead when the reader actually becomes a writer, or "producer"? Is it dead when ideological demands convert novels into "texts"? There does appear to be a definite feeling on the part of those writers directly involved that the anti-representational "textes" of *Tel Quel*, for instance, constitute an entirely

27 See Jean Starobinski, *Les Mots sous les mots: les anagrammes de Ferdinand de Saussure* ([Paris]: Gallimard, 1971).

different form from the *nouveau nouveau roman*'s auto-representation.[28] In the latter, to use Ricardou's terminology, the inner linguistic mirrors are not destructive, but rather the doubling forms the "fiction" itself; the objective is unification, not disruption. Representation is not annulled but turned in on itself, and the "narration" invades and pervades the "fiction."

While extreme forms of this invasion—the devastation of the "fiction"—would signal the destruction of the novel, there does seem to be room still, within the genre, for a movement toward a more productive, active concept of reading, as well as writing. The decentralizing of the traditional realistic interest of fiction, away from the story told to the story telling, to the functioning of language and of larger diegetic structures, is important to the *nouveau nouveau roman*. Language becomes material with which to work, the object of certain transforming operations which give it meaning. There is a self-conscious recognition of the multiple contextual significances yielded by textual selection and organization. As such, this "new new novel" can remain within the novel genre, since these are the very operations or processes that form the link between reading and writing—that is, between life and art, reality and fiction—that seems to be a minimal requirement for a mimetic genre. Metafictionist John Barth has recently stated this same life/art connection in typically lively terms: "Of course form can be passionate; language itself can be passionate. These are not the passions of the viscera, but that doesn't give them second-class citizenship in the republic of the passions."[29]

28 See *Nouveau Roman: hier, aujourd'hui* 2, 348 (Robbe-Grillet and Ricardou on Sollers) and Thibaudeau's remarks in Michel Foucault (directeur), "Débat sur le roman," *Tel Quel* 17 (Printemps 1964), 25–26.
29 In "Hawkes and Barth Talk about Fiction," *New York Times Book Review*, April 1, 1979, p. 32.

Process and Product: The Implications of Metafiction for the Theory of the Novel as a Mimetic Genre

The novel is an invention, something that is made; it is not the expression of "self"; it does not mirror reality. If it is any good at all it mirrors the process of the real, but, being selective, makes a form that allows us to see these processes with clarity.

Gilbert Sorrentino

This study of the forms and implications of metafiction is obviously guided by sustained reference to certain central arguments—that of the parallels drawn by self-conscious texts themselves between the acts of writing and reading, that of the subsequent paradox of the reader (drawn into yet out of the text), that of the responsibility of freedom demanded of the reader. Another issue which was raised earlier and which will be the focus of these pages is that of the difference between what has been called mimesis of process and mimesis of product.

As Claudio Guillén has noted: "The exceptional formal qualities of the verbal work of art appear less remote if only one views poetic 'form' (the achievement of the writer as maker or 'poet') as both a product and a creative process underlying this product—as form-making, that is, or formation; and a cultural structure, in a dynamic sense too, as structuration."[1] Literary history suggests that new critical languages are necessarily developed in order to come to terms with new literary forms. In the case of narrative, this sequence has probably never been more clearly demonstrable than it is at present: the time-honoured critical equation between the novel and nineteenth-century concepts of "realism" is being challenged, assaulted by these ever more self-reflecting metafictions. In order not to displace this literary challenge by attributing it, as is tempting and likely even valid, to yet another of those philosophical, ideological, or scientific redefinitions of the

1 "Introduction" to *Literature as System: Essays Toward the Theory of Literary History* (Princeton: Princeton University Press, 1971), p. 12.

"real,"[2] one might begin by accepting as an axiom the fact that one is dealing here with a methodological problem of *literary* history, and attempt to find solutions within these terms of reference.

This self-conscious variety of narrative appears to be an international phenomenon; it is discernible in the works of the French *nouveaux romanciers*, in those of the Italian *Gruppo 63*, and individual writers from Barth to Borges, from Cohen to Coover, from John Fowles to Julio Cortazar. This is not to say that this operation is new in literature.[3] Shelley's analogy of the Aeolian lyre for the poetic mind was also, of course, the subject of poetic discourse. Nor is the dual interest in the storytelling as well as the story told new to the novel genre, as *Tristram Shandy* bears witness. ("I have a strong propensity in me to begin this chapter [1, 23] very nonsensically, and I will not baulk my fancy.") Nor are those increased demands made on the reader really new, as Wolfgang Iser's *The Implied Reader* (Baltimore: The Johns Hopkins Press, 1974) has revealed. Reading and writing are both active, creative exercises and always have been; it is perhaps merely the degree of self-consciousness regarding their quasi-parallel natures that has increased. In metafiction the reader or the act of reading itself often become thematized parts of the narrative situation, *acknowledged* as having a co-producing function.

In the light of such fiction, it is not surprising to discover an increased critical interest in reader aesthetics. Some of these theories will be examined in a later chapter. Yet, the largely negative reviews of much new metafiction on the basis of its being the death of the novel, solipsistic, and self-destructive, not to say "unrealistic," might suggest that certain of the categories of novel criticism are being revealed as inadequate. The generally accepted concept of novelistic realism which is, in essence, only a period-description, would seem to have been reified and extended beyond its critical range in an attempt to encompass all fiction.

Such a generalization fails to do justice, not only to modern metafiction, but to the novel genre as a whole. It ignores that one fact that is worth keeping in mind at all times—that *Don Quijote* is one of the first of

2 Cf. Robert Scholes, "On Realism and Genre," *Novel* 2 (Spring 1969), 269: "It seems to me that the whole phenomenon known as realism has been governed for some centuries by empirical assumptions and attitudes about the nature of reality, and that these assumptions are now beginning to lose their force just as the theological assumptions that governed what Auerbach called 'figural realism' lost their force with the waning of the Middle Ages. We are at an ideological watershed . . . [and] I believe I see in the writers I have called fabulators the way toward a new reality." See also Murray Baumgarten, "From Realism to Expressionism: Toward a History of the Novel," *New Literary History* 6 (Winter 1975), 416 on the epistemological and ontological realms in narrative.

3 See Stanley E. Fish, *Self-Consuming Artifacts: The Experience of Seventeenth-Century Literature* (Berkeley: University of California Press, 1972) and *Surprised by Sin: The Reader in* Paradise Lost (London: Macmillan, 1967).

the self-informing fictions that thematize the power, the consequences, and the very workings of both the creative imagination and the language of literature.[4] What Ian Watt, in *The Rise of the Novel* (London: Chatto & Windus, 1957), calls the "realism of presentation" of the eighteenth-century English novel of Richardson and Defoe, is actually coeval with the equally potent "realism of assessment" of Fielding and Sterne.

In fact, there would seem to be considerable evidence to suggest that the parodic, self-reflective nature of many of these early narrative works is paradigmatic. In Chapter One, it was suggested that the key to the novel's origins and development might well lie in parody, in the unmasking of dead *literary* conventions and the establishing of new *literary* codes. As Robert Coover writes in his dedication to Cervantes in "Seven Exemplary Fictions," Cervantes' parodies gave birth to the novel and were "exemplars of a revolution in narrative fiction, a revolution which governs us—not unlike the way you found yourself abused by the conventions of the Romance—to this very day."[5] In this light perhaps nineteenth-century French or eighteenth-century English "realism" was not so much the epitome of the novelistic mode, as a stage in the genre's development, a stage containing within itself the contesting seeds of its own transcendence. Even *Madame Bovary* can be, and has been,[6] read as an attack on this very concept of "realism," as an allegory of the power of language and literature. Emma is the naïve realist who, like Don Quijote, believes that words in books refer directly to reality, to experiences "out there" waiting for her.

Yet, the history of novel criticism demonstrates that, while the novel *form* developed further, its *theories* froze in time somewhere in the last century. What was a temporary stage in literature became a fixed definition in criticism. From this point on, any form which revealed a moving beyond that stage could only be dealt with in negative terms (as not really a novel, or at best as a *new* novel or perhaps as a *meta*fiction), rather than being treated in terms of a natural, dialectical development of the genre, as the backgrounded traditions parodied in such forms themselves proposed.

One of the reasons why this kind of fiction has been refused entry to the ranks of the genre seems to be that the theoretical basis of "traditional realism" is what could be called a mimesis of *product*. The reader is required to identify the products being imitated—characters, actions, settings—and recognize their similarity to those in empirical reality, in order to validate their literary worth. Since no codes, no conventions for this procedure are acknowledged, the act of reading is

4 Cf. Michel Foucault, *Les Mots et les choses* (Paris: Gallimard, 1966), p. 62, and Marthe Robert, *Roman des origines et origines du roman* (Paris: B. Grasset, 1972), p. 11.

5 *Pricksongs and Descants* (New York: Dutton, 1969), p. 77.

6 See Leo Bersani's *Balzac to Beckett* (New York: Oxford University Press, 1970).

seen in passive terms. Metafictions, on the contrary, bare the conventions, disrupt the codes that now *have* to be acknowledged. The reader must accept responsibility for the act of decoding, the act of reading. Disturbed, defied, forced out of his complacency, he must self-consciously establish new codes in order to come to terms with new literary phenomena. Since product mimesis alone does not suffice to account for the new functions of the reader as they are thematized in the texts themselves, a mimesis of *process* must perhaps be postulated. The novel no longer seeks just to provide an order and meaning to be recognized by the reader. It now demands that he be conscious of the work, the actual construction, that he too is undertaking, for it is the reader who, in Ingarden's terms, "concretizes"[7] the work of art and gives it life.

The act of reading, then, is itself, like the act of writing, the creative function to which the text draws attention. That this process is now the object of imitation does not alter the essential nature of the novel as a mimetic genre. Metafiction is still fiction, despite the shift in focus of narration from the product it presents to the process it is. Auto-representation is still representation. *All* art has always been what Claudio Guillén calls "an inorganic entity or process endowed with formal qualities and expressive virtualities and thus capable of stimulating in turn a kind of experience that is vital (that is 'life' too)."[8]

Art as mimesis: classical rhetoric granted a certain liberty to the imitators of nature by sanctioning deviations for purposes of instruction or delight. Sidney argued that the poet teaches best because he creates *another* nature, a "heterocosm." Addison's papers on "The Pleasures of the Imagination" paved the way for the non-instrumental Romantic theories of creative autonomy. Within this tradition, the rigidly mimetic theories of "novelistic realism" in eighteenth-century England and nineteenth-century France almost seem reactionary, especially in the light of the freedom and autonomy sought by Cervantes, Sterne, Diderot, and many other early novelists.

Modern metafiction which thematizes its own fiction-making processes signals a contesting of "realism" of this kind. Perhaps it even means a return to what might be considered the mainstream of a tradition of narrative freedom, for it embodies its own theories, demands to be taken on its own terms. The course of literary history is being altered, and, as always, it is being altered by the texts, not the critics. In fact, this new narcissistic fiction is allowing (is forcing?) a re-evaluation of the novels of the past, thanks to its challenging of the inadequate, reified critical notion of "realism" based on a narrow product mimesis alone.

7 *The Literary Work of Art* (Evanston: Northwestern University Press, 1973), p. 352.
8 "The Aesthetics of Literary Influence," *Literature as System*, p. 28.

"The history of the novel," according to Frank Kermode, "is the history of forms rejected or modified, by parody, manifesto, neglect as absurd."[9] If so, why has novel criticism faltered? Why have the "truth to life," the documentation—in short, the (unacknowledged) conventions—of a particular kind of fiction at a particular stage of the development of narrative (the French novel of, say, Champfleury's 1857 *Le Réalisme*), been extended from being parts of a period-description, and been permitted to take over, and indeed to tyrannize the definition of an entire genre?

It could probably even be argued that, in a larger narrative perspective, this so-called "realism" is more an aberration than a norm. Autoreferentiality can be traced back, beyond *Don Quijote* and *Tristram Shandy*, to the epic practice of having a character relate part of his own tale (e.g., Ulysses in the *Odyssey* 9–12) in order to give the illusion of taking attention away from the Homeric voice and to create a *mise en abyme* structure.[10] Actually what happens in this case is that the narrating becomes an *act* like any other within the fiction, a mirroring on a minor scale of the epic narration. The content has expanded to include diegesis or the process of narration itself. This would suggest that a concept of mimesis of process is a constant in literature, and not just a new critical need. The modern diegetic preoccupation may only differ in its explicitness and theoretical self-consciousness within the novels themselves.

Some distinction between the two kinds of mimesis—product and process—does seem desirable, especially because product mimesis, when petrified into a limiting concept of "realism," becomes exclusive and denies the validity of *any* process orientation. Even Aristotelian mimetic theory, essentially objectivist in nature, allowed room for the imitation of creative process, since art was perceived as an active rival of the ordered and ordering processes of nature itself, as the act of creating a totality through a harmonious design to a logical end.

In classical theories of mimesis it is clear that mimetic art involves the creation of a fictive illusion which only simulates a reality. In antiquity, this notion of recognized fictionality was not used to negate ties between the literary and the empirical. It is, nevertheless, difficult today to dismiss the negative connotations of the word "imitation"—artificial, sham, inauthentic—which suggest a lower ontological status: art is inferior to the "life" it copies, and draws any value it has from its proximity to that "life." Yet both Plato and Aristotle were aware of the power and validity of art as mimesis, both in itself and as a force for the education and the shaping of man. In the *Poetics*, Aristotle underplays Plato's distinction between drama and narration (*mimētikon* and

9 *The Sense of an Ending* (1966; reprinted, New York: Oxford University Press, 1970), pp. 129–30.

10 See Gérard Genette, *Figures* 3 (Paris: Seuil, 1972), 241ff.

diēgēmatikon), treating both as forms of a general imitation, in a way that corresponds roughly to the suggested use here of the terms product and process.

What exponents of "traditional realism" ignored, when they turned to classical mimetic theory for support, was that the instinct to imitate is complemented, in the *Poetics*, by an equally strong impulse toward ordering (7: 2 and 4). Aesthetic imitation involves the completed and harmonized integration of parts into an organic whole (8: 4), even if such parts should involve the irrational (24: 10) or the impossible (25: 5). Mimesis is never limited to a naïve copying at the level of product alone.

Yet, as M. H. Abrams has shown at length in his famous analysis of the mirror archetype in *The Mirror and the Lamp* (New York: Oxford University Press, 1953), the mimetic concept of art in criticism after Plato and Aristotle did become restricted, concentrating on product, on the relation of subject matter to empirical reality and truth. It is to *this* general critical tradition and *not* to the natural line of novelistic development in particular that the concept of "traditional realism" as a genre (rather than period) description would seem to belong. In demanding recognition of diegesis or narrative process as part of mimesis, metafiction is in a sense demanding a reworking of the Aristotelian theory. It is not that the emphasis has shifted *from* mimesis *to* the creating imagination, but rather that the critical terms in which we discuss that which is imitated in fiction must be opened again to make room for the new novels being written and read.

Poiesis, the act of making, forms one necessary addition to the novelistic mimetic code, as a process shared by writer and reader. Harold Rosenberg's observation about the visual arts holds true for literature as well: "for all the modernist passion for denuding things of their mystery, art has been unable to relinquish its affinity with man's most mysterious power, and his most precious one: I mean, the power of creation."[11] Now it is the *reader* who is being forced to acknowledge his active creative role.

Of course, he has *always* been the one to activate the latent universe of the novel or short story; metafiction merely makes this fact conscious and functional by revealing the conventions that "traditional realism" sought to conceal, or even deny. The writer has always had to try rhetorically to unite shared language and his private imaginative experience. The reader then approached that same language, bringing to it all his own experience of life, of literature, and of language, in order to accumulate enough fictive referents to bring the autonomous fictional universe into being. This has always been the case. It took, however, the diegetic and linguistic self-consciousness of a Fowles or a Borges to begin to bare this process by thematizing it within fiction

11 "Metaphysical Feelings in Modern Art," *Critical Inquiry* 2, no. 2 (Winter 1975), 218.

itself, thereby revealing that what had formerly been accepted as an unimpeachable canon of "novelistic realism" was really just another set of literary conventions.

What one comes up against, then, is a problem or a block in *literary theory*. This reification of a period-concept of "realism" need not be dealt with in philosophical, psychological, sociological, or ideological terms of reference. There also seems no need to be concerned with definitions of "truth," since the interest here is in textual validity. In his "Des différentes conceptions de la vérité dans l'oeuvre d'art,"[12] Roman Ingarden argued that the term "truth" was best limited to that logical epistemological result of knowledge. He felt that alternate terms should be selected to refer to the other seven kinds of aesthetic "truth" he isolated. The more neutral term of "validity" seems adequate here to account for both the static notion of inner cohesion and ontological autonomy of literature, and the more dynamic one of Aristotelian ordering or mutual motivation of parts of the work of art. If one's roots are in structuralism, as are Barthes',[13] the term is also useful since in the light of the Saussurian sign, the real object outside the linguistic system is not relevant; the adjustment of signified to signifier is. Inner coherence replaces inner-outer correspondence (the achievement of which is, in any case, doubtful).

As many metafictionists have assured their readers, fictional creations are as real, as valid, as "truthful," as the empirical objects of our physical world. The essence of literary language lies not in its conforming to the kind of statement found in factual studies, but in its ability to create something new — a coherent, motivated "heterocosm," or *other* world. Mimetic literature has always created illusions, not literal truths; it has always utilized conventions, no matter what it might choose to imitate — that is, to create. The familiar image of the mimetic mirror suggests too passive a process; the use of micro-macro allegorical mirroring and *mises en abyme* in metafiction contests that very image of passivity, making the mirror productive as the genetic core of the work. In such fiction the reader is made aware of the fact that literature is less a verbal object carrying some meaning, than it is his own experience of building, from the language, a coherent autonomous whole of form and content. This whole is what is meant here by the term "heterocosm." Sartre might protest the "unreal" ordering of experience that occurs in such a fictional cosmos, but as Henry James, among others,

12 *Revue d'esthétique* 2 (1949), 162–80. See also the variants of Frege's *Sinn* and *Bedeutung* distinction in John R. Searle, "The Logical Status of Fictional Discourse," *New Literary History* 6 (Winter 1975), 319–32; in Georges Lavis, "Le Texte littéraire, le référent, le réel, le vrai," *Cahiers d'analyse textuelle*, no. 13 (1971), 7–22; and in Paul Ricoeur, "The Model of the Text: Meaningful Action Considered as a Text," *Social Research* 38 (1971), 529–62, reprinted in *New Literary History* 5 (Autumn 1973), 91–117.

13 "Criticism as Language," *The Critical Moment* (London: Faber & Faber, 1963), pp. 123–29.

has explained, the selection and ordering processes are what make art valid as art. Mimesis is transmutation, not reproduction,[14] whether it be a mimesis of product or process. Diegesis is a part of mimesis, as Aristotle perceived, and so ought to be taken into account in definitions of what constitutes novelistic "realism."

There is, to be sure, no shortage of attempts to define this elusive term. Novelists explain how their particular works are "realistic"— James, Virginia Woolf, Cary, Robbe-Grillet, and so on. Psychologists, philosophers, journalists[15] add their opinions. And, of course, so do the literary critics. Often these latter, the experts, are the least helpful. The inability of many reviewers to treat the new fiction on its own terms is not a result of the outdating of concepts of mimesis and representation themselves (as Jean Ricardou has felt[16]), but rather, it results from that transfer of a period description to a genre definition which threatens to distort the entire history of the novel as a mimetic form. Ricardou has been among the most outspoken of the modern critics of this inadequacy in fiction theory:

Ce que toute une littérature moderne nous a appris de manière décisive, c'est notamment l'idée qu'en un récit, la fiction, loin de signer un quotidien quelconque, se développe selon de singulières lois spécifiques. C'est parce qu'elle diffère du quotidien qu'elle peut agir, non par une analogue illusoire. Attendre d'une fiction qu'elle cesse d'être fiction pour accueillir, tout crus, d'entiers fragments du quotidien, c'est perpétuer un vieil obscurantisme.[17]

In his earlier debate with Greenwood on the topic of "realism,"[18] René Wellek too had fought against this same dangerous reification, urging a restriction of the term "realism" (and *not*, one might note, mimesis) to the nineteenth-century European novel. He did so in order to prevent any generic reduction from denying the creative efforts of *making* a world. Such a reduction also risked endangering the novel's freedom to grow; too often "realism" became identified with truth, with the universal, or with good art in general.

The danger of such generalizing, normative definitions is easily seen. In *The Rise of the Novel*, Ian Watt uses eighteenth-century "formal realism" as a qualitative measure, as the defining characteristic of "the novel." He thereby ultimately forces himself into a position of declar-

14 See Stefan Morawski, "Mimesis," *Semiotica* 2 (1970), 35–58.
15 Respectively, for example, Jerome S. Bruner, "Art as a Mode of Knowing," *On Knowing* (New York: Atheneum, 1968), p. 73; John Casey, *The Language of Criticism* (London: Methuen, 1966), p. 64; and Tom Wolfe, "Why they aren't writing the Great American Novel anymore: A Treatise on the Varieties of Realistic Experience," *Esquire*, December 1972, pp. 152–59 and 272–80.
16 See *Nouveau Roman: hier, aujourd'hui* 1 (Paris: Union Générale d'Editions, 10/18 1972), 376 for one of many such statements.
17 *Pour une théorie du nouveau roman* (Paris: Seuil, 1971), p. 227.
18 *Neophilologus* 45 (1961), 1–20; 46 (1962), 89–97 and 194–96.

ing almost everyone but Richardson as outside the novel tradition. Even Auerbach, in *Mimesis* (Princeton: Princeton University Press, 1953), writes from the implied stance that nineteenth-century French realism is the true modern "realism"; therefore, all "realistic" attempts before Stendhal are but imperfect steps toward the true "realism," and any after, signs of its decline.[19] When "imitation of reality is imitation of the sensory experience of life on earth," as it is to Auerbach, products alone, especially in their visual and oral manifestations, will take precedence over the processes of imagining and writing. (It is interesting to signal, in this regard, the antiphonocentrism of Jacques Derrida's post-structuralism.)

It would seem to be very difficult to keep the term "realism" in a literary context and retain a fixed meaning[20] free from epistemological or ideological connotations. It is for this reason that a name change has been suggested here, a return in the terminology of novel criticism to the term *mimesis* which would, in Aristotelian terms, encompass also the diegetic. The inclusion of this latter element is important since all written narrative differs from that of the oral tradition in that the storyteller, as well as his story, is represented or imitated. (Even the epic, perhaps the closest form to our novel, was for Plato [*Republic*, 3: 393] both diegetic and mimetic, the narrating of a story which was the imitation of an action.) In the basic structure of the novel genre as a whole, the story's diegesis becomes an element in its mimesis. Early novels often thematized and integrated this process self-consciously into their very form: *Tristram Shandy, Vanity Fair, Tom Jones, Jacques le fataliste*. The presence of an authorial narrating figure served as mediator, and the act of narration oriented the reader temporally and spatially in the fictive universe.

The modern novel seems to be the literary heir, less of Richardsonian or Balzacian "realism," than of the critical awareness and diegetic self-consciousness of the eighteenth century. It is also, of course, heir to the Romantic view of the imagination and the creative act. This latter force entered fiction, as has been seen, in the *Künstlerroman*. Although there appeared to be a reaction against the Romantics and back to earlier poets at the start of this century, the same artist-critics who first brought about this revolt—Yeats, Joyce, Eliot, Pound—adopted a Romantic view of the imaginative processes, while combining critical awareness in the *act* of writing with a kind of instinctive subjective consciousness.[21]

19 See also the critiques by Wellek, "Auerbach's Special Realism," *Kenyon Review* 16 (1954), 297–307, and by David Carroll, "Mimesis Reconsidered: Literature, History, Ideology," *Diacritics* 5 (Summer 1975), 5–12.

20 See Roman Jakobson, "Du réalisme artistique" in Tzvetan Todorov (ed.), *Théorie de la littérature* (Paris: Seuil, 1965), pp. 98–108.

21 See Stephen Spender, *The Struggle of the Modern* (1963; reprinted, London: Methuen, 1965), p. 48.

In fiction, this critical awareness or self-consciousness has been more and more structurally internalized, moving from the Preface into the content, and finally into the structure of the novel itself. This movement suggests the need for a broader concept of mimesis which would enlarge the range of objects of imitation from those of the empirical world to include the problems of writing and reading. The novels about novels of the early half of the century — of Gide, Huxley, Flann O'Brien — give way increasingly to novels which thematize *and* actualize the very processes undertaken by both writer and reader.

In the light of literary history, as has been shown, self-reflecting art is not unique to the twentieth-century novel. Its forms, however, do change with the conventions of the genre and of the time, conventions which it challenges and parodies. From Diderot to Gide, the narrator-novelist's intrusion into the characters' heterocosm creates a new illusion, even as it claims to denounce the one on which the "traditional realistic" novel is based.[22] From Gide to Ricardou, the narrator-novelist gives way to the internalized act of narration itself, the process which mediates between reader and text.

This threat to rigid notions of mimesis which are limited to product alone has been effected by the novels themselves, for they contain and constitute their own critical terms of reference. That they must do so in such a deliberate manner is perhaps a comment more on the novel criticism[23] they might be seen to contest, than on the fictions themselves. They are not about "reality," but about the imaginative processes of coming to grips with it in formal aesthetic terms. If this is true, cannot all fiction be so described? Is Flaubert any less a "scripteur" than Robbe-Grillet? Perhaps the definition of this term by Ricardou might apply to earlier fiction writers as well:

l'activité de l'écrivain ne saurait se réduire à celle de ce propriétaire du sens institué qu'on appelait autrefois l'Auteur: elle est celle d'un *Scripteur*. Le scripteur n'est aucunement une neutralité idéale: rien de ce qui le situe dans la réalité, corps, travail, pensée, qui ne le concerne au plus près. Seulement, loin d'être l'objet d'une expression ou d'une représentation, cet ensemble se trouve investi, à des niveaux variés, dans un processus général de *transformation* qu'on commence à entrevoir et qui pourrait se nommer en l'occurence *inscription*. Pris de mille manières dans l'écriture, cet ensemble subit des réorganisations incessantes.[24]

Literature creates its criticism: a change in the language of novel theory was born out of the need to account for the fiction of Joyce,

22 See Jean Verrier, "Le Récit réfléchi," *Littérature* 5 (février 1972), 59–60.
23 Literary history is never static but is a process, a plurality of culturally active currents. See Claudio Guillén, "Second Thoughts on Literary Periods," *Literature as System*, pp. 465–69.
24 Jean Ricardou, "Penser la littérature aujourd'hui," *Marche romane* 21 nos. 1–2 (1971), 15–16, italics his.

Proust, Pirandello, Virginia Woolf. Discussions began to centre around the concept of "subjective realism," and usually they were based on the belief that a new epistemology, a new psychological view of reality had caused, or at least conditioned, the literary change. The proof lay, it was argued, in the manner and subject matter of the novels, as well as in the novelists' own pronouncements.

Yet, what seems equally clear, from these very same testimonies, is that what was seen as a new philosophical and psychological mode was just as much an attempt to abandon the constricting *literary* forms of "realism" and naturalism, while remaining within the bounds of a mimetic genre. Pirandello tried in his novels to free himself of the "stupidissima verosimiglianza, a cui l'arte crede suo dovere obbedire"; Virginia Woolf demanded the novel be released from the tired, constricting conventions of the outdated "realists"; in *Le Temps retrouvé*, Marcel claims that "la littérature qui se contente de 'décrire les choses' . . . est celle qui, tout en s'appelant réaliste, est la plus éloignée de la réalité."[25]

The early *nouveau roman* reveals a tension of transition between a concept of "realism" based on product mimesis alone, and that which includes process, the shared act of creating a fictive universe. Later critics (Barthes, Ricardou, Todorov, Genette) formulated in theoretical terms what the novels had already asserted — that what this fiction was imitating (that is, creating) was not any empirical world, but a view of its own linguistic and literary production. The textual mirror was turned inward and activated, as Roland Barthes explained:

bien loin d'être une copie analogique du réel, *la littérature est au contraire la conscience même de l'irréel du langage*: la littérature la plus "vraie," c'est celle qui se sait la plus irréelle, dans la mesure où elle se sait essentiellement langage, c'est cette recherche d'un état intermédiaire aux choses et aux mots, c'est cette tension d'une conscience qui est à la fois portée et limitée par les mots, qui dispose à travers eux d'un pouvoir *à la fois absolu et improbable*. Le réalisme, ici, ce ne peut donc être la copie des choses, mais la connaissance du langage; l'oeuvre la plus "réaliste" ne sera pas celle qui "peint" la réalité, mais qui, se servant du monde comme contenu . . . explorera le plus profondément possible la *réalité irréelle* du langage.[26]

The familiar categories of novel criticism — and in particular, mimesis — need not be rejected, but merely reworked. Even the most linguistically auto-representational *nouveau nouveau roman*[27] still

25 Respectively: "Avvertenza sugli scrupoli della fantasia," *Il fu Mattia Pascal* (1921; reprinted, Milano: Mondadori, 1965), p. 256; "Mr. Bennett and Mrs. Brown," *Collected Essays* 1 (London: Hogarth Press, 1966), 319-37; *A la recherche du temps perdu* 8 (Paris: Gallimard, 1954), 243.
26 Roland Barthes, "La Littérature, aujourd'hui," *Essais critiques* (Paris: Seuil, 1964), p. 164, italics his.
27 Though not the anti-representational *Tel Quel* texts which claim to be, and indeed seem to be, outside the critical categories of novel and mimesis completely.

creates, through the reader, a kind of fictional world (since novelistic language is a form of discourse and cannot escape referentiality). No matter how diegetic, metafictions remain mimetic — and "vital" — to use Claudio Guillén's term once again. Novelistic "reality" has always been fictive. It is ordered and patterned in a way that life experience rarely, if ever, is. Yet it is a paradigmatic order. One of John Barth's characters even claims that "Art is as natural an artifice as Nature; the truth of Fiction is that Fact is fantasy; the made-up story is a model of the world."[28] Narrative (diegesis, the creative process) is a natural act of the human mind, transferred from life to art.[29] What is new in modern self-conscious fiction is the acknowledged involvement of the reader who is asked, as an early statement by Robbe-Grillet claimed, to invent "à son tour l'oeuvre — et le monde — et d'apprendre ainsi à inventer sa propre vie."[30]

Novel theory which has reified "realism" and has limited mimesis to product alone has ignored the dialectical relationship that must exist between literature and criticism, a relationship that demands a reworking and possibly a transcending of the limits of any theoretical formulation which fails to come to terms with new literary forms. Reader aesthetics has been one reply to the needs of modern metafiction. A related concept of mimesis of process might be another.

The potential methodological value of the return of diegesis to mimesis lies in its allowing room for *meta*fictions, *new* novels, even *new new* novels (that is, post-Cerisy 1971), within the boundaries and terms of reference of the mimetic genre we call the novel — the narrative form born of Cervantes and Sterne, as much as of Defoe and Stendhal. There is no *literary* reason why socialist realism should be considered any more novelistic, any more mimetic, than the fantasy fictions of Borges. By claiming that it is nothing but art, nothing but imaginative creation, metafiction becomes more "vital": it reflects the human imagination, instead of telling a secondhand tale about what might be real in quite another world.

28 "Bellerophoniad," *Chimera* (New York: Random House, 1972), p. 246.
29 See Barbara Hardy, "Towards a Poetics of Fiction: 3) An Approach through Narrative," *Novel* 2 (Fall 1968), 5-14.
30 *Pour un nouveau roman* (Paris: Gallimard, 1963), p. 169.

Thematizing Narrative Artifice: Parody, Allegory, and the *Mise En Abyme*

> (1) fiction must acknowledge its, fictitiousness and metaphoric invalidity or (2) choose to ignore the question or deny its relevance or (3) establish some other acceptable relation between itself, its author, its reader.
>
> John Barth

Barbara Hardy[1] has suggested that narrative is a primary human function, one which is part of life, and which is represented overtly in the form of certain literary genres. If this is so, it would not be "unrealistic" to have novels about the actual narrative processes. Daily we create worlds[2] for ourselves — that is, ordered visions of our lives (real or fantasy); the novelist's act is basic to his human nature, as basic as his desire to imitate. *Diegesis* and *mimesis*, as was argued in Chapter Two, can indeed go together. This fact is most clearly seen in that mode and form of narrative self-consciousness which has been called overt diegetic narcissism. This is at once the most straightforward and the most instructive of the four types outlined earlier, and for this reason would warrant an extended investigation in the next two chapters.

John Barth, one of the most overt of metafictionists, has openly claimed that one way to come to terms with the generally supposed discrepancy between art and the world we live in is to affirm the artificial element in art — "you can't get rid of it anyhow"[3] — and make it part of the point of the work. Certainly, the stories in his *Lost in the Funhouse* once again provide a clear example of diegetical preoccupation in the extreme. Storytelling runs amok: the "Menelaiad" works up

1 "Towards a Poetics of Fiction: 3) An Approach through Narrative," *Novel* 2 (Fall 1968), 5–14.

2 See Marthe Robert, *Roman des origines et origines du roman* (Paris: B. Grasset, 1972), pp. 50ff. for the implications of the Freudian theory of the child's pseudo-biography.

3 Comment quoted by Gerhard Joseph, *John Barth* (Minneapolis: University of Minnesota Press, 1970), p. 8.

to seven levels of narration by section seven and then works back down to one level by the end (after seven, the section numbering also reverses to one). The reader is faced with this:

" ' " ' " ' "Speak!," Menelaus cried to Helen on the bridal bed,' I reminded Helen in her Trojan bedroom," I confessed to Eidothea on the beach,' I declared to Proteus in the cavemouth," I vouchsafed to Helen on the ship,' I told Peisistratus at last in my Spartan Hall," I say to whoever and where- I am. And Helen answered:
 " ' " ' " ' "Love!" ' " ' " ' "[4]

Needless to say, the reader's task becomes increasingly difficult and demanding, as he sorts out the various narrative threads. The universe he thus creates, he must then acknowledge as fictional and of his own making. With this latter recognition his conscious relation to the text alters. With a technique not unlike that of Brecht's alienation effect, the parody and self-reflection of narcissistic narrative work to prevent the reader's identification with any character and to force a new, more active, thinking relationship upon him. It becomes increasingly clear that, though free to interpret, the reader is also responsible for his interpretation. Alfred Appel's remarks on Nabokov and his *Ada* apply to most metafictional diegetic self-consciousness as it relates to the reader's relationship to the parodic text: "Through parody and self-parody, he exorcises the trite terms inherent in each story he chooses to tell, and by parodying the reader's conception of 'story'—his stereotyped expectations and preoccupation with 'plot' machinations—Nabokov frees him to experience a fiction intellectually, aesthetically, ecstatically."[5]

In much metafiction the reader is left with the impression that, since all fiction is a kind of parody of life, no matter how verisimilar it pretends to be, the most authentic and honest fiction might well be that which most freely acknowledges its fictionality. Distanced from the text's world in this way, the reader can share, with the author, the pleasure of its imaginative creation. In forcing recognition of a *literary* code, parody seems to be one important means to this paradoxical kind of narcissistic extramural involvement. The narrator of Nabokov's *The Real Life of Sebastian Knight* informs the reader that the novelist, Knight, "used parody as a kind of springboard for leaping into the highest region of serious emotion," and that he "was ever hunting out the things which had once been fresh and bright but which were now worn to a thread, dead things among living ones; dead things shamming life, painted and repainted."[6]

4 (Garden City, New York: Doubleday, 1968), p. 155. Later page references will be to this edition and will appear in parentheses in the text.

5 "*Ada* Described," *Tri-Quarterly* no. 17 (Winter 1970), 174.

6 (1941; reprinted, Norfolk, Connecticut: New Directions, 1959), p. 91. Later page references will be to this edition and will appear in parentheses in the text.

This is very close, of course, to a theoretical statement of the Russian formalist concept of parody, a concept that seems particularly applicable to metafiction. Parody develops out of the realization of the literary inadequacies of a certain convention. Not merely an unmasking of a non-functioning system, it is also a necessary and creative process by which new forms appear to revitalize the tradition and open up new possibilities to the artist. Parodic art both is a deviation from the norm and includes that norm within itself as backgrounded material.[7] Forms and conventions become energizing and freedom-inducing in the light of parody.

Yet critics of the new novel in France and of similarly narcissistic fiction elsewhere have seen the parodic element of overt self-consciousness as debilitating,[8] as replacing the function of literary criticism[9] itself, or as revealing the limitations, in fact, and not the strengths of imagination and creation. But to see parodic metafiction, as does Earl Rovit, for example, as "the Novel as Jig-Saw Puzzle,"[10] in terms of the piecing together of factory-cut parts, is to underrate the creative function of parody and also to presume that pieces put together anew remain the same — irrespective of context. Parodic motivation is absorbed into a new text and the pieces are reworked, re-signified. Rarely do they form what Rovit sees as "a firm and unyielding regimen of subordination" or an arbitrarily chosen, closed system or even a superimposed external order. (As Sartre once remarked, *all* ordering is fictive.) There is no reason why parody must limit itself to satirical exposure of non-literary external elements — "the false, the ugly, the affected, and the hypocritical" — especially since the parodic code as used in metafiction is both internal and literary. To claim that John Barth is prevented *by parody* from communicating his "unique metaphor of experience" is to ignore the fact that, of all writers, the vehicle, if not the tenor, of Barth's metaphor *is* parody. Like Nabokov, on whose use of parody much has been written,[11] Barth uses parodic

7 See Fredric Jameson's discussion of Tynyanov in *The Prison-House of Language* (Princeton: Princeton University Press, 1972), p. 92; and Victor Erlich, *Russian Formalism: History, Doctrine*, 2nd ed. (The Hague: Mouton, 1965), pp. 92–93, 193.

8 See, for instance, Alfred Chester, "Nabokov's Anti-Novel," *Commentary* 34 (November 1962), 449–51.

9 See Richard Poirier, "The Politics of Self Parody," *Partisan Review* 35 (Summer 1968), 339.

10 "The Novel as Parody: John Barth," *Critique* 6, no. 2 (Fall 1963), 79. The quotations following are also from this article and page.

11 A short list: Alfred Appel, Jr., "*Lolita*: The Springboard of Parody," in L. S. Dembro (ed.), *Nabokov: The Man and His Work* (Madison: University of Wisconsin Press, 1967), pp. 114–15, 124–25, 133, 135, 139; and in the same volume, John O. Lyons, "*Pale Fire* and the Fine Art of Annotation," pp. 157–64; Simon Karlinsky, "Illusion, Reality and Parody in Nabokov's Plays," pp. 183–94; Patricia Merivale, "The Flaunting of Artifice in Vladimir Nabokov and Jorge Luis Borges," pp. 218–19; and also A. Appel, Jr., "*Ada* Described," pp. 168–71, 176–81; William Woodin Rowe, *Nabokov's Deceptive World* (New York: New York University Press, 1971), pp. 21–23.

devices to point to the diegetic, fictive, literary elements of his fiction. He makes the artificial and the creation of it into the significant part of his literary universe. In the works of both of these parodists there often are characters who are aware of their status as fictional entities. Rather than limiting the range and significance of these works, this device is related to what has here been called a mimesis of process: the imaginative effort involved in creating ontological identity becomes fundamental in the text, as in life. As shall be shown shortly, in *The French Lieutenant's Woman*, identity itself — be it the reader's own or that of characters in fiction — is always an artistic construct.

This form of parody, however, is but one way of pointing to artifice. If the historical development of narrative narcissism, as outlined in the Introduction, is accepted, then it is important to note that the first full flowering of the novel genre in the eighteenth century coincides with the revival of the concept of art as an independent and unique function of life, a revival distinguished by a certain critical self-awareness.[12] In the novel this meant that frequently the content's dramatic presentation of the diegetic act became a major controlling factor in the structural, as well as in the thematic, unity of the work.

In this light, the omniscient "authorial" narration so common in the traditional novel of the next century — from Manzoni's manuscript editor to Thackeray's garrulous Master of the Puppet Show — becomes a potentially useful self-reflecting device. The presence of an "authorial" narrating figure as mediator between reader and novel world demands recognition of a subsequent narrative distance. This results in an added emphasis on diegesis, on the act of storytelling. In such fiction, the reader is temporally and spatially oriented in the fictional world by the act of narration itself; the narrating figure is the centre of internal reference.

This can also occur in a first-person narration, and especially when such a form is used parodically in metafiction. In Giuseppe Berto's *Il male oscuro* (Milano: Rizzoli, 1964), for instance, the narrator seems at first to function as would a traditional first-person narrator character who happens to be a patient under psychoanalysis. It is only later in the novel that he self-consciously admits that all he knows about analysis he has really learned from Italo Svevo's novel, *La coscienza di Zeno* and from Svevo's own comments (such as, significantly, the one that Freud is of more value to writers than to sick patients). Berto's novel picks up the motifs of the Oedipal struggle and the search for a cure for seemingly imaginary ills from *Zeno*, but the narrator comes to see that he cannot (except parodically) redo Svevo or even Musil. It is important that he is "cured" when he burns the photos of his dead father along with the first chapters of his "traditional" novel. At this point the

12 See Walter Jackson Bate, *From Classic to Romantic* (1946; reprinted, New York: Harper and Row, 1961), p. 186.

novel about the "obscure malady" also must end. The new parodic form has literally as well as thematically destroyed the old.

V, the narrator of Nabokov's novel, *The Real Life of Sebastian Knight*, claims to have difficulty writing the biography of his novelist brother (the novel we read is more a tale *about* his attempts than the actual biography). He does not want to tell the story of Sebastian's childhood with methodological continuity as if he were a character of fiction. Loathing the "biographies romancées" (p. 20) he chooses, perhaps, the "roman biographié," since he has, after all, taken a "be-an-author" correspondence course (pp. 34–35).

Narratorial (not authorial) self-consciousness such as this often takes the form of a parodic awareness of literary conventions—of the journal (Butor's *L'Emploi du temps*), of criticism (Nabokov's *Pale Fire*), of the epic (Barth's *Giles Goat-Boy*), of biography (Woolf's *Jacob's Room*), of the essay (Borges' *Labyrinths*) and, of course, of the novel. The "rules" of fiction-making come into play as the overt subject matter of much modern metafiction. Barth's story, "Lost in the Funhouse," directs the reader's attention to the conventions of traditional realism — verisimilitude, dialogue, factuality ("Is there really such a person as Ambrose, or is he a figment of the author's imagination?"), and even the actual printing, such as the use of italics for emphasis or the legalistically cautious blanks ("in the town of D--").

Many of the other stories in *Lost in the Funhouse* recount the problems and progress of their own structuring process. How does one begin a story, structure the action, end it, integrate imagery, find the best point of view? "Autobiography," "Anonymiad," "Title," and "Life-Story" address themselves to these directly-asked questions. Barth is one of the most self-conscious of writers today, especially regarding the diegetic process and fictive ontological identity. On the other hand, as the reader is told by the narrator of "Life-Story": "assaults upon the boundary between life and art, reality and dream, were undeniably a staple of his [the writer-character's] own and his century's literature, as they'd been of Shakespeare's and Cervantes's" (p. 129).

However, Sterne is perhaps the most blatant forbear of Barth's brand of parody and self-consciousness about novelistic conventions. The causality of plots, the use of illustrations and footnotes, the demand for moral content, adventures, suspense, the time conventions, the writer's power, the critic's demands, chapter divisions, the use of prefaces, cover pages, digressions, stylistic uniformity—these are only a few of *Tristram Shandy*'s parodied conventions. Sterne's problem in aesthetic terms seems to have been the difficulty of reconciling the planned novel form and its conventions with a content which was concerned with the process of writing and living—that is, with contingency. Not unlike Sartre in *La Nausée*, he solved his problem in a self-conscious parodic manner. Barth's problem is more one of

acknowledging the fictionality of art—as emblematic of that of any of our ordering efforts in life as well—without destroying the validity of all art. In the story, "Title," the reader is told that even the demise of the novel, which is doubtful, would not necessarily mean the end of narrative art. Thanks to parody, the "end of one road might be the beginning of another" (p. 109). The intertextual reference to Barth's own novel, *The End of the Road*, is not, of course, accidental.

A more interesting kind of overt diegetic self-consciousness is that in which the focus is on the process of actually writing the fictional text one is reading at the moment. In Borges' "Theme of the Traitor and the Hero," the narrator begins by informing the reader that, under the influence of Chesterton and Leibniz: "I have imagined this story plot which I shall perhaps write some day."[13] Then, he proceeds to do just that, allowing the reader to observe the creative choices at work: "The action takes place in an oppressed and tenacious country. . . . Let us say (for narrative convenience) Ireland; let us say in 1824." Similarly Italo Calvino's reworking of Dumas' Count of Monte Cristo story in *Ti con zero* allows for Dantes to imagine his escape possibilities from prison by imagining an Alexandre Dumas and two assistants writing variants to be selected for a novel. To plan a book is to plan an escape—for the reader. One of the most extreme versions of this novel of process is Raymond Federman's *Double or Nothing*. But this same mode is thematized in a more simple and accessible form by Nabokov's narrator of *The Real Life of Sebastian Knight*, according to whom the characters of Knight's first novel are "methods of composition": "It is as if a painter said: look, here I'm going to show you not the painting of a landscape, but the painting of different ways of painting a certain landscape, and I trust their harmonious fusion will disclose the landscape as I intend you to see it" (p. 95).

For the reader/critic of metafiction, overt diegetic narcissism seems to involve the thematizing within the story of its storytelling concerns—parody, narrative conventions, creative process—with an eye to teaching him his new, more active role. For the metafictionist himself this thematizing operation is also central. Barth writes that the "regnant" idea linking the stories of *Lost in the Funhouse* is that of turning as many aspects of the storytelling as possible— "the structure, the narrative viewpoint, the means of presentation, in some instances the process of composition and/or recitation as well as of reading or listening—into dramatically relevant emblems of the theme."[14]

Aside from parody in general, the two most frequently used literary devices in this thematization process are the *mise en abyme* (a term for which there is no convenient English equivalent) and a kind of more

13 *Labyrinths*, trans. James E. Irby (New York: New Directions, 1962), p. 72.
14 In "Seven Additional Author's Notes," added to *Lost in the Funhouse* (1968; reprinted, New York: Bantam, 1969), p. x.

extended allegory, two devices which are often hard to distinguish one from the other. Although all the theoretical works of Jean Ricardou dwell to some extent on the *mise en abyme*, it is his *Le Nouveau Roman* ([Paris]: Seuil, 1973) that works out most fully the kinds and their functions ("révélatrice," "antithétique" and so on). Not all of these are of interest in the discussion here, however. A horizontal *mise en abyme* on the level of "fiction," for example, will perhaps call attention to the repetitive, "un-lifelike" nature of the plot, but Ricardou's (interrogatory) efforts at making this narcissistically functional remain somewhat unconvincing: "si la mise en abyme éclaire la fiction, n'est-ce point, dans certains cas, parce qu'elle l'a engendrée à son image?" (p. 53). If, as Ricardou states, the fascination which the adventures of the "fiction" exercise is inversely proportionate to the exhibition of the generative, productive procedures (p. 76), then it will be both the *mises en abyme* which operate on the "narration" level—verbally and structurally— and those which involve both the "narration" and the "fiction," which are of particular interest here. For instance, the narrated description of the engraving of the defeat of Reichenfels, in Robbe-Grillet's *Dans le labyrinthe*, is no less minute and no different tonally or diegetically from the rest of the narration, so the reader is not surprised when the picture functions not only as a horizontal *mise en abyme* on the "fiction" level (male figure with box) but as a vertical one as two levels of fictive reality and narration proceed to merge.

The *nouveau roman* is not unique in its use of diegetic or "narration" level *mises en abyme*. At the end of Borges' "Averroës' Search," the narrator thematizes this concern in telling the reader: "I sensed, on the last page, that my narrative was a symbol of the man I was while I wrote it, and that to write that story I had to be that man, and that to be that man I had to write that story and so to infinity. (The instant I stop believing in him 'Averroës' disappears.)"[15] And so does "Averroës' Search," of course.

One of the most complicated and extended examples of this kind of thematization of overt diegetic narcissism is, once again, in *The Real Life of Sebastian Knight* where each of Knight's novels functions as a *mise en abyme* of Nabokov's novel itself—both of its "narration" and its "fiction." The first, *The Prismatic Bezel*, is a detective tale about a dead man who turns out to be alive. This indeed turns out, for the reader, to be a clue to the status of the hero of the very text he is reading. At any rate, Nabokov's novel is also about a detective (V., Knight's brother) who hunts for clues to a man's life and death. *Success*, Sebastian's second novel, is about the meeting of two lovers in a plot which echoes both the writer's and his brother's attempts to find the fascinating woman of Knight's life. Siller, the character on the train in Sebastian's "The Back

15 In *A Personal Anthology*, trans. Anthony Kerrigan (New York: Grove Press, 1967), p. 110. See also the end of "Everything and Nothing" in this same volume, p. 117.

of the Moon" becomes Silberman who meets V., also on the train. *The Doubtful Asphodel*, the final novel, contains in its plot elements of Sebastian's life (and therefore of V.'s narrative and of Nabokov's novel) which the reader (but not V., seemingly) notices. The reader is further told that at the end of this particular book, "the author seems to pause for a minute, as if he were pondering whether it were wise to let the truth out" (p. 180). In order to understand what "truth," the reader must look at the end of *this* novel where he finds V. writing: "Sebastian's mask clings to my face, the likeness will not be washed off. I am Sebastian, or Sebastian is I, or perhaps we both are someone whom neither of us knows" (p. 205). When the reader learns that Sebastian was planning (but, *according to V.*, never wrote) a "fictitious biography," he is left to decide if what he has read — Vladimir Nabokov's novel — is supposed to represent V.'s biography of Knight, or a fictionalized autobiography by Knight, or Knight's latest novel. It is not a matter of life or art, but of which kind of art. The same mechanism operates in other of Nabokov's fictions. In *The Eye*, for instance, what appear to be psychological problems turn out to be *mises en abyme* of problems of composition.

Often the *mise en abyme* contains a critique of the text itself; as in Borges' world of Tlön, a "book which does not contain its counterbook is considered incomplete."[16] In Barth's "Title" there are at least three *mise en abyme* levels: the narrator's problems with his companion, his problems with the story he is telling and therefore with his reader, and finally, his problems with his society and the literature to which he contributes. Even more blatantly, the narrator of "Life-Story" tells the tale of a writer who, suspecting that he is a fictional character, wants to write a story about a writer who also has this feeling: "Another story about a writer writing a story! Another regressus in infinitum! Who doesn't prefer art that at least overtly imitates something other than its own processes?" (p. 117). Obviously Barth does not, but also, the processes of art as thematized in the text are always presented as "vital," humanly real in themselves and for themselves.

The reference above to the "regressus in infinitum" suggests that there may exist more than just a simple mirroring *mise en abyme*. And such is indeed the case. Lucien Dällenbach's extensive study of this reflexive modality, in *Le Récit spéculaire* (Paris: Seuil, 1977), traces the term itself back through its critical heritage in the works of C. E. Magny and P. Lafille in the 1950s, to Gide's own use, taken from the heraldic image of an escutcheon bearing in its centre a miniature replica of itself. Dällenbach feels that the mirroring image is central to the concept of the *mise en abyme*, but that there are three distinguishable kinds. One is a simple reduplication, in which the mirroring fragment has a relation of similitude with the whole that contains it. A second type is a

16 "Tlön, Uqbar, Orbis Tertius," *Labyrinths*, p. 13.

repeated reduplication "in infinitum" in which the above-mentioned mirroring fragment bears within itself another mirroring fragment, and so on. The third type of doubling is labelled "aporistique," and here the fragment is supposed to include the work in which it itself is included.

The detailed typology with which Dällenbach follows this diachronic analysis is based on three structural levels of reflection. For example, the *mise en abyme* might consist of an *énoncé* which reflects the text's *énoncé*, its story. This could take the shape of any kind of plot *résumé*, in narrative or in any other art form. For instance, in Hubert Aquin's *Trou de mémoire*, it is Holbein's painting of the "Two Ambassadors" which fulfils this function in a very self-conscious manner. At this level it is also important to note the position of the *mise en abyme* in the text, and the direction in which it points, for it can direct the reader to future events, yet unread, or to past ones, both within and preceding the text. Dällenbach's second level of reflection is of even more interest to a study of overt narcissistic fiction for in this case an *énoncé* reflects on the *énonciation* or the process, the production, carried out by the agents — both author and reader. A third level, in which it is the code itself (either narrative or linguistic) that is reflected, is obviously that at which both overt and covert modes of metafiction can operate.

At a certain point, however, the *mise en abyme* becomes so extended *in size* that it is better described as a kind of allegory. In "Lost in the Funhouse," the narrator recounts the difficulties he (Ambrose) has writing a story called "Lost in the Funhouse" about Ambrose's being lost in the funhouse, of course. The narrator becomes confused, forgets the direction of his narration, becomes lost in "Lost in the Funhouse" which is itself lost in the middle of the collection, *Lost in the Funhouse*. All of this play functions in addition as an allegory of the position of the reader who is lost in the funhouse with Ambrose as he tries to find his way out of the mirror-maze of the story. At the end he is told that Ambrose "will construct funhouses for others and be their secret operator — though he would rather be among the lovers for whom funhouses are designed" (p. 97) — that is, among the readers. Barth once wrote about a modern "literature of exhaustion," one that, by such means as the parody and the internal mirrorings and allegorizings that have been discussed here, sought to use up all the possibilities of art — but never succeeded. Narcissus lives on, or in Barth's own terms: "exhaustion is just an invitation to administer artifical resuscitation to the *apparently* dead. But I want the result to be real life, not some Lazarus-like life."[17] The implications of this identity of art and of the artistic process as "real" are what must now be faced and investigated.

17 "Hawkes and Barth Talk about Fiction," *New York Times Book Review*, April 1, 1979, p. 32, my italics.

Freedom Through Artifice: *The French Lieutenant's Woman*

> Fiction that insists on created actuality is
> its own reality; has its own vitality and
> energy.
>
> John Hawkes

One of the best metafictional examples of extended thematized allegory of the shared creative process involved in writing and reading is to be found in John Fowles's novel, *The French Lieutenant's Woman*. This novel is worth closer investigation here because it also brings to the fore many of the other motifs and devices of the overt kind of diegetic narcissism that has been the topic of discussion in the last chapter. For this reason, it stands almost as a model. It also clearly demonstrates the distinguishing differences (thanks to the thematized role of the reader) between modern metafiction and earlier forms of novelistic self-consciousness.

Overwhelmed by the self-aware Chapter Thirteen of the novel, the reviewers, while labouring the obvious Victorian parody, the motif of existential freedom, and the theme of social evolution, denounced the self-conscious coyness of Fowles himself, whom they apparently took to be the narrator of the novel—an error about which college freshmen are constantly being warned. That the narrator is *not* Fowles is what makes an otherwise commonplace literary device both interesting and problematic. Here we are dealing with a number of worlds within worlds. The core or most traditional novelistic universe is that of the characters. Outside and including that is a world in which exist the man in the train, the impresario—in other words, the narrator's personae who enter, at times, the core world. Outside that is the diegetic world of the narrator's voice. But beyond even that stands John Fowles—the man who masterminds both the creation of the Chinese-box structure

and the tensions which exist between these worlds and which are functional within the novel as a whole. In each universe, there is a *mise en abyme* of a creator figure—Sarah, the personae, the narrator—and outside the last of these worlds stands the author, *outside* it. Realism, as the novel reveals and as the narrator suggests in Chapter Thirteen, has once more been redefined—with the aid of the *nouveau roman*—and the allegorical structure of this novel and its preoccupation with imaginative process belie the narrator's modest opinion that this cannot be a novel in the modern sense of the word.

One of the thematized concerns of the novel that is openly theorized upon in Chapter Thirteen is the problem of the real versus the imaginary. The narrator realizes that, like Sarah and himself, the reader constantly fictionalizes his own life, that the act of making fictions is a natural and "vital" human function. All novelists, we are told, also "*wish to create worlds as real as, but other than the world that is.*"[1] The narrator continues: "We know a world is an organism, not a machine. We also know that a genuinely created world must be independent of its creator; a planned world (a world that fully reveals its planning) is a dead world. It is only when our characters and events begin to disobey us that they begin to live." The Romantic awkwardness of this formulation can perhaps be avoided by translation into more formalistic terms: there is a certain inner logic, or motivation, which comes with the process of creating the novelistic universe and which makes imperious demands upon the novelist, forcing him to abandon any plans conceived *before* putting pen to paper.

The narrator hastens to assure his reader that he is not being unduly artificial or coy, for the act of creating a self-contained world analogous to our own is a very natural act—for each of us. He writes: "I have disgracefully broken the illusion? No" (p. 97). Yet one could reply, yes, only to establish a new illusion in which he is a part—a wider heterocosm. When he remarks, "My characters still exist, and in a reality no less, or no more, real than the one I have just broken," then one could just as easily claim that *his* new reality is the reader's new illusion. For the reader, fiction *is* "woven into all"; on another level he is, however, drawn into the reality of the creative process, while remaining distanced from the illusion of the product created, the character's world.

Despite his intentions in the chapter—to unfold Sarah's true state of mind—the narrator finds that "possibility is not permissibility," that his character refuses to allow him his creator's liberty, *and* that he is morally as well as aesthetically bound to obey her. Fowles's narrator here is in a tradition of earlier self-conscious writers—Unamuno, Pirandello, Gide—who rejected the theological and artistic implica-

1 *The French Lieutenant's Woman* (Boston: Little, Brown and Co., 1969), p. 96, his italics. All further page references will be in parentheses within the text. Note that spellings are Americanized in this edition.

tions of the novelistic illusion: first, that the novelist is a god who—like God—creates what and how he pleases, since art imitates life and its myriad possibilities; and secondly, that the reader is reading a verisimilar "slice of life" to which, paradoxically, he need not seriously respond, since it is "only a novel," only entertainment, only fictive. In traditional product mimesis, art has its significance in the fact that it mirrors the real. However, a dichotomy exists, since this very mirroring is once removed from reality and is therefore inferior to it. In one sense, then, the moral stress of much mimesis or realism is only ostensible. Fowles, in breaking down this dichotomy, works to establish a different moral and human connection between art and life for the novel genre.

What is of interest is the way in which Fowles effects this new and broader reconciliation. Most of the reviewers and critics of the novel have dwelt lovingly on the Victorian parodic elements—which, it must be allowed, are dutifully pointed out by the modern narrator himself. Fowles's debts to Scott, George Eliot, Thackeray, Arnold, Dickens, Froude, and Hardy are perhaps more or less evident; but his narrator too hides nothing, mentioning Cervantes, Proust, Brecht, Ronsard, Flaubert, Milton, Radclyffe Hall, Catullus, Jane Austen, Arnold, Goethe, Dana, Tennyson, Hardy, Dickens—and so on. If he can be accused of playing literary games, the reader is at least carefully taught the rules. Even the characters' thought patterns provide a *mise en abyme* of the novelist's creative process. As Charles looks at Sarah: "it was suddenly, out of nowhere, that Emma Bovary's name sprang into his mind." "Such allusions are comprehensions: and temptations" (p. 120), adds the wary narrator.

Such intertextuality has a function within the novel similar to that of the Victorian parody as a whole. Fowles's use of this parody establishes, as the Russian formalists agreed, a new seriousness, a new code with which he attempts to deal with the ambiguities of both fiction and reality. Out of a temporally and philosophically superseded literary mode comes the illumination of a new form which goes one better than the ideal of Conrad and Ford: not only will Fowles make the reader "see," but he will reveal to him the mechanisms of vision-creating. He will let him see through the spectacles of books in order to let him see more and see differently. Historically, Fowles has no choice; he writes after the *nouveau roman*. While retaining all the moral and social concerns of James and the English novel tradition, he knows that a new, equally "vital" form must emerge from its antiquated conventions. If he self-consciously imitates George Eliot, it is as a way to Roland Barthes.

At various times, Fowles has compared *his* (and not his narrator's) handling of the parodic material to Stravinsky's eighteenth-century reworkings, to the use of Velasquez made by Picasso and Francis

Bacon, to Prokofiev's "Classical Symphony."[2] His earlier works reveal the same functional role of parody. In *The Collector*, it is the fiction of Fowles's own generation of "angry young men" and *The Tempest* as well which are played upon parodically. *The Magus* is constructed upon the forms of the *Bildungsroman*, the gothic tale, the masque, psycho-drama, and fantasy (such as *Le Grand Meaulnes*). He admits to earlier unpublished efforts in the modes of Gide, Flaubert, Lawrence, Defoe, Hemingway, Chandler, and Hammett. A more recent work, *The Ebony Tower*, confirms both the literary and broader human functions of parody. The old artist of the title story manages to "buttress" and "deepen" his art through parody. His visitor, a younger painter, sees that "behind the modernity of so many of the surface elements there stood both a homage and a kind of thumbed nose to a very old tradition,"[3] and that this is precisely what his own abstract modern art lacks. None of Fowles's novels lacks such support.

Obviously this parodic rehandling functions thematically and structurally on a purely introverted aesthetic level within *The French Lieutenant's Woman*. However, it also has an extramural role, directing the reader to the moral and social concerns of the novel—concerns which critics seem to have felt were somehow independent of these "coy" self-reflective modalities. The theme of the changes over a century of social evolution would be blatant and unsubtle, *if* Fowles were claiming that modern man is freer and better than the Victorians whose style he is parodying. The narrator certainly makes the reader aware of the temporal telescoping, but he is not telling him that change is improvement or even that he *is* so very different from the Victorians. "I suspect," writes the narrator in a related context, "we are in reality dealing with a human constant: the difference is a vocabulary, a degree of metaphor" (p. 268). It is not the *fact* of temporal telescoping, then, that is significant, but the *function* of it. This is the point at which literary parody takes on moral and social dimensions; the *reader* of this novel is never allowed to abstain from judging and questioning himself by condemning or writing off the novel's world as "just" Victorian (as well as "just" fiction). The real and the imaginary, the present and the past, merge for the reader.

This moral function is directly related to the structural and thematic use made in the text of the concept of existential freedom. In his first two novels, Fowles mocks the existentialist pretensions of G. P. and Nicholas Urfe, while presenting aesthetic metaphors or allegories of existential freedom within the novels' fictions. In *The French Lieutenant's*

2 See "Notes on Writing a Novel," *Harper's Magazine*, July 1968, pp. 89–90; "On Writing a Novel," *Cornhill Magazine* 1060 (Summer 1969), 287–88; and in Richard Boston, "John Fowles, Alone but Not Lonely," *New York Times Book Review*, November 9, 1969, p. 2.

3 (Boston: Little, Brown and Co., 1974), p. 18.

Woman it is the ironic, parodic function of the modern narrator to suggest that existentialism is the only view possible for a modern individualist who *will* see Sarah as Sarah, and not as the French Lieutenant's Whore. In *The Aristos*, Fowles's remarks suggest that existentialism is, for him, a philosophical counterpart to his own novelistic use of parody: "Existentialism is not a philosophy, but a way of looking at, and utilizing, other philosophies. It is a theory of relativity among theories of absolute truth."[4] Fowles was attracted to the English Victorian age, he claims, not because of its differences from the present, but because it too was "highly existentialist, in many of its personal dilemmas."[5] He did not choose it to make trite and obvious moral statements about the superiority of modern existentialism. It is a vehicle rather for both the aesthetic and moral preoccupations of the novel.

When Ian Adam notes that Sarah is not a fully developed character—and then asserts: "The quarrel becomes not one with an existentialist heroine but with her existence. My final reservation about an important novel is aesthetic rather than moral"[6]—he is attempting to separate the inseparable. In the face of Mrs. Poultenay's servant Millie and her "ten miserable siblings," the narrator has come to loathe the dishonest paintings of the "contented country laborer and his brood" by George Morland and Birket Foster. "Each age," claims the narrator, "each guilty age, builds high walls round its Versailles; and personally I hate those walls most when they are made by literature and art" (p. 158). The bowdlerized fiction of the time is therefore abandoned for the "cold reality" of the Commission Reports. The narrator chooses to blur the distinctions between real and fictional in order to stress the necessary link between moral and creative honesty and freedom.

In *The Aristos*, Fowles claims that freedom is inherent in the best art, as it is in the best science. Both are essentially demolishers of tyranny and dogma (10:181); this is a positive stating of Marx's social and linguistic observation that forms the epigraph to Chapter Thirty: "But the more these conscious illusions of the ruling classes are shown to be false and the less they satisfy common sense, the more dogmatically they are asserted and the more deceitful, moralizing and spiritual becomes the language of established society" (p. 243). There is an obvious connection between the desire for power over someone and a lack of freedom—be it from a Marxist, existentialist, or aesthetic perspective. Marx provides the epigraph to the entire novel: "Every emancipation is a restoration of the human world and of human relations to man himself."

4 (Boston: Little, Brown and Co., 1964), 6: 105. Other section references will be in parentheses in the text.
5 "Notes on Writing a Novel," p. 90.
6 In Patrick Brantlinger, Ian Adam, Sheldon Rothblatt, *"The French Lieutenant's Woman*: A Discussion," *Victorian Studies* 15 (March 1972), 347.

In the core universe it is the ironically named Mr. Freeman and his daughter who pose the greatest threats to Charles's freedom, asking him to pay the price of "the best of his past self" to enter their bourgeois world. Charles perceives the need to "reject the notion of *possession* as the purpose of life" (p. 295), yet in his attempt to release himself from the constraints of his age, to become a free outcast like Sarah, Charles must face another reality. He wants to *possess* Sarah sexually. That he does so only physically and not in any more significant way, and that he does not see that sexual possession is as potentially negative and freedom-denying as any other act of possession, is made clear at the end of the novel. But even after the seduction scene, Sarah's "You cannot marry me" means "you may not," a refusal Charles is not capable of even imagining — as witnessed by his letter to her about "*our* future" (p. 370, his italics). Sarah chooses the freedom of fantasy over the bondage of marriage: "I wish to be what I am, not what a husband, however kind, however indulgent, must expect me to become in marriage" (p. 450).

It is one of Sarah's moral functions in the novel to teach Charles this lesson. She sends him her Exeter address and he sees at once that he must make a choice: "He had not the benefit of existentialist terminology; but what he felt was really a very clear case of the anxiety of freedom" (pp. 340–41). After the seduction, Charles believes that the "false version of her betrayal by Varguennes, her other devices, were but stratagems to unblind him" (p. 368), but he does not recall that Sarah's fictional identity was created *before* his arrival in Lyme and therefore had another function for Sarah herself, as free woman and as fiction-maker.

That the narrator should characterize her by "passion and imagination" (p. 189) reveals his intuition of the strong ties between the moral or sexual and the artistic. The Victorians saw passion, the reader is told, as a censurable sensuality, imagination as the merely fanciful. Much of the core universe of the novel is about passion and morality; much of the self-conscious storytelling of the wider world is here concerned with imaginative process as a serious and natural human faculty. Imagination and its articulation in verbal fiction constitute profoundly necessary acts for Fowles, and therein lies the importance of language as man's most precise, inclusive, and most evolved human tool, shared by literature and life, art and society.[7] The existential theme of freedom takes shape on the aesthetic level; the only boundaries to a novel are words. Anything that language can do, the novel can do. Fowles feels that the novel is the ultimate free literary form: "This is its downfall and its glory; and explains why [it has] been so often used to establish freedom in other fields, social and political."[8]

7 See *The Aristos*, 7: 163; 177; 178; 180; 198, and *The Ebony Tower*, pp. 186, 277–80.
8 "Notes on Writing a Novel," p. 92.

In a short piece, "Is the Novel Dead?,"[9] Fowles contrasts this imaginative freedom of the writing and reading of words to the tyranny of the film-maker's imagination upon that of his passive viewer. Television's threat is not directed towards fiction, he feels, but towards something much more essential to human development and contentment—"the right, the power and the need to exercise the individual imagination" of both writer and reader. This recalls Sarah's alleged moral purpose in *her* fiction-making. She freely creates an identity, telling Charles that she has lost her virginity, in order to be different: "I did it so that people *should* point at me, *should* say, there walks the French Lieutenant's Whore—oh, yes, let the word be said. So that they should know I have suffered, and suffer, as others suffer in every town and village in this land" (pp. 174–75). Charles is quite right in saying: "you cannot tell me it is your duty to offend society" (p. 181), but not for the reasons he presumes. Sarah's identity as the fallen woman is a *fiction*, yet it may perhaps even attain the status of social reminder, a result more morally commendable at least than the separation of art and reality effected by Victorian painters.

However, the implications of the fiction-making process are "vital" and moral in a more subtle way. "I said earlier," recalls the narrator, "that we are all poets, though not many of us write poetry; and so are we all novelists, that is, we have a habit of writing fictional futures for ourselves" (p. 339). In positing the relationship between fiction-shaping and reality in these terms, the narrator hearkens back to a kind of classical aesthetics. In the *Poetics*, Aristotle saw art as forming, guiding, and developing the concrete into a unified meaning and completeness. Art as mimesis had a cultural and moral function—to shape and form man. As in this novel, moral worth is inseparable from action and events, our own fictionalized ones or those in art. The diegetic narrative act, which Aristotle saw as mimetic as well, is a moral act and it is as such that it is overtly thematized in Fowles's novel.

The laying bare of the mechanism of fiction-making—the element of the trickster, the charlatan, the magus—has always existed in the novelist's role. And the narrator here reveals it most fully, jumping easily in one page over twenty months in time (as does Stendhal), having his characters share time and space with historical realities (as does Scott), footnoting his use of certain epigraphs, clarifying points by quotation of further documentary evidence, and so on. What is interesting is that by using these conventional novelistic devices which are usually employed to authenticate the core universe, the narrator manages to achieve opposite results, validating instead his wider universe. The voice of the narrator is not an exterior authenticating authorial one; it is the voice of a character.

9 *Books* 1 (Autumn 1970), 2–5.

In *The Magus*, Nicholas Urfe realizes that he has created an imaginary god-like novelist to order his own life, to turn it into a fiction in which he is a character. Charles, on the other hand, here tries to be that god himself, to control, to possess. His various fantasies turn out to be unrelated to his reality, however, and it is only in the church in Exeter that he has a "glimpse of another world: a new reality, a new causality, a new creation" (p. 365). But this new fictive universe is again one in which Charles feels the need to be in control, ushering Sarah to Winsyatt, around Europe, and so on. The narrator is always especially careful to separate the unlikely nature of the content, from the valid process, of Charles's fantasizing.

It is not until the end of the novel that Charles perceives that fiction-making is a freedom-inducing act, not an act of possession, of planning, of control, as it is here. Giving himself up to thoughts of his future with Sarah, Charles here dreams of his wedding trip: "Moonlight, the distant sound below of singing gypsies, such grateful tender eyes . . . and in some jasmine-scented room they would lie awake, in each other's arms, infinitely alone, exiled, yet fused in that loneliness, inseparable in that exile" (p. 400). The descent into romantic cliché tonally underlines the narrator's—and soon Sarah's—rejection of a fiction that does not respect the integrity of the protagonist. Sarah rightly refuses and fears the demands of his love upon her freedom, demands she senses without ever having received Charles's revealing letter.

This freedom and integrity is ultimately also what the narrator's dandified impresario persona denies. From his vantage point outside his persona's "heterocosm," the narrator does not like this character, for "he very evidently regards the world as his to possess and use as he likes" (p. 462). This is not to say that the narrator condemns *himself* for being a creator, although any creator who does not respect the inner logic and motivation of his characters is, as has been noted, morally suspect. In the first "on stage" appearance of his persona on the train, the narrator describes this figure's look as being like that of some omnipotent god: "Not at all what we think of as a divine look; but one of a distinctly mean and dubious (as the theoreticians of the *nouveau roman* have pointed out) moral quality" (p. 405). By creating for his prying persona, in Unamuno fashion, this inner but other world somewhere between his own and his characters', the narrator breaks through the illusion of mimetic mirroring by decompartmentalizing what was traditionally considered to be a simple relationship of author to reality. *Neither* of these two particular entities appears in the complex Chinese-box structure of the novel.

The arbitrary persona gives way to the narrator who recognizes the aesthetic demand for a sense of unity of interconnection within the novel world. He must respect the literary integrity of his characters, as

an allegory of his respect for that of other human, non-fictional beings. Charles, when playing fiction-maker himself, "became increasingly unsure of the frontier between the real Sarah and the Sarah he had created in so many such dreams" (p. 428). Indeed, the "real" Sarah is the greatest fiction-maker of the novel, creating her own identity, an identity which, suitably, is not complete in any of Charles's versions: "the one Eve personified, all mystery and love and profundity, and the other a half-scheming, half-crazed governess from an obscure seaside town. He even saw himself coming upon her again—and seeing nothing in her but his own folly and delusion" (p. 429). She is a little of each, and more; she is No One's Woman.

Fiction-making as a potential mode of control, of freedom-denying, is indeed linked in the core world to sexual possession and even love. However, it is also connected to a broader social concern. This is clear in the epigraph to Chapter Thirty-seven—Marx's comment about the bourgeoisie's forcing all nations to adopt its mode of production and thereby to become bourgeois as well: "In a word, it creates a world after its own image" (p. 280), like an omnipotent creator. In rejecting the Freemans' bourgeois values, Charles chooses first his gentlemanly liberty and later the greater freedom which Sarah forces him to face.

Earlier, when Charles had stood at the window of Grogan's office, looking out into the night where Sarah was, he "felt himself in suspension between the two worlds, the warm, neat civilization behind his back, the cool, dark mystery outside" (p. 151). Charles is indeed suspended between two worlds—Ernestina's and Sarah's—both of which are potentially worlds within himself as well. He first hears Sarah's tale from his fiancée and responds: "I wish you hadn't told me the sordid facts. That's the trouble with provincial life. Everyone knows everyone and there is no mystery. No romance." Tina rightly mocks him, "the scientist, the despiser of novels" (p. 10). The irony is that to the end no one will know Sarah and that to label, to know the "facts," is not at all to destroy the mystery.

At the start, though, Charles had looked to the malleable young Tina for a cure to his restless boredom. Unable to indulge his "Byronic ennui," he had reverted to convention, since in essence he shared his wife-to-be's world view: "Life was the correct apparatus; it was heresy to think otherwise" (p. 78). Sarah, of course, is that heretic in this society. Charles's early response to her is ironic: "here, if only some free man had the wit to see it, is a remarkable woman" (p. 182). In fact, the "free man" here is doubly ironic. Charles is engaged (*his* intended meaning) but he is also not free existentially at this stage. Secondly, Ernestina *Freeman* and her father would *not* have "the wit" to see it, although Charles still does.

It takes Sarah's speaking eyes to make him perceive in his fiancée a certain shallowness, a cuteness he took for acuteness. Tina, in fact,

gives the novel its title: "They call her the French Lieutenant's . . . Woman" (p. 9), but it is Sarah who demands that "Whore" be used, for she is free of the frivolity, the prudery, and even most of the feminine vanity of Ernestina. The la.ter is presented as almost a Victorian cliché; she would like children but "the payment she vaguely divined she would have to make for them seemed excessive" (p. 29). Sarah, however, suspects that there is more to sex than a "bestial version of Duty," but the Victorian Charles still presumes her disgust after his seduction. There is great irony in Charles's earlier response to Sarah upon hearing her story: "He was at one and the same time Varguennes enjoying her and the man who sprang forward and struck him down; just as Sarah was to him both an innocent victim and a wild, abandoned woman" (p. 176). That Charles *is* her Varguennes is underlined by Sarah's writing to him in French (p. 208).

Yet Sarah has something beyond her sexual power to separate her from other women. Charles is surprised by her directness of look, of thought, and of language: "less an equality than a proximity, a proximity like a nakedness, an intimacy of thought and feeling hitherto unimaginable to him in the context of a relationship with a woman" (p. 182). Sarah leads him to believe that she is indeed the French Lieutenant's Whore, an identity the reader and Charles both later discover to be fictional. However, this role does allow her a means of self-definition: "If I leave here I leave my shame. Then I am lost" (p. 180). When Charles assures her that she has done her penance and is forgiven, she voices the fear implicit above: "And may be forgotten." It is only at the end of the book that Charles tells her he will never forget her; again it is through her fiction-making that she has effected this permanence. After Charles has seduced her, she admits to wishing it so and, indeed, long imagining such an event (p. 352). Now that she knows that he once loved her, she implies, she can live on with rich food for more imaginings, with none of the constrictions Charles's love would impose upon her. To Charles's vanity and resentment at being the dupe of her imagination, she replies: "Today I have thought of my own happiness" (p. 356). It is only after her disappearance that Charles begins to see that beneath "all her stories and deceptions she had a candor . . . an honesty" (p. 417). The sexual conflict here is not just a narrative cliché; it is closely related to power and fantasy.

Despite appearances, it is Sarah who is the named protagonist of the novel, the veiled Isis, the dark Maker of the epigraph to the theoretical thirteenth chapter. She acts out, on the level of the fiction, an allegory of the narrator-novelist's freedom of creation of the novel itself. Why choose a female for this role? Perhaps because in the novel the narrator, who continually forces the reader to unite the moral and the artistic in a contemplation of the meaning of freedom, is writing of an age in which "there was an enormous progress and liberation in every

other field of human activity; and nothing but tyranny in the most personal and fundamental" (p. 267) and woman was the victim. In *The Aristos*, Fowles himself presents woman as a symbol of the challenge of the Fall, of the belief that humanity can develop by consciousness and imagination to achieve new powers (4: 24).

Sarah is the narrating novelist's surrogate within the core fictional world. Like him, she has existence only within that fictive universe; the narrator is not Fowles himself, and Sarah too can be known by no outside structure ("outside" here being the Victorian world of the core), for she creates her own story, her own identity. There is no doubt that Sarah "lies" in order to bring Charles to a realization of the "truth," just as the novelist was traditionally condemned for creating lies in making fictions for his readers. At the start Charles looks at Sarah's "unforgettable" face and sees "no artifice there, no hypocrisy, no hysteria, no mask" (p. 10), just as up to Chapter Thirteen, despite several hints to the contrary, the reader is almost convinced of the narrator's typical Victorian conventionality, almost unaware of the modern mask. As Sarah frees Charles from illusion by fiction-making, so the narrator frees the reader from his illusions about fiction-making.

At times, Sarah is not unlike the narrator's impresario persona. She is a consummate actress, carefully setting the scene for her revelations to Charles (p. 123), pricking her finger on a hawthorn (p. 180) for sympathy and Hardyesque symbolism. The narrator had earlier explained that in order for him to be free himself, he must grant each of his characters his freedom: "There is only one good definition of God: the freedom that allows other freedoms to exist" (p. 97). This is the meaning of power and of the god-game. The novelist is a creating god-figure, but freedom, not authority, dominates his image. It is this freedom that Sarah too has, and in order to retain it, she too must give her creature his freedom. Her freedom lies in her existence in another world, as an imaginative construct, a fiction of her own making: "I think I have a freedom [other women] cannot understand. No insult, no blame, can touch me. Because I have set myself beyond the pale. I am nothing, I am hardly human any more" (p. 175).

Like the narrator, Sarah too pretends not to know things she has really plotted very carefully. When Charles comes to her room in Exeter she stammers: "Forgive me. I . . . I did not expect" (p. 346). Yet the reader has seen her plan the seduction—the fragile white night-gown, the green shawl to set off her hair (pp. 277–78)—and he has now to see it all work: Charles is excited by the fragility of her gown, amazed at the beauty of her hair against the green of the shawl, and weakened by concern for her "injured" ankle. She is a fine impresario for her own show.

Yet the qualities which allow her to be so are qualities that the reader comes to associate in the novel with the artist and his art: "that fused

rare power that was her essence—understanding and emotion" (p. 58) and an "instinctual profundity of insight" (p. 53). It is not surprising that, like the parodic novelist whose surrogate she is, Sarah sees the world through books. Given her education and situation, she has read more than most women. Novels and poems "served as a substitute for experience. Without realizing it she judged people as much by the standards of Walter Scott and Jane Austen as by any empirically arrived at; seeing those around her as fictional characters, and making poetic judgements on them" (p. 53). It is only at the end of the novel, as Charles realizes, that she can fully articulate her intuition. Her time in the Rossetti house "deepened her clarity of insight; had now anchored her, where before had been a far less secure mooring, to her basic conception of life and her role in it" (p. 451)—that is, the role of creating fictions and thereby granting freedom.

The Pre-Raphaelite Brotherhood plays an interesting role in several of the novel's universes. For the narrator, they stand out, against the backdrop of that schizophrenia of the Victorian mind, as those "who tried—or seemed to be trying—to be one-minded about both art and life" (pp. 368–69). The narrator has attacked the claustrophobic and unrealistic (and therefore immoral) art of the period: "Hide reality, shut out nature. The revolutionary art movement of Charles's day was of course the Pre-Raphaelite: they at least were making an attempt to admit nature and sexuality" (p. 176). This they did, but they also possessed two other qualities which would render them attractive to the narrator and to his creator. First, they were seriously dedicated to the artistic life and saw one of their responsibilities as artists as being the duty to paint contemporary life and its problems—social and moral; witness Ford Madox Brown's "Work" and Rossetti's "Found." Fowles's own use of Marxist epigraphs suggests a similar concern. Secondly, the Pre-Raphaelites often paradoxically chose their subjects from the past to do this, as do Fowles and his narrator, and were themselves inspired by literature.

Sarah's world is like that of the Brotherhood, for she shocks social propriety as much as does the "celebrated, the notorious" Rossetti. She tries to reassure Charles of her innocent status in the artist's house by mentioning the name of another inhabitant—likely Swinburne. Although Charles suspects her of a certain naïveté with regard to her fellow housemates, he fails to see why she is at home here. He does not know of the Pre-Raphaelites' respect—not to say idolatrous admiration—for their models: Rossetti and Lizzy Siddal, Morris and Jane Burden, later Rossetti and Jane (then Jane Morris). In fact, the descriptions of Sarah in the novel resemble those of the paintings of Jane—the hair, the mouth, the voluptuousness combined with the dreamy, the intense with the languid. Jane Burden, like Sarah, was of a lower class as well.

The other marginally Pre-Raphaelite figure who enters the novel is Ruskin, whom Charles glimpses ("the famous lecturer and critic . . . widely respected and admired"), but whose presence in the Rossetti "den of iniquity" he cannot comprehend. It is Sarah, the artist surrogate, who makes the connection with Ruskin: "I have since seen artists destroy work that might to the amateur seem perfectly good. I remonstrated once. I was told that if an artist is not his own sternest judge he is not fit to be an artist. I believe that is right. I believe I was right to destroy what had begun between us. There was a falsehood in it, a --" (p. 448). Here she uses Ruskin's term "inconsistency of conception": "the natural had been adulterated by the artificial, the pure by the impure." Sarah attributes the negative part to herself, to her fictions, but Charles now sees that it is he and his language that are guilty of artificiality, of betraying "a hollowness, a foolish restraint." But even now he has not perceived Sarah's role: "you cannot answer me with observations, however apposite, on art." Sarah rightly replies, as would the narrator, that they were intended to apply to life as well (p. 449).

Charles suspects that Sarah is manipulating him, feigning contentment, suffering still, "and that was the mystery she was truly and finally afraid he might discover" (p. 453). This is likely true; Sarah told Charles after her seduction that she had that day thought only of her own happiness, but should they meet again, as now, she would think only of his. If she is to give Charles his freedom, it will be at her own expense: "something of the terrible outrage in *his* soul was reflected in *her* eyes" (p. 454, my italics). In those eyes he sees "a spirit prepared to sacrifice everything but itself—ready to surrender truth, feeling, perhaps even all womanly modesty in order to save its own integrity" (p. 465). Sarah is free and will force Charles to be so, to react against her fiction-making, to refuse to let *her* possess *him*.

Why must he leave? Why are there two endings? In life there are infinite possibilities, yet this is not life, but fiction, and the novelistic universe has its own logic and inner coherence which "fix the fight" for the reader. This is not a Victorian novel and cannot have a conventional closed ending. The flipping of a coin or the turning back of a clock do not have any final effect on the reader, who is still prey to that "tyranny of the last chapter" (p. 406), however it was chosen. Were Charles the protagonist (and of a Victorian novel), the first ending would be possible, but even then violence would needs be done to the text. Since Sarah is the named protagonist, the painful freedom-granting second ending of a modern novel is the only probable one.

Fowles, as well as Sarah and the narrator, has fixed the fight for both Charles and the reader long before this final scene. The reader, like Charles, has been manipulated, controlled within the coherent world of the text. Early in the novel, Sarah warns Charles: "What has kept me alive is my shame, my knowing that I am truly not like other women. I

shall never have children, a husband, and those innocent happinesses they have" (p. 175). Instead she chooses fantasy, freedom, and her integrity. After her seduction she tells Charles that he cannot marry her, that is, she will not let him. She begs him to leave her—unlike Ernestina—because she loves him enough to bring him and leave him to his own painful freedom. He says to himself in the church after the seduction: "You know your choice. You stay in prison, what your time calls duty, honor, self-respect, and you are comfortably safe. Or you are free and crucified" (p. 362). He then has a vision of Sarah, not as his wife, significantly, but as someone to uncrucify him, to allow him to be free and happy. But he learns that *he* must make the liberating move, and that freedom is painful.

Perhaps the best indication of the textual impossibility of the first ending is the existence of the very similar scene between Charles and the red-haired prostitute, Sarah, and her daughter. It is true that in both cases he amuses the child with his watch and chain, but despite the glaring ironic similarity of situation, the language of the earlier scene denies any link to this Victorian conventional ending. With the first girl's child, Charles has an intuition about life, about time as "here and now," rather than as a road going forward to the future and back to the past. Making this existential realization, he feels his sense of irony return as "a kind of faith in himself." He feels "suddenly able to face his future, which was only a form of that terrible emptiness. Whatever happened to him such moments would recur; must be found, and could be found" (p. 320). Indeed they are found—in the second ending where Charles at last has "an atom of faith in himself, a true uniqueness" (p. 467) in his empty future.

He sees now that Sarah is not the Sphinx, that she cannot choose for him, that life too "is not a symbol, is not one riddle and one failure to guess it, is not to inhabit one face alone or to be given up after one losing throw of the dice; but is to be, however inadequately, emptily, hopelessly into the city's iron heart, *endured*. And out again, upon the unplumb'd, salt, estranging sea" (p. 467). The echoing of Charles's favourite poem, Arnold's "To Marguerite," in the last line reaffirms his realization that his freedom is both necessary and inevitable, no matter how much he might wish the contrary ("Oh might our marges meet again!" wrote the poet). For this desire is rendered vain in Arnold's poem by "A God," and in Fowles's novel by three gods—Sarah, the narrating novelist, and Fowles—whose worlds each logically allow only this ending, both in structural, artistic terms and in thematic, moral ones. As is usually the case in metafiction, what first appear as allegory, *mise en abyme*, parody—that is, as signs of self-conscious literary introversion—function as the means by which new extramural connections are forged between art and life. Self-reflective fiction, even in its most overt diegetic form, does not mean the death of the novel as a mimetic genre, but perhaps rather its salvation.

Actualizing Narrative Structures: Detective Plot, Fantasy, Games, and the Erotic

> I would advise in addition the eschewal
> of overt and self-conscious discussion of
> the narrative process. I would advise in
> addition the eschewal of overt and self-
> conscious discussion of the narrative
> process.
>
> John Barth

Fowles's novel is explicitly and self-consciously auto-referential. Its thematization of the role of the reader and of the ontological status of the text works both to create and to break down artifice. The reader has his orders and is not allowed to ignore them; like Charles's, his freedom is a real, though an induced one. But what if the author decides to *assume* that his reader already knows the story-making rules? He would still imbed certain instructions in the text, but these would not be in the obvious form of direct addresses. Therefore this would be a more "covert" version of diegetic self-reflectiveness. The act of reading becomes one of actualizing textual structures, and the only way to approach these narcissistic forms (as well as their implications) would be by means of those very structures. At the diegetic level there appear to be certain models favoured by metafictionists as internalized structuring devices which in themselves point to the self-referentiality of the text. It should be noted that the four models singled out earlier— detective plot, fantasy, games, and the erotic—are in no way exclusive, but represent only four of the most visible forms presently in use in metafiction.

1. THE DETECTIVE STORY

In order to understand the internalized functioning of this model in metafiction, one must isolate first the three major characteristics of detective fiction that are relevant to this discussion: the self-consciousness of the form itself, its strong conventions, and the important textual function of the hermeneutic act of reading.

To begin with, the detective story is almost by definition intensely self-aware. Often this will take the form of a writer of detective stories within the novel itself: Latimer, the academic turned novelist in Eric Ambler's *A Coffin for Dimitrios*, is offered a banal plot for a novel by one Colonel Haki. However, through this latter fellow, he takes up instead a real life investigation which ends in the death of the hunted man, Dimitrios. Only then is Latimer free to write his next novel. However, he rejects the tale the reader has been reading, which he deems unsuitable—messy, not tidy and artistic enough. In fact his projected plot opening is not unlike the Colonel's suggestion, previously scorned as banal. Similarly, though in a less complex manner, the murderer's manuscript at the end of Agatha Christie's *And Then There Were None* calls the reader's attention to the text's *mise en abyme*:

> It was my ambition to *invent* a murder mystery that no one could solve.
> But no artist, I now realize, can be satisfied with art alone. There is a natural craving for recognition which cannot be gainsaid.[1]

In this same novel there is a good example of the other kind of self-consciousness that abounds in the genre—the characters' belief that certain things occur in life (that is, that novel), others in fiction. Just before he dies, the first victim merrily refuses to leave the island: "Ought to ferret out the mystery before we go. Whole thing's like a detective story. Positively thrilling."[2] In *Have His Carcase*, Dorothy Sayers' detective-novelist heroine, Harriet Vane, agrees with the sleuth, Lord Peter Wimsey: "One wouldn't make an intending suicide take a return-ticket in a book, but real people are different."[3]

This last point brings up the second above-mentioned concern, the strong conventions of order and logic in detective fiction which Harriet Vane knows are to be obeyed because the *reader* expects them and needs them in order to read the work, in order to participate in the case. It is this very store of infinitely reworkable conventions that is acknowledged and exploited, "re-contextualized," by metafictionists such as Robbe-Grillet and Borges. The third point of interest arises from this active participation of the reader in detective fiction. The act of reading is here an act of interpretation, of following clues to the answer of a given problem.[4] The hermeneutic gaps are textually functional in an explicit manner here, but the process is emblematic of that of reading any novel. It is this realization that covertly narcissistic metafiction exploits. Often a detective story will explicitly thematize this hermeneutic paradigm. In a double *mise en abyme* (Ellery Queen

1 In *Christie Classics* (1924; reprinted, New York: Dodd, Mead, and Co., n.d.), p. 317.
2 Ibid., p. 205.
3 (1932; reprinted, New York: Avon, 1968), p. 82.
4 See Frank Kermode, "Novel and Narrative" in John Halperin (ed.), *The Theory of the Novel: New Essays* (New York: Oxford University Press, 1974), especially pp. 159–68.

[really Messieurs Lee and Dannay] always writes about himself in the third person), Ellery's novel, *The Finishing Stroke*, contains within itself a quotation from his first novel, *The Roman Hat Mystery*. This citation is presented as a "Challenge to the Reader" at the start of the third book. The reader is informed that he now knows everything that the chief sleuth does and can proceed by a series of logical deductions and psychological observations to the solution of the mystery.

A reality of all reading, this can also be allegorically worked out, as in several of the Simenon novels. In *The Methods of Maigret*, for example, the discreet, self-effacing, intelligent Inspector Pyke is the reader's surrogate, as he follows Maigret around trying to discern his famous methods. Pyke impassively sifts his every gesture and word, much to Maigret's annoyance, for Maigret yearns to discover his colleague's thoughts about himself and the case at hand. Like the reader's, these thoughts are inaccessible.

The logical deductions demanded of the reader place him more often, however, in the shoes of the detective himself, be he an active investigator or an arm-chair wizard. False trails may be laid for both of these interpreters but the evidence discovered must be shared by the sleuth with the reader; it is not fair of Watson in the Sherlock Holmes tales to withhold details from the reader, for instance. If the latter is the sleuth's surrogate, then perhaps the author is the criminal's. G. K. Chesterton's Father Brown stories make this allegory clear. In "The Blue Cross," the detective, Valentin, realizes that the criminal is a creative artist and he, the chasing detective, merely a critic. Flambeau, the master criminal, artistically attempts to match his crime to the season or the landscape (see "The Flying Stars"). He continues to function as the imaginative force even after giving up a life of crime, leaving the critic's work always to Father Brown. (In a fit of moral and perhaps creative frustration, Valentin, on the other hand, turns clever criminal in "The Secret Garden.")

It is perhaps not hard to see now why this genre should appeal to metafictionists as a structuring model. It also appeals on the overt level, of course, as witnessed in Nabokov's parody, in *The Real Life of Sebastian Knight*, of the detective plot in his hero's mystery novel, *The Prismatic Bezel*, itself seemingly a parody of Agatha Christie's *Three Blind Mice*. The entire novel (Nabokov's) is itself based on the detective structure as the narrator seeks the "truth" about the novelist, Knight, and the reader seeks the "truth" about the novel he reads. Is it fictive autobiography? Pure fiction? Biography? But, as Nabokov writes in *The Eye*: "The stress is not on the mystery but on the pattern."[5] His *Despair* is about a failed murder; *Lolita* and *Pale Fire* end in murder. The stylized properties of detective fiction—when either parodied overtly or

5 (New York: Phaedra, 1965), p. 10.

covertly used as structural principles—are employed to point to the text in its existence as literature, as patterned, ordered art.

Two of the writers of metafiction who most interestingly use this model are Robbe-Grillet and Borges. The latter, as well as having anthologized and translated detective stories, has written a volume of them himself—*Seis problemas para don Isidro Parodi*—whose punningly named hero is unavoidably an arm-chair detective, since he is in jail. In his other short metafictional pieces, Borges usually internalizes a puzzle or enigma structure, and often the mystery variant of it, as in the case of "Death and the Compass." Lönnrot, the detective, sees himself as a "pure thinker" (à la Dupin) and divines the "secret morphology" of the crimes—crimes which he has brought about himself. His enemy, Red Scharlach, had read in the papers of Lönnrot's abstruse theory to account for a murder of a rabbi. It was based on Hasidim texts and so Scharlach had plotted the equally abstruse trap for the detective with his own plan. Like the reader, Lönnrot feels the obvious—and incidentally, true—explanation for the first murder to be "possible but not interesting" and so, like the author, sets up the rest of the narrative. The detective predicts—in time and place—the final murder of the series, unaware that it is his own. As he wanders in what is to be his death-place, Triste-le-Roy, the strange house seems to him larger than it is, due to the "penumbra, the symmetry, the mirrors, the years, my ignorance, the solitude"—an allegorical description of the effect of this self-mirroring story on the reader.

Although Wallas, the hero of Robbe-Grillet's *Les Gommes* (Paris: Minuit, 1953), lives out the rigid conventions of the *roman policier*, the novel goes beyond those properties to a metafictional reworking. In "Sur quelques notions périmées," Robbe-Grillet noted that both this novel and *Le Voyeur* (where the reader has to decide if, as well as how, a crime has been committed) contain "une trame, une *action*, des plus facilement discernables, riche par surcroît d'éléments considérés en général comme dramatiques. S'ils ont au début semblé désamorcés à certains lecteurs, n'est-ce pas simplement parce que le mouvement de l'écriture y est plus important que celui des passions et des crimes?"[6] In later theoretical statements, Robbe-Grillet equates *écriture* and *lecture*, but even here, in these early novels, the equation of writing and reading is implied.

Critics have pointed out both the *roman policier* elements and the use of the Oedipus myth in *Les Gommes*. Often they do so as if the two structures functioned separately, when in fact it is their interplay that is crucial to the act of reading and interpreting the text. From early on the reader is made aware of the fact that Daniel Dupont is still alive, a fact unknown to the detective investigating his death, Wallas. As he reads, he also learns, before the event and even before Wallas, that it is

6 In *Pour un nouveau roman* (Paris: Minuit, 1963), p. 32.

Wallas who will be Dupont's actual murderer. It is in the mechanism of this learning process that the murder mystery conventions and the myth's structure come into play—and interplay.

Through the detective plot clues, the reader follows Wallas as he tries to discover the murderee as well as the murderer. Why does Laurent not have possession of the murdered body? How could Dupont have died as he did? There are too many accounts, including conflicting newspaper stories, one of which has the victim as one *Albert* Dupont, who indeed dies the *next* night. But the reader also has another set of clues to interpret. Why has Wallas' watch stopped at 7:30 p.m., Monday? Why is Wallas confused about the day of the week— Monday or Tuesday? Why is he unsure of his goal? Does he really resemble the suspect, André WS? Is he André WS? Why is one bullet missing from his gun, a gun exactly like Dupont's?

It is only through the interaction of these clues with the Oedipus myth structure that the crime's inevitability appears to the reader. Gradually details mount up: the statue of the Chariot of State on the way to the rue de Corinthe, the drunk with his riddle (what animal is a parricide in the morning, incestuous at noon, blind at night?), the eraser with its middle letters of "DI" in a word of seven or maybe six letters (like the police phone number of 124-24-- OEDIPUS, OEDIPE), the picture of the ruins of Thebes, the bronze statue of a blind man, the rue Bergère where Wallas notices his swollen feet, sore from walking. These details serve to give context to the most important of the myth's uses: Wallas recalls having been in this town earlier with his mother. At first he cannot remember the circumstances—a visit? an inquiry about a legacy? It is only at the point at which he recalls that they were really seeking his unknown father that the detective clues fall into place and the reader knows, even before the repetition of the exact description of the killer's preparations in the study, that Wallas will murder Dupont (who may indeed have a son, the reader is told). Alone, neither the mystery plot nor the myth would have guided the act of reading sufficiently to allow the reader's prior knowledge of the crime (and the detective's ironic lack of it). As Jean Ricardou states: "l'activité d'Oedipe est une opération aléthéique: elle *dévoile* ce qui a eu lieu; l'activité de Wallas une opération productrice: elle *engendre* ce qui n'était pas."[7] Whereas Oedipus moves from error to knowledge, Wallas moves allegorically from fiction (Dupont's feigned death) to reality (his real death). Since the investigation precedes and brings on the crime, it is the reader who must indeed endeavour to interpret the meaning of the internalized structures.

In addition, the Prologue-Epilogue-five chapter (act) structure contributes to the already strong self-reflectiveness of the text as a text. One finds, for example, in section two of the prologue, that as Garinati

7 *Le Nouveau Roman* ([Paris]: Seuil, 1973), p. 33.

follows Bona's precise directions and instructions for the killing, several significant images (all the more noteworthy in a book of few metaphors) appear: the plan is said to be like perfectly adjusted machinery which bears no surprises; in fact, all Garinati needs to do is follow the text, reciting phrase after phrase, like an actor reading his script, in order to fulfil the word and have Lazarus rise from the tomb. Of course, the reader only needs to do the same to discover a Dupont rising from his tomb. Just as Wallas gives up trying to explain his interpretation of the case to Laurent in carefully chosen words and instead falls back on clichés and ready-made formulae, so Robbe-Grillet uses the clichéd structural conventions of detective fiction in such a way that the act of reading becomes one of active participation, of "production." And this is one of the aims of covertly narcissistic texts.

2. FANTASY

It is interesting to note that metafictionists who use the detective structures also often use those of fantasy literature. Borges professes to intense interest in both Chesterton and Poe (who wrote those horror fantasies but who also "invented" the detective story); Nabokov was influenced, he claims,[8] by Wells as much as by Conan Doyle. The next chapter will examine the linguistic relation between the referents of fictional language as they accumulate for the reader, building up the novelistic world. This is true of *any* narrative, but is especially clear in the conscious realization of the process itself in narcissistic texts. In fantasy literature, the fictiveness of these referents is axiomatic: the time and space of such narratives need not correspond to those of the reader's experience.

In the kind of metafiction which structures its temporal and spatial relations with the reader on the model of fantasy literature, the act of reading is presented as going one step beyond the one suggested by the detective model above. It involves not just the interpretation of clues and the construction of an ordered plot. It also involves (perhaps at a more fundamental level) the very act of imagining the world, of giving shape to the referents of the words that go to make up the whole of the world that is the "concretized" text being read. Again, this is true of all fiction, but, while accepted as axiomatic in fantasy, it is made self-evidently so in metafiction using this model of covert diegetic narcissism.

All literature could be said to be "escape" literature: readers as well as authors want to create worlds as real as, but other than, the world that is, to use the narrator's terms in *The French Lieutenant's Woman*. In fact, all reading (whether of novels, history or science) is a kind of "escape"

8 Interview with Alfred Appel, Jr., in *Novel* (Spring 1971), reprinted in Nabokov's *Strong Opinions* (New York: McGraw-Hill, 1973), pp. 174–75.

in that it involves a temporary transfer of consciousness from the reader's empirical surroundings to things imagined rather than perceived. Perhaps it is the imposed order and coherence, as well as the fictiveness, of the worlds created by the imagination that separate them from other linguistic constructs. The act of reading partakes of man's lived life; what he reads competes, during that act, with the empirical world he inhabits. If this is seen as desirable, then one speaks of the freedom, the liberation of the mind through art; if it is not, then one talks of literature as "escape" in derogatory terms. Theoreticians of the *nouveau roman* were quick to claim the freedom-inducing properties of the new fiction; because of its linguistic and fictive[9] natures, the novelistic universe can and does compete with the empirical. And its paradigm is the world of fantasy.

The reader's act of forming the universe of fantasy (or of metafiction using fantasy as a model) is like that of forming all novelistic worlds in that it provides the freedom — or the "escape" — of an ordered vision, perhaps a kind of "vital" consolation for living in a world whose order one usually perceives and experiences only as chaos. That the order here is of a fictive universe does not matter; the need and desire for such order is real, as is the need for freedom, for the liberation of the imagination from the bondage of empirical fact.

Not only have works of metafiction and fantasy become simultaneously plentiful recently (the Tolkien fad being only one manifestation of the latter), but they have both often been denied the critical treatment allowed to "serious" literature. However, neither represents a current outside the central mode of literature or fiction (that is, realism), as some have claimed.[10] Fantasy is indeed the "other side of realism" and represents historically a parallel and equally valid literary tradition. The most extreme autonomous universes of fantasy are still referential; if they were not the reader could not imagine their existence.[11] This has always been the case. In diachronic terms, the same external and internal forces and concerns that spawned traditional realistic fiction could be said to have created Science Fiction. Did the interest and curiosity in exploration promote only true travel tales (and

9 See Roland Barthes, "Introduction à l'analyse structurale des récits," *Communications* no. 8 (1966), 26–27 and Jean Alter, "Perspectives et modèles" in *Nouveau Roman: hier, aujourd'hui* 1 (Paris: Union Générale d'Editions, 10/18, 1972), 52–53.

10 See Patricia Meyer Spacks, "Power and Meaning in *The Lord of the Rings*" in Neil D. Isaacs and Rose A. Zimbardo (eds.), *Tolkien and the Critics* (Notre Dame, Indiana: University of Notre Dame Press, 1968), p. 99 and in the same volume, Burton Raffel, "*The Lord of the Rings* as Literature," pp. 232, 240, 246.

11 See Witold Ostrowski, "The Fantastic and the Realistic in Literature," *Zagadnienia rodzajów literackich* 9, no. 1 (1966), 63: "A work of completely fantastic fiction would have to present creatures that are completely different from us and modes of existence and action with their space and time settings completely alien to us. To tell a story about them the writer would have to use a new, non-human language and then the story would be unintelligible, unimaginable, and awfully uninteresting."

so *Robinson Crusoe*) or can one include Gulliver's imaginary voyages? The positivistic, scientific materialism of the last century brought both *L'Assomoir* and *Frankenstein*.

From the point of view of the reader it is no easier to create and believe in the well-documented world of Zola than it is for him to imagine hobbits or elves: the imaginative leap into the novel's world of time and space must be made in both cases. Any literary landscapes, inhabitants or events can be made credible. "A dream world may be full of inexplicable gaps and logical inconsistencies;" explained Auden, "an imaginary world may not, for it is a world of law, not of wish. Its laws may be different from those which govern our own, but they must be as intelligible and inviolable."[12] Like Tolkien's Middle Earth, Borges' self-reflective world in "Tlön, Uqbar, Orbis Tertius" has its own history, geography, culture, its own inhabitants, myths, and language.

The invented autonomous cosmos of fantasy becomes a model in metafiction for the temporal and spatial structuration of both the universe of the work and its very narration—and this is so from the perspectives of both writer and reader. Moving from the views of Pnin and Humbert Humbert, émigrés who see America as an invented land, through the fictive countries of Padukgrad of *Bend Sinister* and Zembla of *Pale Fire*, Nabokov in *Ada* proceeds to rework both time (Veen's time) and space (Terra versus Antiterra), making Van's world as real as the novel's and both as real as the reader's.

The complex interplay of dream and reality, fiction and fact, structures Borges' already-mentioned "Tlön, Uqbar, Orbis Tertius." A metafictional allegory of all reading and writing processes, it presents the story of the creation of another cosmos which decidedly seduces and takes over the existing real one. Italo Calvino's *Le città invisibili* (Torino: Einaudi, 1972) is a more extended version of this same mode. In it Marco Polo provides the Kublai Khan with descriptions of the cities of his empire that the discoverer has already visited (and some he will visit in the future). Soon the ruler notices that these cities, each with a seductive female name, resemble each other, as if the traveller were merely shifting common elements around. He is annoyed then because he feels mocked by Marco Polo's lies: these cities have never existed except in words, or if they did, they no longer do. The stories that follow this outburst (such as "Olivia") reveal, on the contrary, that falsehood is never in words but in things. Later the explorer points out that the ear, not the voice, determines the nature of the tale: like the reader of Calvino's stories, the listener of Marco Polo's constructs the cities in his imagination, feeling free to wander about or leave at will. Kublai Khan remarks that Marco has never spoken of his own city, Venice. With a smile, the storyteller asks what else he has ever spoken of. Each description of each city has said something about Venice. Yet

12 "The Quest Hero" in Isaacs and Zimbardo (eds.), *Tolkien and the Critics*, p. 50.

he avoids speaking of it directly for fear of losing it. Fictive referents are more real to the imagination than are real ones. Stories are only stories—and therein lie their enormous power and value.

This same diegetic concern is revealed more covertly in Calvino's earlier works, *Cosmicomiche* (Torino: Einaudi, 1965) and *Ti con zero* (Torino: Einaudi, 1967). In these stories, the author becomes intrigued with the imaginative possibilities for narrative which lie latent in scientific theories of creation (of the universe, the earth, the body) and in mathematical and logical concepts of time and space.[13] In most of the tales the narrator, one Qfwfq, tells of the time when he was only consciousness, straining to achieve bodily form. The referents of the scientific theory are real enough, but in the context of Qfwfq's narration they become fictive,[14] the fuel for imaginative flight.

Taking the human reader into account, Qfwfq tries to explain his pre-human state as consciousness straining to perceive the new forms of nature by assembling sensations which allow a visual or aural image to form. Then, of course, comes the problem of naming objects and states. Fantasy, Calvino reveals, shares with science the burden of inadequate linguistic resources which threaten to block actual perception; Qfwfq's situation differs in that he can express his states *afterwards* without the danger of language guiding or tyrannizing what he actually perceives. In metafictional terms, the interest is in the structural similarity between the efforts of the humanoid consciousness toward perception, meaning, and naming and the imaginative processes of the reader of fiction who must not—once the text has established itself—allow real referents to blind him to what is really a fictive world. The naming process is done anew in each work.

Qfwfq is content to allow his reader liberties with his story: the process of narration, though guided by him, is open. In *Ti con zero*, in a story about the origin of the birds, the narrator tells the reader, if he does not like the far-fetched (and textually self-conscious) means by which Qfwfq has arrived at the land of the birds, that he can make up another. The important thing is to have him arrive there somehow. Umberto Eco's "opera aperta," the freedom within a certain order, here takes on diegetic form.

Indeed, in many tales, Qfwfq is presented as the order-maker, the one who tries to discover meaning through system in the chaos of life data—human and pre-human. The act of reading these texts is analogous to this process, as Calvino suggests in "Priscilla," in the second

13 See, for a full discussion of this point, Gian-Paolo Biasin, "$\frac{4}{3}\pi r^3$ (Scientific vs. Literary Space)," *Versus* 19/20 (1978), 173–88.

14 Science fiction, according to Kingsley Amis, is "that class of prose narrative treating of a situation that could not arise in the world we know, but which is hypothesized on the basis of some innovation in science or technology, or pseudo-science or pseudo-technology, whether human or extra-terrestrial in origin." *New Maps of Hell* (New York: Harcourt, Brace, 1960), p. 18.

section of *Ti con zero* which ends with a narrating voice desiring (this is intercellular love) to capture his beloved at last in words, and at least on the page unite "io" and "Priscilla."

Calvino's metafictional fantasies range over time and space both, as do those of Alejo Carpentier, although these are even more directly concerned with narrative time. One of his books, *Guerra del tiempo*, takes its title from Lope de Vega's image of the soldiers in the "war of time." One story in this volume begins in the time of the *Iliad*, Book One, with Agamemnon's ships taking on soldiers to go to Troy, and it continues in section two as the (now) Spanish ships prepare to leave for the new world. In section three, the soldier seen in the first two is now in sixteenth-century France, bidding farewell to his jealous virginal sweetheart; in four, the now Teutonic soldier goes off to a brothel in frustration before leaving; in five, before finally leaving for Troy, he goes home, only to find his sweetheart in his bed. Rumour has it too that Helen is happy with Paris anyway.

The temporal and spatial circling is both a fantasy structure and a metafictional device which points to the literary and fictive ontological status of the text. Carpentier's next tale in the volume is a fragment of a text, beginning at Chapter Four. Already the reader is made aware of the textual identity of the story. It turns out to be essentially a multicultural coming together of all the flood myth heroes, their gods, and their creation myths. In some cultures man is born of woman (Noah), in others of pebbles (Deucalion), in others, of palm seeds (Amaliwak). This latter, ignoring his counterparts' advice, scatters seeds to repopulate the earth, but a vague story of a woman's abduction divides the crowd into factions and war results. The temporal play here is intratextual, as this tale links up with its seemingly independent predecessor. The act of reading becomes one of ordering as well as imagining, sense-making as well as world-building.

Narrative has the power to reverse time: its words progress in a linear fashion in space and time but the referents of those words can be temporally reversed. In another story, "Journey Back to the Source," Carpentier forces, through the structures of fantasy, this very realization upon the reader. An old man pokes amid the rubble of a building being torn down. When the workers leave, the house puts itself back together, like a movie in reverse. Don Martial lies on his death bed. The candles begin to lengthen and he is now in bed with a woman. At dawn the clock strikes six p.m. The woman is a necessity for the Don, since his wife has died. Coming home one day, he finds his wife and her relatives. Martial (not Don Martial now) is an ardent lover of his wife, but after an argument, they put on their wedding clothes and go off to be married in order to regain their freedom. Presents are returned. Rings are taken back to have inscriptions removed, and a new life begins for Martial. One night after too much drink, the clock seems to

strike five, then four, then three, but the hero pays no heed. He has a party when he reaches his minority; his signature now is no longer valid. After entering school, he learns less and less, while enduring his puberty and adolescent sexual obsessions. Furniture grows taller; he sits on the floor and plays with toys. Once he is given sweets and locked in a room with Melchior, the groom, so that he will not see the coffin. He then visits his sick father. Once an admirer of Melchior, he soon forgets him and plays only with the dogs. Achieving ultimate liberty he talks his own language. Then he feels only hunger, thirst, heat, pain, cold; his field of perception is reduced. After closing his eyes he enters a warm damp body, slipping towards life. At this point, birds return to eggs, fish congeal to roe, the marble appears on a ship returning to Italy, leather gloves grow hair, the bricks return to clay and the house disappears. The angry demolition crew returns and marches in protest to the park where the men sit as the sun goes from east to west, from life to death.

In this short narrative, Carpentier can allegorically present the power of language and of narrative in an emblematic fashion. It is not only in fantasy that time is so controlled: Scott, Balzac, Stendhal—all jumped over fictional years in mere lines of narrative, or in the space between chapters. Characters appear in other places without the reader's having observed their travels. The "fantastic" temporal and spatial self-involvement of metafictional works of the covert diegetic mode is ultimately emblematic of the imaginative leaps in time and space required in the reading of *any* fictional work. Such narcissism brings to the reader's attention the fact that fantasy is not a deviation from either reality[15] or the conventions of realism.[16] Any text— realistic or fantastic—uses certain conventions in order to create its own reality.

It was suggested earlier that narrative is a basic human faculty, transferred to art from life. Storytelling is imaginative, ordered construction in language. Fantasy, as a human psychological impulse, is the source of the inventive energy that created man's earliest myths as well as his most self-conscious modern art: nature is humanized, assimilated to human forms.[17] Bergson felt that the "fonction fabulatrice" was a human necessity, giving the mind instinctual images free from the perception of the empirical world or reason. Jean Bellemin-Noël has noted that: "ce ne sont peut-être pas les longs romans réalistes, ceux qui se soucient de copier peu ou prou le réel de notre monde quotidien, qui nous disent le plus long sur ce qui constitue au fond

15 See Michel Butor, "Science Fiction: The Crisis of Its Growth" in Thomas D. Clareson (ed.), *SF: The Other Side of Realism* (Bowling Green, Ohio: Bowling Green University Press, 1971), pp. 157–65.
16 See Rudolf B. Schmerl, "Fantasy as Technique," ibid., pp. 110–15.
17 See Northrop Frye, "Myth, Fiction, and Displacement," in *Fables of Identity* (New York: Harcourt, Brace and World, 1963), p. 31.

notre réalité la plus profonde, notre vrai rapport au monde: ce sont les contes de la nuit, du délire et de la fantaisie."[18] In "The Relation of the Poet to Day-dreaming," Freud saw the importance of fantasies driven by unsatisifed wishes—in this case, wishes for an ordered meaningful universe, the totality one can probably only find, or rather create, as a reader or a writer of fiction.

All novelistic fiction-making and world-ordering find paradigms in the reading of fantasy, and it is this realization that the covert diegetic mode of metafiction exploits. This productive labour is no longer the explicit subject of overt teachings to the reader; the text now forces him to read with his imaginative and ordering faculties alert and at work.

3. GAME

While the detective and fantasy structures are the most frequently used in this mode of narcissism, the game model appears often enough to warrant attention. At Cerisy in 1971, Robbe-Grillet gave the theoretical and ideological justification for the conceptual model of the "jeu" in the *nouveau roman*.[19] With the disappearance of the old myths of "profondeur" (and the bourgeois order of values) came the loss of the sense of the "sérieux" behind art. Behind the "jeu" there is nothing; it is all surface, like a game of cards in which each card has no meaning in itself. However, the player organizes his cards into a "hand" and, within the context of the game's code or rules, gives them their significance. This is not a hindrance to the player's freedom, but rather it is the very "champ de cette liberté," allowing him to project his personal ordered creation and meaning upon the chaos of the world. If the cards he plays with are words, then his task is even more creative: "votre organisation du jeu dans votre main, la bataille sur la table seront en même temps la création des règles, la création du jeu et l'exercice de votre liberté, donc aussi bien la destruction des règles, pour laisser de nouveau le champ libre à l'homme libre qui viendra encore après."

In using a game model, metafiction calls attention to a free creative activity (as in fantasy) within self-evolving rules, an activity that is the same in all fiction reading. The reader must either learn the code (that is, create it) or be unable to bring the fictive world into play. As Claudio Guillén has observed,[20] the early Robbe-Grillet, in trying to divorce seeing from knowing, engages his reader in a sort of "metaphysical" game, a fluid contest with changing rules and high stakes. The links here with the detective structure are clear. Since Poe first codified "The Gold Bug," the deciphering of codes by the sleuth and the reader has

18 "Notes sur le fantastique (textes de Théophile Gautier)," *Littérature* 8 (décembre 1972), 23.

19 *Nouveau Roman: hier, aujourd'hui* 1: 127–28.

20 "On the Concept and Metaphor of Perspective," *Literature as System* (Princeton: Princeton University Press, 1971), p. 355.

been a major motivational force in the action of interpretation—or in the game plan. The murder of *The Finishing Stroke* is committed with the aid of the Phoenician alphabet as a code to lure the ingenious Ellery Queen. Parodic metafictional structures also demand that the reader learn rules, codes—literary this time—in order to understand the text. Nabokov has called parody a game, but a serious, if delicate one.[21]

One of the favourite metafictional game structures seems to be that inherently narrative one—chess—with its characters of all classes, its intrigues, and action. This is used either covertly as a structure, as in Sollers' *Drame*, or in a more overt manner, while still remaining structural, as in Nabokov's *The Defense*. Here, Luzhin, the chess master, reads Jules Verne and Conan Doyle, attracted to "that exact and relentlessly unfolding pattern" which he finds in their plots. Like the chess player, the reader too develops a strategy. The chess-board of dark and pale squares of the ground below the window out of which Luzhin throws himself to commit suicide, is also the black and white of the printed page—all that is left of the hero. An ardent chess player and problem-deviser himself, Nabokov denies that his novels are plotted like games,[22] while admitting that his (narcissistic) narratives do have inexorable rules of logic (as do all literary universes) that govern their proceeding.

In Calvino's *Le città invisibili*, Kublai Khan tries to understand by analogy the cities of his empire (in order to possess them) through the means of chess playing. He presumes a coherent, harmonious, codified system which, he learns, does not exist in the cities at all, although it does in Marco Polo's and Calvino's literary narratives.

Robert Coover uses a multidimensional game image to structure his novel, *The Universal Baseball Association, Inc. J. Henry Waugh, Prop.* An accountant, paradoxically fascinated by the laws of chance and probability, Henry begins his real life after work as he sits down to his creation—a dice game of baseball, complete with league records, politics (since officers are elected every four years for each club), rewards, penalties, personnel (old players die; rookies break in). A gradual process begins: the fantasy game comes to impinge more and more on his working life. Reality begins to copy art: Pete in the bar reminds him of Jake, one of his creations. Although this game serves as an allegorical comment on American life and values, it is of interest here because it is an extended internalized structural metaphor of the novel, as well as an overtly metafictional allegory of the creative process.

Henry's invention of his players (dialogue, looks, mannerisms) and their contexts (favourite songs, love affairs, batting averages) is a *mise en*

21 *Strong Opinions*, pp. 75–76.
22 The critics continue to disbelieve him and attempt to prove otherwise. See, for instance, Andrew Field, *Nabokov: His Life in Art* (Boston: Little, Brown, 1967), pp. 138–39, 175–77, 326–27, 166–67.

abyme of the authorial act of creation that brought Henry into being as well. The *process* of creation is explained by the narrator:

Henry was always careful about names, for they were what gave the league its sense of fulfilment and failure, its emotion. . . . You roll, Player A gets a hit or he doesn't, gets his man out or he doesn't. Sounds simple. But call Player A "Sycamore Flynn" or "Melbourne Trench" and something starts to happen. He shrinks or grows, stretches out or puts on muscle. . . . Strange. But name a man and you make him what he is. Of course, he can develop. . . . But the basic stuff is already there. In the name. Or rather: in the naming.[23]

This game (about a game, baseball) or this fiction (within a fiction, the novel) begins to structure and dominate the "fiction" as well as the "narration" of the text. Henry lives more and more for his league, losing his job, alienating his few friends. Finally, in an echo of Doomsday, Damonsday CLVII ends the game and the Association and the novel of the same name. The game has become itself self-reflective, for on Damonsday new players act out the ritual death of the great Damon Rutherford, once Henry's favourite (until an unlucky throw of the dice killed him in his prime). Henry too has disappeared. In the last chapter there is no narrative framework, just the game itself; no dice, just the action. Chapter *eight* is the last, ending with the Damonsday game also awaiting, of course, the last, the *ninth* inning. Both structurally (covert) and allegorically (overt) the game image works to guide the act of reading—of interpreting, ordering, imagining.

This guiding is made even more self-reflective in Sanguineti's *Il giuoco dell'oca*, which the reader is instructed to order by shooting dice himself. The usual linear plot of fiction is replaced (as in Marc Saporta's *Composition N° 1,* though by a different mechanism—unbound pages) by an accumulative collage effect of verbal images taken from printed sources, unitable (by the reader) only by *motif* and theme, and the narrating "I" who alternately lies in a coffin and sits writing at a desk, "la faccia al pubblico," blurring (by his myopic vision and the poor light of his candle) the visual images that are here verbalized. The dedication to the novel includes Breton's "ce n'est que superpositions d'images 'de catalogue." Also a parody of the convention of the "trionfo della morte," of Dante's voyage in the Malebolge, and of the picaresque tradition,[24] this novel reveals its ideologically operative aim (as did Robbe-Grillet's theorizing) through its equating of the act of reading with that of writing. On the back cover of the 1967 Feltrinelli edition are these instructions to the reader:

E chi avrà fatto tutte queste fermate e avanzate e ritorni e pene e pagamenti, innante e indietro quante fiate correndo come un matto con i suoi dadi e gli occhiali, e il naso

23 (New York: Random House, 1968), pp. 46–47.
24 See Renato Barilli, *L'azione e l'estasi* (Milano: Feltrinelli, 1967), p. 166.

puntato e il mente proteso, sì che giunga primo o postremo alla conclusione del giuoco, ne *avrà tratto il giovamento che pare trarne l'autore*, al lume di quella candela, con la testa tutta piegata sopra il tavolo, lì sopra i suoi fogli, lì sopra i suoi libri con le figure, sopra il suo teschio giallo.

The final section (111) ends with the narrator's decision to write the name of the ship *we* have all been sailing—the title of the novel is then given—followed by another word which he wants placed a little below, in the middle:

"FINE."

In Sanguineti's novel, a game system of self-signifying units organized by the reader replaces traditional novelistic structure, but the narrative of the writing—and reading—of the novel remains intact.

4. THE EROTIC

Although less frequently used to specifically metafictional ends, the erotic or sexual metaphor is also found occasionally as an actualized structure in narcissistic texts. Reading becomes, like the fiction-making that is the author's, an act of possession, of control, as in *The French Lieutenant's Woman*. In *Lolita*, Humbert Humbert learns at last that he can only possess Lolita, only make her live, imaginatively, in a diegetic erotic[25] version shared with the reader.

That very special kind of relationship between reader and writer could be considered erotic by nature: Barth's genie, in *Chimera*, expounds on the mutual involvement and active participation of both parties, each necessary for the text—and each other—to live. Sex is a metaphor for this union of processes in Coover's phallic-laden myth parodies in *Pricksongs and Descants*, or "death-cunt-and-prick songs," as one character calls them. As Robert Scholes has remarked, sex itself is here "the door that connects fictional form and mythic idea."[26]

William Gass's novel, *Willie Masters' Lonesome Wife*,[27] provides a more extended structural use of the erotic model in metafiction. In this textually intriguing work—with its unnumbered pages, different page forms and tints, different print sizes and colours—Gass mirrors the loneliness of the writer in that of sexual intercourse for the heroine who livens up the act by inventing fictional worlds (imagining herself as Madame Bovary). Just as she *is* her body, so "the poet is his language. He sees his world, and words form in his eyes just like the streams and trees there. He feels everything verbally"—as does the reader. She sees herself as only "a string of noises": "These words are all I am." "Not even the Dane is any more than that," she adds.

25 *Lolita* is not pornographic in design or intent, although it is erotic. See Nabokov's "On a Book Entitled *Lolita*" in *Lolita* (New York: G. P. Putnam's Sons, 1955), p. 315.
26 "Metafiction," *Iowa Review* 1 (Fall 1970), 113.
27 (New York: Alfred A. Knopf, 1968), unnumbered pages.

Gass also draws the reader directly into the text by trick footnotes, one of which ends with a verbal rape: "Now that I've got you alone down here, you bastard, don't think I'm letting you get away easily." The narcissism of the text, like that of sex, is here explicit. For instance, after a great proliferation of asterisks, the reader is told: "the stars interfere with reading, pester the eye. (Why don't you go to a movie?)." One page is smudged: "The muddy circle you see just before you and below you represents the ring left on a leaf of the manuscript by my coffee cup. Represents, I say, because, as you must surely realize, this book is many removes from anything I've set pen, hand, or cup to." Aware of the illusion involved in reading, yet insisting that "the acts of the imagination are our most free and natural," Gass plays with that "artificial" yet "vital" paradox present in all narcissistic fiction. Another representation of a coffee cup ring encircles the message: "You have fallen into art—return to life." Although the text deliberately works at being discontinuous, Gass ironically undercuts this as a mere illusion for novelistic art. The final page presents a coffee ring around the navel of a photographed woman—a direct and unifying link to the second sentence of the novel: "there'll be rings on my belly where men have set down drinks"—as there are rings on the manuscript of the narrator.

That the erotic forms the metafictional underpinnings of this novel is what guides the reader through the labyrinthine print of the text. But all novels are erotic in another way—they seek to lure, tantalize, seduce the reader into a world other than his own. Only by forcing the act of reading to become one of imaginative possession, analogous in degree of involvement and active participation to the sexual act, can literature bring itself to life. This is the point that metafiction of this mode brings to the reader's attention.

Far from sharing the fate of a drowned or dead Narcissus, covertly self-reflective narrative often presents the story of its own coming to life, its own creative processes, through the actualized structures of these various models. Detective plots, fantasy, games, the erotic—all these function as self-reflective paradigms, making the act of reading into one of active "production," of imagining, interpreting, decoding, ordering, in short of constructing the literary universe through the fictive referents of the words. Reader and writer both share the process of fiction-making in *language*. And it is this process that must now be investigated.

The Language of Fiction: Creating the Heterocosm of Fictive Referents

> These people aren't real. I'm making them up as I go along, any section that threatens to flesh them out, or make them "walk off the page," will be excised. They should, rather, walk into the page, and break up, disappear.
>
> Gilbert Sorrentino

The theoretical implications of modern metafiction reach out in several significant directions, and many questions come to mind. If literary critical notions of novelistic mimesis must be expanded to include that creative and "vital" process shared by writer and reader, then what subsequent effect will this expansion have on the critical view of the nature of literary language and of the fictional, autonomous identity of the narrated world? If, as recent structuralist theories have suggested, language constructs and directs our world and the limits of what we can conceive and communicate, then can there be such a creature as a transparent linguistic text in the traditional realistic mode? Or does metafiction teach that a text can exist only as language and can function only insofar as it mediates linguistically between writer and reader?

Of all the literary genres, the novel is the one which has perhaps most resisted being "rescued" from the myth of the instrumentality of language. Poetry escaped with the aid of the Symbolists, the New Critics, and others, but the critical fate of the novel has been less open. Part of the problem is no doubt the result of the extended length of the genre. New Critical methods are not totally successful with larger verbal structures, partly because of memory limitations. Since a novel is never a coherent spatio-temporal unit in the reader's mind, as a lyric poem might be, the critic, in discussing its language, must decide whether he will isolate passages for commentary, trace linguistic threads through the work, or use some other method.[1] Metafiction often resolves this

1 See, for example, Roger Fowler and Peter Mercer, "Criticism and the Language of

dilemma in part for the critic by bringing the formal language issue into the foreground, into the thematized content itself.

Whereas poetic language is now more or less accepted as autonomous and intransitive, fiction and narrative still suggest a transitive and referential use of words. This is no doubt in part due to the fact that the novel is written in prose, and prose is usually considered a discursive medium for ideas. It is also associated with ways of verifying facts, since it often records or describes actual events. However, this superficial explanation alone does not suffice to account for the intransigent belief of many critics[2] and readers that the referents of fictional language are real, that is, that they are of necessity part of the empirical world, as if there actually were a stable and objective reality "out there." As a reader begins a novel, he does indeed read referentially in that he refers words to his linguistic and experiential knowledge; gradually, however, these words take on a unity of reference and create a self-contained universe that is its own validity (and "truth"). The fictions and essays of Jorge Luis Borges, for example, stand as allegories and statements of this, the reading (as well as writing) side of *poiesis*. What happens is that the referents of the novelistic language (which, as shall be demonstrated shortly, are fictive and not real) gradually accumulate during the act of reading, gradually construct a "heterocosm," that is, another cosmos, an ordered and harmonious system. This fictional universe is not an object of perception, but an effect to be experienced by the reader, an effect to be *created* by him and in him.

Given the great number of narcissistic texts which thematize the creative process, novelists themselves would seem to be aware of the emblematic or paradigmatic nature of the *act* of creating ordered fictive worlds through language — be it by the author or by the reader. In their basic relations to themselves, comments Robert Musil's narrator in *Der Mann ohne Eigenschaften*, most people are narrators. What they like is the orderly sequence of facts, because it has the look of a necessity. By means of the impression that their lives have a "course," most people manage to feel somehow sheltered in the midst of chaos.

As Frank Kermode has pointed out,[3] fictions are indeed man's way of dealing with the discrete brute facts of chaotic reality. He constructs ordered worlds, mental structures which humanize time by giving it the form of narrative plots. The novelistic universe draws at least some of its potency from this paradigm, and so Kermode fears that the self-reflective literary forms of today reveal a loss of confidence in our

Literature," *Style* 3 (1969), 45–72; David Lodge, *Language of Fiction* (New York: Columbia University Press, 1966), p. x; and Ian Watt, "The First Paragraph of *The Ambassadors*," *Essays in Criticism* 10 (1960), 250–74.

2 See, for a blatant example, Jean-Paul Sartre, "L'Ecrivain et sa langue," *Situations* 9 (Paris: Gallimard, 1972), 40–82, as well as his famous "Qu'est-ce que la littérature?" in *Situations* 2 (Paris: Gallimard, 1948), 57–330.

3 *The Sense of an Ending* (1966; reprinted, New York: Oxford University Press, 1970).

"human concords." Although he remarks upon the progression from a literature which assumed it was imitating an order to one which assumes it must create its own order, Kermode does not go on to note that, as has been suggested here, the process *per se,* the act of creating any new ordered world, is in itself a human act of great intrinsic interest and quite in accord with those human concords, if at another level of realization. The act of creation becomes paradigmatic of all human acts of constructing ordered visions. The writer and reader share this process in and through the novelistic text.

Narrative itself could be seen, then, as a natural mental act, as much a part of life as art. We do not, it is true, take leave of fiction-making when we abandon fairy tales and childhood games. We always tell stories — to escape, to remake, to alter our past and our future. To teach this is the thematized function of the protagonist, Sarah, in John Fowles's novel, *The French Lieutenant's Woman.* The novel is not a copy of the empirical world, nor does it stand in opposition to it. It is rather a continuation of that ordering, fiction-making process that is part of our normal coming to terms with experience.

In John Barth's novel, *The End of the Road*, the mythic world-creating, or the storytelling capacity of the mind, is thematized overtly as the basis of "mythotherapy." In life, as the doctor explains to the hero, Jacob Horner, "there are no essentially major or minor characters. To that extent, all fiction and biography, and most historiography, are a lie. Everyone is necessarily the hero of his own life story . . . we're the ones who conceive the story, and give other people the essences of minor characters."[4] For Barth, as for Fowles, the narrative heterocosmic impulse is related to human choice and existential freedom. "So in a sense," continues the doctor, "fiction isn't a lie at all, but a true representation of the distortion that everyone makes of life."

Jacob, who is significantly a teacher of the English language — the means by which he creates his fictions — is in the grip of a Pirandellian relativity paradox. To turn experience into linguistic speech, he reflects:

—that is, to classify, to categorize, to conceptualize, to grammarize, to syntactify it — is always a betrayal of experience, a falsification of it; but only so betrayed can it be dealt with at all, and only in so dealing with it did I ever feel a man, alive and kicking. It is therefore that, when I had cause to think about it at all, I responded to this precise falsification, this adroit, careful *myth-making*, with all the upsetting exhilaration of *any artist at his work*. When my mythoplastic razors were sharply honed, it was unparalleled sport to lay about with them, to have at reality.[5]

Jacob perceives that language, by its creative power, is the key to this myth-making; by its structures, it is the means to the only lucidity man

4 (1958; reprinted, Garden City, New York: Doubleday, 1967), p. 83.
5 Ibid., pp. 112–13, italics mine.

can ever know. Novels such as this which show a character looking at—that is, creating—the novelistic world, mime the mind's ordering process of coding and decoding, ciphering and deciphering. And the essence of literary language lies not in its conforming to the kind of statement found in factual studies, but in its ability to create something new, a coherent, motivated universe. Svevo's hero in *La coscienza di Zeno*, thinking that he can be the novelist of his own life, learns that to recapture the past is to structure it, to falsify it, to invent it, in short, as if it belonged to someone else. Later, in "Il vecchione," the only part of the past that Zeno actually can recall as real is what he wrote down — that is, in part invented due to his linguistic limitations: a native Triestine-speaker, Zeno can only relate in Italian those parts of his world for which he has sufficient vocabulary.

As the "content" of a work of art, the heterocosm is not necessarily to be judged by its relationship to extralinguistic, extraliterary reality. What Mukařovský claimed for poetry holds true for fiction: "the question of truthfulness does not apply in regard to the subject matter of a work of poetry, nor does it even make sense. Even if we posed the question and answered it positively or negatively as the case may be, the question has no bearing on the artistic value of the work; it can only serve to determine the extent to which the work has documentary value."[6] The heterocosm has inner motivation and validity; its relationship to "truth" may be irrelevant, for the *reader*, at least.

This idea of a heterocosm that the reader and writer create together is not merely a concept of just *another* world. The *cosmos* is "the world or universe as an *ordered* and *harmonious* system" (*Oxford English Dictionary*). Even in classical mimetic theory, mirrors are seen to create worlds even as they imitate (as Plato explains in the *Republic* 10). Literature remains a self-sufficient aesthetic system of internal relations among parts that aim at an Aristotelian harmony which the reader actualizes. Along with the ordered and self-informing characteristics of the novelistic universe (as created in the act of reading), the reader must also come to terms with its fictive nature. Since fiction is not a way of viewing reality, but a reality in its own right, the fictive heterocosm will have its own rules which govern the logic or motivation of its parts. It will have rules or codes of which the reader becomes gradually aware as he proceeds.

As well as being ordered and fictional, the heterocosm is constructed in and through language, and both author and reader share the responsibility for this work. For the *reader*, literature has a particular context created by those relationships activated between words. Also, the actual referents of those words are not necessarily real in the

6 "Standard Language and Poetic Language," in Seymour Chatman and Samuel R. Levin (eds.), *Essays on the Language of Literature* (Boston: Houghton Mifflin, 1967), p. 246.

context of empirical reality. The result of the potential dual remove from the "real" is the liberation of the reader from the world he knows only through the senses. The fictiveness of the referent of the novel's sign is responsible for this freeing of language from being a mere counter to any reality outside fiction. It is simplistic to claim that detective stories are "unrealistic," as does one critic,[7] because, although full of murders, no one really dies. Surely, this is true of all fiction: no one fictional event is more or less real than any other.

This is not to deny the novel's "vital" connection, that is, its link to life. It has been claimed that novelists feel that they use language only as the verbal mediation of a devised succession of events.[8] Yet, as David Lodge responded to this view: "whatever novelists 'feel,' it is axiomatic that it is only through language that they are communicating."[9] Lodge accepts Wittgenstein's view that consciousness is conceptual or verbal; we know preverbal experience exists, but we cannot be conscious of it without verbal concepts. Articulation is understanding. The primacy of language in the creative *and* cognitive processes is what Nabokov, Joyce, Beckett, and even Flaubert have suggested to their readers.

What has here been referred to as the "linguistic heterocosm," however, does have its own ontological status as a self-sufficient artifact to be brought to life, or "concretized," by the reader. It does not partake of the contingency of life, however much it may thematize it or borrow from it in its genesis: witness *La Nausée*, once again. This heterocosm is a totality in a way that lived life is not.[10] This has always been the case. "En voyant reparaître dans *Le Père Goriot*," wrote Balzac, "quelques-uns des personnages déjà créés, le public a compris l'une des plus hardies intentions de l'auteur, celle de donner la vie et le mouvement à tout un monde fictif."[11] The concept of an autonomous and coherent fictional universe is implicit, then, in even that rigorous nineteenth-century period-concept of novelistic "realism." The ontological independence of the fictional world depends, not on "truth," but rather on the notion of validity or motivation, on both that dynamic logic and that formal coherence within the text. That Gregor Samsa turns into an insect is made logical and credible within the literary world of Kafka's *Die Verwandlung*. The functional logic of this change in appearance cannot follow the logic of literal or even of one-to-one symbolic representa-

7 Katherine Lever, *The Novel and the Reader* (New York: Appleton-Century-Crofts, [1960]), p. 26.
8 E.g., Malcolm Bradbury, "Towards a Poetics of Fiction: 1) An Approach through Structure," *Novel* 1 (Fall 1967), 50−51.
9 "Towards a Poetics of Fiction: 2) An Approach through Language," *Novel* 1 (Winter 1968), 160.
10 See Georges Lukács, *La Théorie du roman* ([Neuwied am Rhein]: Editions Gontier, 1963), p. 28.
11 Quoted by Michel Butor, "Balzac et la réalité," *Répertoire* 1 (Paris: Editions de Minuit, 1960), 86.

tion. But this different order of logic does not at all invalidate the paradigmatic function of the reader's (and the author's) construction of the heterocosm. That mimetic art/life (or "vital") connection continues to operate; it functions as a way of linking two worlds — that lived in and that living through the reader.

In most novels, it is the narrator who provides the reader with the most explicit bridge into a novelistic universe, since, for the reader, his living in that world is simultaneous with his writing of it: "as long as I live or write (which in my case means the same thing)," comments Tristram Shandy (III, iv). The narrating historian of Gabriel García Márquez's heterocosmic Macondo (in *Cien años de soledad*) presents to the reader real historical events (the Colombian civil wars) as if lived for the first time in his fictional world where fantastic things occur equally logically; time and space have no meaning outside the text itself.

Fantasy literature is in this sense the extreme form of all novelistic creation, as the last chapter suggested in another context; new viable worlds must be created, but the medium is the language of *this* world, the use of which might be said to limit the novelist's ability to evoke in the reader the figures of his imagination. But *all* novelists must convince the reader of the reality of their fictive worlds during the reading act; and they must do so through language alone. Fantastic novels may perhaps demand an increased effort on the writer's part because of the axiomatic imaginary character of their worlds. Or is the opposite true? Do the reader's expectations as he reads a fantasy novel perhaps facilitate the task by also making axiomatic the fictiveness of the referents of the language? No one demands that Tolkien's Middle Earth be a counter to our empirical world, just that it be a coherent heterocosm. Tolkien himself wrote that the successful story-maker creates "a Secondary World which your mind can enter. Inside it, what he relates is 'true': it accords with the laws of that world. You therefore believe it, while you are, as it were, inside."[12] This is true of even the more radical fantasy worlds such as that of Ambrose Bierce's "The Damned Thing" where there are colours human eyes cannot see and sounds human ears cannot hear, or in David Lindsay's land of Tormance (in *A Voyage to Arcturus*) where the human hero, Maskull, has to grow new non-human organs to cope with the geographical and emotional peculiarities of each region.

However, the more traditional novel within a mimetic code has to battle constantly with the very demands for empirical counters that fantasy literature can evade. Perhaps the self-conscious thematization of this battle in modern metafiction is aimed at forcing recognition of the fact that the referent of fiction is not necessarily the same as that of nonliterary language. Prose may be the form of our newspapers and our letters, but there is an important difference in context between my

12 "On Fairy-Stories," *The Tolkien Reader* (New York: Ballantine, 1966), p. 37.

letter to my parents and Richardson's Pamela's to the Andrews. My letter will be judged by informational or expressive criteria—the accuracy and interest of its details, my sincerity as writer; but the details and form both of Pamela's letter have a structural function in the plot and character motivation of the novel. They have no necessary relationship to real referents outside the text of the novel. In literature, the language creates its object; it does not have to describe an object outside itself. Literary language has a kind of fundamental reality of its own, marking, as Blanchot has suggested,[13] not the presence of real objects, but their absence.

This problem cannot be resolved in purely linguistic terms since my letter and Pamela's can and must be treated without their contexts, that is, in the same manner linguistically. A word—"dog" for instance—in either letter consists of the written representation of an acoustic image and a concept of dog-ness, as opposed to cat-ness, perhaps. Within a Saussurian or Hjelmslevian frame of reference, it is this signifier and signified that are important for signification, and not the denotative relationship of sign and referent.

Jean Ricardou feels that the confusion of traditional realism is one between the signified of a literary sign and its referent: "je songe à tous les gens qui pensent à propos de tel roman: moi, à la place de tel personnage, j'aurais fait autre chose. . . . Eh bien, ces gens font en quelque sorte passer un personnage du domaine du signifié à celui du référent."[14] However, Ricardou has ignored a more basic point—that the signified of the literary language is the same as that of ordinary language; it is the nature of the *referent* that has changed. Such people as he mentions confuse, not signified and referent in this case, but real and fictive referents.

This latter distinction was made by Georges Lavis in 1971 in "Le Texte littéraire, le référent, le réel, le vrai,"[15] in response to Arrivé's contention (in *Langue française* 3 [septembre 1969]) that the literary text had no referent. At the level of *langue*, Lavis claims, using Saussure's definition of reference, there are real referents which can be either physical (*table, front*) or non-physical (*honnêteté*). There are also fictive referents which are physical (*licorne*) or non-physical (*ubiquité*). At this *langue* level, fictive referents are not real because they are non-existent in empirical reality.

On the level of *parole* this issue is more complex. Referents can again be real, as in most ordinary language usage, or fictive (physical or not). Here, however, they are fictive either because they are lies (false

13 "La Littérature et le droit à la mort," in *La Part du feu* (Paris: Gallimard, 1949), pp. 327–34.
14 *Nouveau Roman: hier, aujourd'hui* 2 (Paris: Union Générale d'Editions, 10/18, 1972), 43.
15 *Cahiers d'analyse textuelle* no. 13 (1971), 7–22.

referents) or because the objects are imagined. It is this latter instance that is of interest here (although one might note that the denigration of fiction in earlier centuries as "lies" has its root in the question of false and fictive referents). In the literary text there are no such things as real referents for the reader: all are fictive—*table, front, licorne, honnê-teté, ubiquité*—and some doubly so (e.g. *licorne*). The *reader* accepts this once he accepts the fact that what he is reading is an imaginative construct. That the *author* may or may not have had real referents in mind can never be determined with certainty.

Norman Mailer's *The Armies of the Night* (New York: New American Library, 1968) acknowledges these kinds of referents; its two parts are the novel as history and history as a novel. Genres are not just classificatory devices; they also enable the reader to orient himself and to understand the context in which he must interpret the work. "Dans le roman," wrote Blanchot, "l'acte de lire n'est pas changé, mais l'attitude de celui qui lit le rend différent."[16] It is very relevant to the reading experience whether or not the referent is believed to be real or fictive—that is, whether one is reading about the "real" world or creating an imaginary one for oneself.

That reification of what was essentially a temporally limited concept of "realism" into a definition of the entire genre has resulted in the positing of the referent of fiction as real, with the underlying assertion and apologia for the novel, that if something "really happened" (or could be made to seem so), it was then its own justification and verification.[17] This "referential illusion" destroys the integrity of the sign, cancelling out the Saussurian signified by presuming direct collusion between referent and signifier. This substitutes a kind of incomplete denotation (sign/referent becomes signifier/referent) for connotation in order to create what Barthes called an "effet de réel."

Yet, even early or very traditionally realistic novels have thematized this effect as fallacy. Don Quijote and Emma Bovary are literary examples of what happens when the referent of fiction is presumed to be real and operative. Emma is the most serious of realists, for she truly believes that art—even the romantic literature she reads—is a vehicle for experiences which really exist and/or can be made to exist in her world. Her belief raises the question of how *both* ordinary *and* literary language can ever correspond to the precise nature of non-verbal realities. It is not that Emma reads the wrong books, as some have suggested, but that, like Cervantes' hero, she reads believing the referents to be real.

It was suggested in Chapter Two that literature can really only have validity, and now it can be seen that this is so, because "truth" would

16 "Le Langage de la fiction," in *La Part du feu*, p. 82.
17 See Roland Barthes, "L'Effet de réel," *Communications* no. 11 (1968), 88: "l'*avoir-été-là* des choses est un principe suffisant de la parole."

demand a real referent, not a fictive one which, at the level of *parole*, is either a lie or imaginary. To read a literary text for "truth" is to read it as a non-literary text. Whether we call the parts of the heterocosm unreal "mental forms" or "subjectified objects," it is the fictiveness of the language's referents that effects the freeing of the reader from what Georges Poulet calls the "usual sense of incompatibility between [his] consciousness and its objects,"[18] for it is the *objects* of consciousness whose ontological status has changed in literature.

What Lavis calls fictive referents, Paul Ricoeur calls "non-ostensive"[19] ones — those which project a fictive universe, aware always of its verbal reality. This too is Blanchot's belief:

la phrase du récit nous met en rapport avec le monde de l'irréalité qui est l'essence de la fiction et, comme telle, elle aspire à devenir plus réelle, à se constituer en un language physiquement et formellement valable, non pas pour devenir le *signe* des êtres et des objets déjà absents puisque imaginés, mais plutôt pour nous les *présenter*, pour nous les faire sentir et vivre à travers la consistance des mots, leur lumineuse opacité de chose.[20]

In fiction the fictive referent and the signified must not be confused, for the former lies *outside* the linguistic sign and in the imagination of the reader.[21] This is not in any way to place the referent above the sign in importance, obviously. Two signs may have the same referent (for example, mutt and dog) but, since the signified marks the distinctive features of the sign, the pejorative connotations of mutt are revealed through it and not the referent. In cancelling out this important role of the signified, realist dogma postulates a common real referent that all readers share, despite individual ideolects. And in doing so realism actually mitigates the possibility of a "vivid" imagining of the text.

It is only by the gradual cumulative constructing of the heterocosm through its (acknowledged) fictive referents that readers can be said to share a text or a novelistic universe. At first the reader can only read referentially but, both because he *expects*[22] a fictive world and because of the accumulated weight of fictive referents, he gradually comes to create a world. An imaginary mental image is symbolized rather than just signified.

Georges Lavis suggests:

18 "Phenomenology of Reading," *New Literary History* 1 (Autumn 1969), 55. Poulet, however, attributes this change to different causes.
19 "The Model of the Text: Meaningful Action Considered as a Text," *Social Research* 38 (1971), 536. Ricoeur links this concept further to Heidegger and Wilhelm Von Humboldt.
20 "Le Langage de la fiction," p. 83.
21 Hence, Ricardou's inability to see the distinction: within the framework of structural linguistics in which he operates, the referent is irrelevant. In the act of reading a novel, however, it is too relevant to ignore.
22 See Jonathan Culler, *Structuralist Poetics* (London: Routledge and Kegan Paul, 1975) on the literary "competency" of the reader.

Le référent dans un roman, c'est donc l'ensemble des actions, situations, personnages, objets, sentiments... qui constituent la fiction du récit, mais qui, en dépit de leur caractère fictif, me sont présentés comme réels. Ce référent—d'une manière analogue à ce qui se passe pour le discours quotidien—se trouve limité et précisé par son contexte naturel qui est l'ensemble du récit. Mais, par ailleurs, ce référent—dans la mesure où il est fictif, ou, plutôt, *dans la mesure où moi, lecteur, je prends conscience qu'il est fictif*—acquiert, comme le référent du discours poétique, une généralité qu'il n'a pas, ou pas souvent, dans le discours quotidien; et, par là, il fait appel, d'une manière plus large, à ma connaissance du monde, à mon expérience d'être humain.[23]

If this is so, once the reader is aware or at least *made* explicitly and purposively conscious of the fictiveness of the text's referents—as he is, most blatantly, in much metafiction—the novel acquires a certain generality (as well as an aesthetic purity usually associated only with poetry). What appears as aesthetic introversion (fiction for fiction's sake) is revealed as an extroverted, indeed paradigmatic, phenomenon.

Although the novel, then, has no responsibility to the real, although "*le réel romanesque n'est pas opérable*,"[24] there are still retired cavalry officers who write to Simon that they lived his *La Route des Flandres*, the novel Ricardou claims is not at all representational. At Cerisy in 1971, when this question arose, Ricardou's reply was typically dismissive because to him, and possibly to Simon, such personal experience is irrelevant: "Ce qui est donné par Simon, ce sont les référents de la fiction: cela ne veut nullement dire que la fiction obtenue par le texte est l'équivalent du référent donné à titre documentaire."[25]

This consciousness of the possible tension in the reading experience between real and fictive referents is perhaps most clearly seen in the novelist's use of real place names in novelistic settings. Robbe-Grillet admits that he has used Hong Kong and New York as explicit locations for the action of his fiction, but adds: "Je savais désormais qu'il ne pouvait plus être question de représentation, et je pouvais nommer une ville réelle tout en produisant par mon propre texte une ville parfaitement imaginaire."[26] Lest this appear to be a new and radical stand, it is worth recalling Kafka's vision of Prague. In his Preface to *Roderick Hudson*, Henry James wrote that he actually felt that the naming of a real place in the novel, instead of being economical and realistic as intended, was limiting and unnecessary.

The autonomy of the referents of literary signs in relation to real referents is, therefore, not a modern radical realization of recent

23 Lavis, "Le Texte littéraire, le référent, le réel, le vrai," p. 19, my italics.
24 Roland Barthes, *S/Z* (Paris: Seuil, 1970), p. 87, italics his.
25 *Nouveau Roman: hier, aujourd'hui* 1, 30. Note the contradiction to his later comment quoted above that this was rather a signified/referent confusion. Here he seems to have slipped outside the more rigid linguistic code.
26 *Nouveau Roman: hier, aujourd'hui* 2, 166.

criticism. Self-informing, self-reflective metafiction merely points self-consciously to what is a reality of the novel genre, a reality that the structuralists have also made manifest. So too have linguistic philosophers such as Wittgenstein who worked to end the confusing of the *meaning* of a name with the *bearer* of a name,[27] and to suggest that the interpretation of art is justified by its internal, not external, relations. All language will have an effect of some kind on the reader, because it is an experience and not merely a store of easily extractable meaning. Yet, there does seem to be a difference in the reader's imaginative process, an increase in the active element of that experience, if the referents are acknowledged as fictive—by the word "novel" on the book's cover, or even more overtly, through narcissistic thematization.

These fictive referents form an increasingly complete heterocosm of referential totalities by means of a process of semantic accumulation. Nothing is in these referents that has not been expressed—explicitly or implicitly—in the text itself. Therefore both the ontological and epistemological natures[28] of the heterocosm (of its characters, events, and so on) are fundamentally different from those of the real world. No matter how "prosaic" the language, no matter how close to banal reality the story, the language of fiction is transformed because it invites the reader to, in Blanchot's words, "réaliser sur les mots eux-mêmes la compréhension de ce qui se passe dans le monde qu'on lui propose et dont toute la réalité est d'être l'objet d'un récit."[29]

It is the reader's genre expectations and his imaginative creating of the fictional universe through the referents of the language, and *not* the subject matter or any supposedly real referents, that determine the validity and even the status of the novel's reality. In *The French Lieutenant's Woman*, Sarah's "true story" is revealed to be fictional, and it is through the very realization of both that fictiveness and its validity, that Sarah can free Charles at the end of the novel—in a *mise en abyme* of the liberation of the reader by the novelist.

Novels such as this one which acknowledge their fictiveness textually and thematically do not represent the death of the genre. Rather, like fantasy fiction, they become emblematic of what is a literary reality of the novelistic form. All fiction obviously retains the representational orientation of words, but it *also* creates a heterocosm through those words because the representation is of a fictive referent; it creates a second symbolic system which increasingly dominates in the act of reading. Fiction conserves an interest in reference without sacrificing the essential non-instrumentality of its language.

27 See John Casey, *The Language of Criticism* (London: Methuen, 1966), p. 3.
28 See Lubomír Doležel, *Narrative Modes in Czech Literature* (Toronto: University of Toronto Press, 1973), pp. 5–6.
29 Blanchot, "Le Langage de la fiction," p. 84.

Literary language signifies and creates; it does not imitate or even describe. Reading is therefore an active, creative, and demanding process. Once again, it is Blanchot who expresses this best:

Qu'est-ce qu'une oeuvre? Des mots réels et une histoire imaginaire, un monde où tout ce qui arrive est emprunté à la réalité, et ce monde est inaccessible; des personnages qui se donnent pour vivants, mais nous savons que leur vie est de ne pas vivre (de rester une fiction). . . . Mais la fiction n'est pas comprise, elle est vécue sur les mots à partir desquels elle se réalise, et elle est plus réelle, pour moi qui la lis ou l'écris, que bien des événements réels, car elle s'imprègne de toute la réalité du langage et elle se substitue à ma vie, à force d'exister.[30]

Even if an author of a determinedly naturalistic novel should choose to draw upon, for reasons of economy, his reader's knowledge of extraliterary realities, he can really only do so in the sense of his text's having an "analagon"[31] in the world outside it; such a relationship is metaphoric rather than referential (that is, with a *real* referent). On the other hand, a theory of fantasy literature must also draw upon a concept of fictive referents (at the level of both *langue* and *parole*) because surely vampires, devils, unicorns, and hobbits exist only in words. Only language can allow us to conceive of the absent, the unreal, the supernatural.[32] This importance of the absent, of the fictive does not obviously imply that *writers* of metafiction have no interest in or response to the world outside their art. All this view of reference suggests is that for *readers* the meaning of each word increasingly takes its context from other words in that same work; the locus of reference gradually changes from the readers' linguistic, literary, and existential experience in general, to include their experience of that text in particular. This last stage leads to the creation of the "heterocosm."

Language has the power to make the reader formulate meaning and build these imaginary worlds. It also possesses inherent limitations, however. These are the recurring themes in what was called, in the typology of Chapter One, the overt kind of linguistic narcissism. The narrator of Borges' "The Aleph" despairs: "All language is an alphabet of symbols whose use presupposes a past shared by all the other interlocutors. How, then, transmit to others the infinite Aleph, which my fearful mind scarcely encompasses? . . . What my eyes saw was simultaneous: what I shall transcribe is successive, because language is successive."[33]

It is not just that a writer can be either amazed and heartened or resigned and despairing at what language can or cannot do. Nor is this

30 "La Littérature et le droit à la mort," p. 341.
31 See Claude Duchet, "Une Écriture de la socialité," *Poétique* 4, no. 16 (1973), 450.
32 See Todorov, *Introduction à la littérature fantastique* (Paris: Seuil, 1970), p. 87.
33 *A Personal Anthology*, trans. Anthony Kerrigan (New York: Grove Press, 1967), pp. 149–50.

a new concern of novelists. Joyce used *Ulysses* to demonstrate that, since English was insufficient for his imaginative needs, he must create neologisms: "I'd like a language which is above all languages, a language to which all will do service."[34] Nor is it a new thematized concern in fiction: Emma Bovary and Don Quijote both attest to the powers and terrors of literary language.

What is new perhaps in the metafictional use of this linguistic theme is that new role of acknowledgement and active involvement that is textually pointed out to the reader. The act of reading is no longer safe, comfortable, unproblematic; the assaulted reader's confidence in, and certainty of, his very language is undermined. At the very end of a long and (as a metaphor) comprehensible description of the "Library of Babel," Borges' narrator parenthetically addresses his reader: "(An *n* number of possible languages use the same vocabulary; in some of them, the symbol *library* allows the correct definition *a ubiquitous and lasting system of hexagonal galleries*, but *library* is *bread* or *pyramid* or anything else, and these seven words which define it have another value. You who read me, are You sure of understanding my language?)."[35] In the overt variety of linguistic narcissism, at least, this questioning and reworking on the level of language is pointed out to the reader directly or is thematized in some way. In the covert equivalent, however, the reader again is expected to have learned and mastered the demanding new techniques.

There are at least three ways in which a novel or short story can be self-conscious about its existence as language. In the simplest form, the work can parade its parodic play on a certain style of writing, as Fowles's text does in *The French Lieutenant's Woman* or as Nabokov's does in *Lolita* in which Humbert's poem read by Quilty ("Because you took,/because you took advantage of my disadvantage") parodies T. S. Eliot, or in *Ada* which opens with a parody of a version by a bad translator (a "transmongrelizer") of Tolstoy's opening of *Anna Karenina*. The heroine's name, for example, is given as Anna Arkadievitch, not the correct feminine Anna Arkadievna.

In a second manner, the novel can be aware of its existence as a written or printed text in words. There is both what one might call a static and a dynamic version possible in this form. In its static form, one might find a text which is intensely aware of its medium. Barth's subtitle to *Lost in the Funhouse* is "Fiction for Print, Tape, Live Voice" and indeed while some are definitely pieces meant for print (the narrator of the "Anonymiad" cures his own goat hide on which to write the story), others lose much meaning in print and have to be imagined spoken. The story, "Lost in the Funhouse," on the other hand, plays

34 Quoted by Richard Ellmann in his *James Joyce* (New York: Oxford University Press, 1959), p. 410.
35 *Labyrinths*, trans. James E. Irby (New York: New Directions, 1962), pp. 57–58.

with the actual conventions of printing ("A single straight underline is the manuscript mark for italic type, *which in turn* is the printed equivalent to oral emphasis of words"[36]). Many of Borges' pseudo-essays with their fictive footnotes and editorial commentary reveal an intense awareness of the text as text. The allegory of the black and white printed page that Ricardou sees in Roussel's "Parmi les noirs" and in Poe's "Arthur Gordon Pym"[37] and which can also be detected in Camus' "Le Renégat ou un esprit confus,"[38] is to be found as well in Ricardou's own opening to *Les Lieux-dits* ("A peine franchie, sous les nuées, cette sombre ligne de faîte, tout le pays, en contrebas, dispense ses reflets"). As he so carefully explains himself: "La première [phrase] figure le texte lui-même: les nuées répercutent la blancheur du papier en haut de la page initiale; la sombre ligne de faîte fait allusion à la première ligne d'écriture au sommet du texte."[39]

There also exist more dynamic varieties of this manner of overt linguistic narcissism. The marginal commentary included in *Ada* is not just a static acknowledgement of the novel's textual identity, but also forms both a kind of active critique of the storytelling and a dramatic verbal dialogue between Ada and Van from a later point in narrative time.[40] The reader also becomes more actively involved in the dynamic self-awareness of the *process* as well as the *fact* of sentence-composing when Barth's narrator in "Title" makes him fill in blanks as he reads: "Why do you suppose it is, she asked, long participial phrase of the breathless variety characteristic of dialogue attributions of nineteenth-century fiction, that literate people such as we talk like characters in a story?" (p. 107). Thematically the structures of language are linked to those of fiction and life experience both: "The novel is predicate adjective, as is the innocent anecdote of bygone days when life made a degree of sense and subject joined to complement by copula" (p. 109). The reader is explicitly told that building worlds with words as material can only create an artifice. Unlike wood and iron which are "first-order reality," "words are artificial to begin with." In other stories, such as "Life-Story," it is the writer figure who is acutely aware of his progress in writing words on paper, and thus he draws the reader's attention to the linguistic creative act in time and space ("while in the introductory adverbial clause it seemed obvious to him that . . .

36 *Lost in the Funhouse* (Garden City, New York: Doubleday, 1968), p. 72. Other page references to stories in the collection will appear in parentheses in the text.

37 "L'Activité roussellienne," *Pour une théorie du nouveau roman* (Paris: Seuil, 1971), pp. 91–117; and "Le Caractère singulier de cette eau," *Problèmes du nouveau roman* (Paris: Seuil, 1967), pp. 193–207.

38 See the author's " 'Le Renégat ou un esprit confus' comme nouveau récit," *La Revue des lettres modernes, Albert Camus* 6 (1973), 67–87.

39 *Le Nouveau Roman* ([Paris]: Seuil, 1973), p. 71.

40 Douglas Fowler disagrees. In his *Reading Nabokov* (Ithaca, New York: Cornell University Press, 1974), p. 188, he asserts that Ada is "intended to be a text, by Nabokov *on* Nabokov, and has dismissed all dramatic resources in order to be a text."

by the time he reached the main clause he had to admit that . . ." [p. 125]). Again it is the thematized concern for the reader's act that tends to distinguish this linguistic self-awareness from that of, say, Diderot or Sterne, although the devices employed may be similar.

The third and perhaps most obvious type of overt language concern is to be found in the various forms of thematized (not actualized) word play, usually puns or anagrams, which call the reader's attention to the fact that this text is made up of words, words which are delightfully fertile in creative suggestiveness. The frantic "self-recorded fiction" of Barth's story "Autobiography" punningly explains to the reader: "I must compose myself. Look, I'm writing. No, listen, I'm nothing but talk" (p. 36). The tale ends with the text, still punning and still frantic, trying to terminate itself:

Basket case. Waste.

Shark up some memorable last words at least. There seems to be time.

Nonsense, I'll mutter to the end, one word after another, string the rascals out, mad or not, heard or not, my last words will be my last words [p. 39]

In Nabokov's *Lolita*, Humbert Humbert uses language—its semantic richness, its punning and anagrammatic fertility—to build a protective defence, to control his confession.[41] But it is in *Ada* that word play takes on its most important narcissistic function, as shall be seen again in Chapter Eight. Van wants to write a poem to "Ada, our ardors and arbors" at Ardis; Van's father, Demon ("a form of Demian or Dementius"), collected, the reader is told, old masters and young mistresses: "He also liked middle-aged puns."[42] Van himself has "word dreams."

Most important are the thematized word games that function as *mises en abyme* to teach the reader how to read *Ada* and to direct him to the main themes of the novel. At a picnic, Ada plays a thematically revealing game of anagrams which proceeds from *insect* to *scient* to *nicest* to *incest* (p. 91). Similarly games of "Flavita" (from the Russian game, *alfavit*, or Scrabble) turn into preludes to sexual dallying between the siblings (pp. 234–40). Though not quite a game, the code devised by Van and Ada for their love letters becomes textually functional and emblematic when the narrator (Van) then forces the *reader* to employ it to read *his* text (p. 168).

In *The Black Prince*, Iris Murdoch's narrator describes *Hamlet* as the play in which Shakespeare "has performed a supreme creative feat, a work endlessly reflecting upon itself, not discursively but in its very substance, a Chinese box of words as high as the tower of Babel, a

41 See Alfred Appel, Jr., "*Lolita*: The Springboard of Parody," in L. S. Dembro (ed.), *Nabokov: The Man and His Work* (Madison: University of Wisconsin Press, 1967), p. 113, and G. D. Josipovici, "*Lolita*: Parody and the Pursuit of Beauty," *Critical Quarterly* 6 (Spring 1964), 35–48.

42 *Ada* (New York: McGraw Hill, 1969), p. 4. Other page references will be in parentheses in the text.

meditation upon the bottomless trickery of consciousness and the redemptive role of words in the lives of those without identity, that is human beings. *Hamlet* is words, and so is Hamlet."[43] Sometimes, however, it is less the creative force of language that is narcissistically thematized, than its ordering and sense-making capacity—for writer and reader both.

The title of Murdoch's *A Word Child* is derived from the saving discovery of language by her orphan-bastard protagonist, Hilary Burde: "I was not, except in some very broken-down sense of that ambiguous term, a love child. I was a word child."[44] A reader of foreign languages, Hilary loves in them the rules of grammar and proceeds, like Barth's Jacob Horner, to structure his life like a rigid grammatical code—certain people to be seen at certain hours of certain days, with fillers such as riding the Inner Circle Tube Line. Similarly, tyrannical Hilary believes these rules will also govern the lives of those with whom he comes into contact: "I relied upon routine, had done so perhaps ever since I realized that grammatical rules were to be my salvation. . . . Routine, in my case at least, discouraged thought. . . . The patterned sameness of the days of the week gave a comforting sense of absolute subjection to history and time, perhaps a comforting sense of mortality" (p. 27).

While, as narrator, Hilary Burde's comments on language reflect as well on his activity as writer, they also form an almost allegorical commentary on the act of reading. He comments: "I loved words, but I was not a word-user, rather a word-watcher, in the way that some people are bird-watchers" (p. 28). The reader, of course, is both a word- and a Burde-watcher. Like the reader, Hilary is "one for whom the spoken and the written word are themselves different languages" (p. 28). It is not surprising that one of the characters should claim to read Hilary "like a book," as, of course, does the reader.

All novels, however, force the reader to work, in the sense that he must imaginatively create a fictional universe out of the accumulation of fictive referents. If this is so, then one of the things modern narcissistic fiction has achieved is to have helped, through its thematization of this process, in the unmasking of what might be called the referential "illusion" of novelistic realism. A concept of fictive referents based on the reader's generic expectations allows for a theory of the autonomous nature of the universe of fiction without falling too far into the trap of the poetic-ordinary language controversy of European structuralism and North American New Criticism.[45] Many writers have insisted on themes of misunderstanding, non-communication, and confusion based on the inadequacy of language in *life*. In literature words create worlds; they are

43 (London: Chatto & Windus, 1973), p. 164.
44 (New York: Viking Press, 1975), p. 21. Other page references will be in parentheses in the text.
45 See the thorough discussion of this controversy in Mary Louise Pratt, *Toward a Speech Act Theory of Literary Discourse* (Bloomington, London: Indiana University Press, 1977).

not necessarily counters, however adequate, to any extraliterary reality. In that very fact lies their aesthetic validity and their ontological status.

The Theme of Linguistic Identity:
La Macchina Mondiale

> When we sing the father hymn, we notice
> that he was not very interesting. The
> words of the hymn notice it. It is
> explicitly commented upon in the text.
> Donald Barthelme

Certain texts explicitly point to the fact that they are texts; in other words, their identity is a linguistic as well as a narrative one. While it is obviously true that all literary texts are composed of words, the overt variety of self-consciousness about the processes of language thematizes both this fact and awareness of it. The focus can be either the immense potency of words in creating worlds or the inadequacy of language—as a means of communication, cognition or creation—in art, and by extension, in life. This kind of narcissism is no less "vital," no less connected to "life," for its linguistic self-recognition.

As was the case in Chapter Four's discussion of this kind of overt auto-referentiality on the level of narrative, the most effective method of analyzing the extended thematization of linguistic identity is by the detailed study of one particular text which can then act as a model both of the form (and techniques employed) and of its implications for the theory of fiction and for the act of reading. An Italian novel has been chosen for several literary historical reasons. It is not only in French or American literature today that one finds blatant linguistic self-awareness. Italian fiction too shares this self-regarding penchant, and not only in the more extreme forms of the neoavant-garde. Paolo Volponi's novels are all, for instance, important statements of the thematized concerns of much recent Italian fiction—such as the nature of creativity and the constructing through language of autonomous fictive worlds. They are especially significant in their parodic response to the neorealistic heritage of Italy, for there that nineteenth-century novelistic "illusion" has continued to thrive. Italian metafiction is thus

more explicit in some ways and provides a particularly clear illustration of the issues involved. Volponi's second novel, *La macchina mondiale*, is therefore of interest because it specifically employs the various overt techniques of linguistic self-consciousness discussed in the last chapter—stylistic parody, static and dynamic awareness of the textual medium, and thematically functional word play. These are used to bring to the fore the linguistic and formal themes which many critics have been disinclined to attribute to anything outside the French *nouveau roman*.

This novel has no blatant narrating novelist à la Fowles, but rather presents the reader with Anteo Crocioni, a self-taught peasant, writing two simultaneous works: first, a journal, which is the text given to the reader, interspersed with quotations from the second, Anteo's treatise on his own mechanical theory of the creation of the world and its implications in the forming of an academy of friendship. However, once again there appears that complex Chinese-box *mise en abyme* structure typical of so much metafiction, for the "Avvertenza" informs the reader that the treatise is a real one, written (according to Paolo Volponi[1]) by a friend of the author, a certain P.M.V. These initials (plus the facts that this man, like Volponi, is said to be a *Marchigiano* living in Piedmont, and is a man of about Volponi's own age) suggest a certain self-conscious game-playing on Volponi's part, as does the syllabic similarity between An/te/o Cro/cio/ni and Pa/o/lo Vol/po/ni. The important point lies, however, not in any autobiographical mirroring on any level, but in the fact that Anteo's theories of the mechanical nature of creativity on a *scientific* level gradually modulate into *aesthetic* propositions which are seen to be shared not only by Volponi himself, but by, more importantly, his earlier and later writer-heroes, Albino Saluggia[2] and Girolamo Aspri.[3] To each of these men, it is imagination that is the form-making faculty and Anteo clearly demonstrates the imaginative freedom of "Kantian man"[4] in rising above nature and society by creating purposiveness within his creative vision. His failure is that he relates the teleology of art to a purpose outside his art—to a socio-scientific theory. It is only in the end when he sees that he has created in words a fictive (artistic) construct and when he renounces his operative intent, that he can really attain that "purposeless purposiveness" that is the novel he has written and just completed.

1 In an interview with Corrado Stajano, "Paolo Volponi: il contadino in gabbia," *Tempo settimanale*, 30 giugno 1965, p. 37.
2 See *Memoriale* (Milano: Garzanti, 1962), p. 176, where the reader is told that man is no longer made in God's likeness, but rather in the likeness of machines, that is, of a totally different race.
3 *Corporale* (Torino: Einaudi, 1974), pp. 28, 76. All further page references will be in parentheses in the text.
4 See Murray Krieger, "Fiction, History, and Empirical Reality," *Critical Inquiry* 1 (December 1974), 353.

Herein lies Volponi's parodic response to the social and political intentions of the language-oriented neoavant-garde (as Chapter Eight will show) as well as to those of the neorealistic tradition in Italy. The broader Chinese-box of P.M.V., as established in the "Avvertenza," functions as a guarantee of the autonomy of the inner world, and not as a naturalistic proof of its direct link to any external life situation. As with much self-conscious fiction, this novel finds its mimetic justification in its relating of the act of reading to that of writing—two creative processes thematized and allegorized within the structure and content of the novel itself.

Although the reader is witness to Anteo's attempts at finding precise verbal terms and at telling everything in the proper order in his journal, it is the act of writing the treatise (the book within the book) that he is made constantly aware of. At the end, however, when Anteo remarks that he is content and proud that no one has ever tried, at least in San Savino and probably even in the Marche and all of Italy, to do what he tried to invent and create,[5] the reader is led to note that what is true of Anteo's creation is probably true of Volponi's as well.

Volponi's own fascination with self-consciousness of this sort is seen in his delight in one particular figure in Masaccio's painting, "Resurrezione del figlio di Teofilo e san Pietro in cattedra" (Cappella Brancacci, Chiesa del Carmine, Firenze). It is the one figure of all Masaccio's silent men who actually seems about to speak, who alone lifts his eyes upward to look at the viewer. It is, in fact, the figure that is the painter's self-portrait.[6] This same narcissism is evident in some of Volponi's early poetry, but especially in his other fiction. Albino's madness in the first novel is also a visionary one, that of a poet transforming objects and creating for them a web of analogies.

Volponi's third novel makes even more explicit the self-consciousness of *La macchina mondiale*. Volponi himself saw *Corporale*'s plot as a discourse on language and on novelistic structures,[7] as well as a social and moral comment on the post-atomic bomb world. The discussion in this novel between Overath and Girolamo, the narrator, is revealing, for in it Girolamo denies that he is a poet, and that his idea of a bomb shelter is "poesia." In response to Overath's questioning, he also denies that it is a novel or a diary, in fact, that it is any kind of literature. Overath then argues against his claim that it is a "teorema" because if it were it would have to have meaning for everyone; otherwise it would be a mad game. Girolamo then pointedly inquires: "E invece cos'è la cattiva letteratura?" Overath replies that bad literature is

5 *La macchina mondiale* (Milano: Garzanti, 1965), p. 274. All further references will be in parentheses in the text.
6 Paolo Volponi, "Il principio umano della pittura-scienza," Introduction to *L'opera completa di Masaccio* (Milano: Rizzoli, 1968), p. 8.
7 Gian Carlo Ferretti's interview about the author's work in progress in his *Volponi* (Firenze: La Nuova Italia, 1972), p. 2.

the history of this society, "la degna storia di questa società" (p. 445). In Part Two of *Corporale*, Girolamo becomes his fantasy—Joaquin Murieta, Mexican revolutionary—and the first-person narration changes to third-person. Or, as Joaquin notes in his diary, in this part of his life (and of this novel), there is no protagonist, that is, someone with a central idea who determines and judges (pp. 155–56).

Perhaps the most interesting piece of self-consciousness in this last novel is a description of the earlier one, *La macchina mondiale* — given in the form of Girolamo's lie to Corboli about why he wants to live in the Marche countryside. He claims to want to write a novel, to write the truth about a peasant from that area of central Italy. He will write about a man working his land but who is a man of a superior destiny too. He plans to include all the relevant historico-economic information regarding institutions, families, in fact, everything about that rural society (p. 303). As Overath had remarked, Girolamo's bomb shelter (the real reason for wanting to live in the area) is literature—Volponi's—just as Girolamo's fictional novel here is Volponi's as well.

Volponi's thematized concern in this earlier second novel is explicitly with the means used to create such fictional worlds as these. This does not mean merely the author's interest in the juxtaposition of the technological abstract language of the treatise with the more lyrical tone of Anteo's journal expression. That language is central in a more important way to Volponi's own theory of narrative is clear in his own early turning to verse, and his refusal to write prose because, as he admitted, his literary and cultural level at that time did not give him a language sufficient to order things fully.[8] In fact, he went on to state, he only attempted *Memoriale* when he was almost forty, when he felt himself finally in possession of an active linguistic instrument, capable of an order of original values and able to maintain an autonomous structure beyond either any lyricism or any narrative mechanism. In his second novel, language *is* the novel, with a precise and essential significance. Anteo, like his creator (and, of course, like the reader), needs a language to order things as well as to create his world.

The reader notices a curious and almost untranslatable metaphor in the first pages of the novel: Anteo feels as if he lives on "una *lingua* di terra ancora *disarticolata* ed ancora con gli *accenti* dei vari fenomeni naturali che vi battono sopra" (p. 8, my italics). Similarly the mechanical joints of an animal's body, as soon noted by Anteo, are *articulated* joints (p. 30), so that the union of *language* with a *mechanical* theory of *nature* is made early in the novel. As he writes the treatise too, the ink, he fears, "avesse potuto *disarticolarsi*, liberarsi e cambiare una delle sue molecole" (p. 46, my italics).

Like Volponi, Anteo looks to language as an inherently ordering phenomenon. He orders words by sounds—"colto, coltivo, coltura,

8 Volponi's 1963 autobiographical sketch, reprinted in Ferretti, *Volponi*, p. 79.

coltivare, continuare, confortare; auto, automa, autore, automatico; genio, geniale, genitale, generare" (p. 30)—and understands that words placed together like this are articulated according to their syllables and their sounds in such a way that a construction already exists. Moreover, this is an autonomous construction, one that has no need of support from his thoughts, but rather forms its own thought by means of its power, its design, and its structures. Indeed it becomes a new and perceivable thing beyond the meaning each word first had on its own (p. 30).

Like modern French theoreticians, Anteo has discovered that language orders, that it is not merely instrumental but is in itself an autonomous system. Anteo's own word play is not at all gratuitous within the context of the novel. Words, seemingly arbitrarily connected (by sound), set out the themes to come: "colto" is "cultivated"—both for land and for men; "coltivo" means "arable" and that which is already cultivated; "coltura" is again cultivation of land, but also both the learning of man's mind, and his breeding. Anteo, the farmer, sees that one can cultivate ("coltivare") both land and friendship; hence his academy of friendship. And, it is only in continuing ("continuare") his endeavours that he can find any comfort ("confortare") for himself and for others. The "auto, automa, autore, automatico" connection suggests to him his entire theory of mechanical evolution and creation by the *automi-autori*. This shall be considered in more detail later.

The "genio, geniale, genitale, generare" group of associations is more complex. "Genio," as in "il genio militare," is significantly the engineering corps of an army. Of course, it also suggests Anteo's "talent" which he feels entitles him to "genius" status, and metaphorically to an understanding of the "genio" or "spirit" of language, the law, the land, or whatever. "Geniale" means both clever and friendly, and ironically also means nuptial, as in "letto geniale"—the possible link with "genitale" and of course with "generare," the procreative, constructive force both of his theories and his life; his wife's denial of this in the murder of their son therefore decides his own suicide. From his desire to be cultured ("colto"), though a mere farmer ("colto, coltivo, coltivare"), Anteo is drawn to his theory of the *automa-autore* and then to his final self-destruction. The verbal play here is functional in a microcosmic, narcissistic manner.

The same is true in *Corporale*, although Girolamo's word associations are more frequent. He too, however, sees language as a means of ordering the chaos of life (p. 142). Volponi himself has claimed that the autonomous novel form has the capacity to revivify that part of reality that is structured and developed through language.[9] Obviously lan-

9 Interview with Ottavio Cecchi, "Lo 'Strega' e la macchina," *Rinascita*, 10 luglio 1965, p. 28.

guage has both aesthetic and social (even moral) functions in all narrative and in a very particular thematized manner in *La macchina mondiale*.

According to his wife, Anteo is a no-good, lazy fellow who lies about whole days staring into space or writing his mad treatise. Anteo, on the other hand, feels that the petty demeaning work at which his father slaved was much worse than that of finding a language to express a significant world vision. His theories are not useless or inhuman; on the contrary, their aim is to better a dehumanized, uncreative society. He seeks to discover and then to give *thought* to machines as well. Then he feels man should begin to construct as many machines as possible in order to help, to exalt, and even to supersede man. Otherwise if man continues to make more and more machines for purposes restricted by the rules society has established, these machines will only be bestial — that is, monotonous, inert, immutable (pp. 77–78).

Anteo explains to his friend, Liborio, that man must be liberated, must free himself from the prison of society (its rules and its language) so that he can perform actions which today are not even foreseen by the very words he uses. Anteo sees that in his society, even words are fictions and the concepts behind them are hypocritical (p. 215). He intuitively makes the link between language and what Wittgenstein called the "form of life"; he learns that every language contains within it certain designs or forms by which man apprehends his world. Therefore as a social rebel, Anteo must rebel in his language usage as well.

His mechanical philosophy is also — paradoxically — a "vitalistic" protest against the mental fixity and ignorance of his society. Most of his neighbours reject him; Liborio, the priest and his only friend, sees that, while he himself represents faith within the church, Anteo is "liberty" (p. 49), despite his very necessary solitude which is, ironically, a result of his desire for science to work, through invention and through the academy of friendship, to become an instrument of liberation (p. 163).

Anteo does not want to explain the origins of man and his position in the world out of scientific disinterestedness: he wants to single out the formulae needed for man's liberation and for the creation of a new academy of friendship for all men — once these same men have acknowledged the validity of his psychological arguments and his scientific code, and have accepted a theory of automatism which respects and makes use of the integrity and dynamism of each element involved (p. 8).

Anteo's relationship to the *automa-autore* (and his to P.M.V. and to Volponi) centres on the coherent world each creates and inhabits. The working of these superior machines, according to the treatise, is perfect insofar as it exempts its *autore* (author, creator) from any direct intervention. However, he is always indirectly present in that the administrators have had full liberty of action — but only the liberty to

serve the law that governs the universe. Only by faithfully serving such a law can the *automa-autore* satisfy his function; outside of this he will find nothing but self-destruction (p. 69). This last prophetic notion refers as well to the end of both Anteo's life and also the innermost fictive world of the novel.

Anteo rejects the servility and misery he sees around him in a society where, as he says, bread and life have the meaning and position that are really due to the freedom to live and to construct (p. 72). To be free is to live, and—for Anteo—to live is to construct, to create. In a double sense, since his life depends on Volponi's creating, he can say at the end of his life (and of Volponi's novel) that he feels he has expressed in his life—in full awareness and with sufficient "liberty" and "purity"—the infinite progression of each "particle" and "molecule" and "body." He feels he has attained great scientific results solely by means of his own life, by means of the constructing of the ideas that sustained it (p. 275). As a fictive character on one level, and as a social rebel on another, Anteo enjoys an unparalleled liberty. Each of the socially unacceptable, pathological "case histories" that Volponi chooses as hero for his novels functions within his own world in the same way that Volponi wishes his novels to function within the reader's world—that is, as a challenge.

Anteo uses language as his main instrument of social protest, telling the court officials that he refuses to understand their bastardized words, because they exchange and use words like cards and at the end of the game, they count up the points. He accuses them of having the dirtiest cards that anyone ever used to play with, and concludes that they are, in effect, without a language—"senza lingua" (p. 261). In a lecture in 1965, Volponi himself echoed these sentiments claiming that his novel—its language, its narration—was outside the rigid, static *status actualis* of society and its language.[10] Like Volponi, Anteo attacks institutions through their all too revealing language and wants to create a new language for the constructs of his imagination.

Writing novels for Volponi is, like the writing of the treatise for Anteo, a subversive activity. The writer is free enough from the rules of society to act as its conscience. This is perhaps where Volponi's parodic and problematic response to the radical *Gruppo 63* is most clear. Is Anteo's scientific theory a parody of that "literature of the laboratory" which paradoxically has extramural political and social intentions? Yes—but the creator of the *automa-autore* still believes in imagination's control over technology, in the anthropomorphizing, not computerization, of the world by man. More significantly, his revolt against society is more than just a linguistic contesting of the system; in fact, it reveals the limits of what Volponi has called the neoavant-garde's dogmatism and delight in forming precepts.[11] As a metafictionist, Volponi prefers

10 In Ferretti, *Volponi*, p. 57.
11 In Stajano, "Paolo Volponi: il contadino in gabbia," p. 38.

to reform from inside conventions, experimenting linguistically and stylistically through parody in a very self-reflexive manner. What begins as a linguistic revolt becomes part of a broader cultural one, based not on the neoavant-garde political and ahistorical semantic upheaval, but on literary, historical, moral, and social grounds. In fact, Anteo's *scientific* failure can be read as a gloss on Volponi's discussion in an interview in *L'Unità* of the dangers of limiting the revolt to linguistic terms. He feels that many of the radicals (who theorize on the rediscovery of reality as a hidden physical material), through the use of all the possible expedients of "the laboratory," actually limit themselves. They believe that once the instrument of research has been invented, the reality itself has been conquered. To Volponi, this is really only another form of the usual bourgeois concept of science and technology as ends in themselves. He links, therefore, this new type of literature which is an end in itself to the "prosa d'arte."[12] In other words, it is not so very radical. (Chapter Eight will investigate this accusation more closely.)

Volponi's own professed intentions for reform are also Anteo's, but *his* revolt is the whole novel, and not only Anteo's *mise en abyme* theoretical treatise, just as Masaccio's revolt was the whole of his art. Both Anteo and Volponi aim, as many metafictionists so explicitly do, at the reader's literary, moral, and social prejudices and blindnesses. Volponi's visionary heroes seem to resemble saints or poets in their possibility of being above reality, or perhaps living in a superior or at least different reality (a fictive linguistic world) of their own making. The theme of all his novels is that the possibility of freedom is anchored in our "culture" and is indispensable for judging or changing the world, and for constructing a new one. That "culture" both contains and is constituted by language is a theme that requires closer attention.

Why does Anteo write the journal, create his heterocosm? Is it because (as in Volponi's novel as a whole) in many of the facts of his life lie the proofs of the scientific theories of his treatise? Anteo writes of the dynamics and the consequentiality of every one of his compositions (in words and numbers) with the "inventions" he kept discovering (like all good "inventors") around him and which he linked up to each other and to his own life (pp. 14–15). Anteo sees as well as Langer or Wittgenstein the inevitable connection between language, creation, and reality. From this intuition, Anteo reasons that to reform society he must reform the language it uses. Like the catechism which, according to church dogma, contains all the answers (p. 12) and like the university professor's insistent view that he cannot listen to Anteo because it would be useless to discuss matters for which there were no doctrinaire answers already given (p. 164), the language of a society reflects, or rather *is*, its limitation.

12 In Ferretti, "Il Gruppo '63 e l'area dello sperimentalismo" in his *La letteratura del rifiuto* (Milano: Ugo Mursia, 1968), p. 287n.

Anteo comes to realize that the referents of words are often not at all real but fictive and that, like his own mechanical vision, society's world view creates a coherent fictional universe—this time, alas, far from his own experience of those words and their referents. In a long denunciation of the court's verbal testimony against him (p. 79), Anteo claims the words therein establish facts that never existed in the reality created by those words—that is, implying certain motives and consequences. He feels that if one adopts words "bloccate dall'uso," blocked by the use made of them by a certain society, one will never conquer the rules— the blocks—of that society. These are blocks which any society builds around itself to impede the flux of reality, to transform it. For this reason he plans to write his treatise "in modo diverso," in such a way that he can use words in a new sense, avoiding the meaning they carry in a history he rejects and wants to conquer. Otherwise, he fears, his treatise would merely be another testimony in support of the view that he is really a lazy good-for-nothing, a lunatic, a persecutor of his wife, and an enemy of the priests and of God. This key passage reveals Anteo's understanding of the nature of the referents of words and the autonomous worlds created by them. Written in ordinary language (that is, with accepted real referents) the work will merely prove to others that he is quite mad. Volponi suggests that if Anteo persists in viewing it as science and not as art, the true realm of fictive referents, he indeed might be.

Anteo knows that language and the question of reference are greater problems than most people—other than novelists—realize. He attacks the speech of the Christian Democrat spokesman, Dr. Colombari, who claims everyone knows the meaning of those words (family, work, religion) which Anteo disputes. They just mean what they say (p. 153). Anteo rejects this simplistic view of reference; each *family* is different, and *work* and *religion* are, to him, merely instruments of oppression. Anteo tries to break the linguistic prison of society's hypocrisy and simplistic mimetic view of reference, and he offers the only alternative he sees—a communist utopia that seems at least closer to his own linguistically inspired, academy-of-friendship, social ideal.

Society's view of Anteo, however, is ironically accurate at least once. The court-appointed lawyer defends Anteo with the idea that his theories are the fruit of his madness, composed essentially, in their absolute vacuity, of *"espressioni e solo di espressioni, cioè di parole* più o meno stravaganti, ermetiche e confuse, dalla cui resonanza l'autore è suggestionato e rapito. Il suo è quindi un pensiero autistico, organizzato con onomatopeie, assonanze, stereotipie, bizzarrie" (pp. 260–61, my italics). What the lawyer is saying, in essence, is that Anteo is an artist, not a scientist, and that his figurative, extravagant language creates an autonomous world. What the court does not see is the social and moral intent behind that created universe—the same extroverted

impulse that can be seen in many seemingly introverted metafictions. While Anteo creates a visionary world that is admittedly fictional, it is out of a desire to free himself and so to help others—in this case, to help found a universal academy of friendship.

Language has a moral and social dimension, even when (or perhaps especially when) its referents are fictive. Language is, to Volponi, an evaluating, ordering, and liberating force. But Anteo, the free but outcast rebel, must go his way alone and poorly equipped verbally— "con pochi strumenti e poche parole" (p. 32). He must forge a world to fit his vision. Science becomes poetry as fictive referents create a whole fictive utopian world which challenges the social, psychological, historical, literary, and linguistic assumptions of the rejected society.[13]

Anteo's universe is the creation of a paranoid not unlike Don Quijote,[14] a man who creates for himself a complete system—biographical and linguistic—in which he can live. The reader in the act of reading shares in the creating of that system, in which he temporarily is also living. The language that creates and *is* Anteo's world is apocalyptic, rigorously rational, yet intensely lyrical, archaic in its distance from the society it exists to oppose. As in all metafiction, however, this novel and its language are not estranged from the reader's reality. Anteo's is no more an artificial language than any other novelist's; it too is verified against (because it refers to) Anteo's vision, which in turn, however, illuminates a possible new mode of structuring reality for his reader.

Language is not merely utilitarian to Anteo, but is itself the very close connection between the creation of his visionary world and his living in the social world. Volponi's heroes often reason from the syntax of the language to the syntax of reality. In all fiction, as in Anteo's visionary treatise, the people, things, events are inseparable from the words. The artist, like Anteo the scientist, must make a world, not merely describe one (real or potential), through technical skill with words. The fictive universe and the language that creates it have moral meaning, but the "analogon" with reality may be more in the process of making fictions through that human language, than in any structural or detailed mimesis of character, event, or object.

Therefore, the question of what language to use in creating a fictive free world is tied to a larger concern for the nature of creativity, a concern shared by most metafiction. People in society, Anteo realizes, are unthinking and unimaginative and *therefore* inhumane. He knows that they have never even thought about an academy of friendship. Nor have they ever tried to understand human destiny. In fact they never even really look at others—except perhaps as enemies or lovers

13 See Vito Amoruso, "La violenza dell'utopia" in his *Le contraddizioni della realtà* (Bari: Dedalo Libri, 1968), pp. 308–309.
14 See Pier Paolo Pasolini, "Un 'piccolo vangelo' anarchico," *L'Europa letteraria* 6 (maggio-giugno 1965), 92.

or parents, that is, blinded by some prevailing emotion, rather than as objects of their possible mediation or creation. No one ever sees himself as an artist who might "*fare qualcosa di diverso*, muoversi, esistere, compiersi" (p. 20, my italics). The verb *esistere* here is contrasted in the novel to mere *vivere* (to eat, to reproduce, to merely live) by the presence of a dynamic organic creative element: "per esistere occorre ogni giorno ricostruirsi, cioè obbedire ad una legge superiore che governa l'universo incarnato e vivente nei corpi di materia organica" (p. 22). Anteo's utopia would harness this creative force in a *collective* effort to make *science* the basis of life (p. 78); Volponi's would make *art* the basis of an *individual* effort, for the reader.

To see little or no connection between the treatise and Anteo's story would be to fail to understand a central point of the novel—that regarding the nature of creativity—as well as the explicit lesson of the protagonist. Anteo claims (p. 79) that he wants the treatise to be free, the words to be new. He wants to write science as science demands—in such a way that it becomes art, "la più dolce delle poesie." Then it will be for each person new, different, rich in infinite "liberations." Only then, he feels, can he overcome the image formed of him by the "vecchi segni," the old signs he equates with "i poveri servi della miseria." Only then will he really be, in the eyes of all, a philosopher and inventor. His treatise will be true science and *therefore* true poetry (p. 81). Both are manifestations of the creative impulse, an impulse even the professors do not comprehend: they find his work beautiful but not mechanical, more poetry than engineering (p. 170). Only by such creative, dynamic means, suggest author and character both, could society be reformed—morally and linguistically. The aim of science, writes Anteo, is to help us to express ourselves in the best possible way and therefore to correct and modify ourselves to the point of total reform of law and even each "forma preesistente" (pp. 247–48).

Volponi's own belief in the close links between art and science can be seen in his interest in Masaccio's painting in which art, science, and social criticism are united. Fifteenth-century painting is, to Volponi, revolutionary in its view of the artisanal, mechanical nature of art which is founded on science. "Popular" workers in the "mechanical" arts were elevated to the dignity of those in the liberal arts, with the result that a double social and cultural integration was possible. That fifteenth-century ideal of a secular culture (to oppose the theological one) was attained at the same time as was the cognitive, scientific ideal—made manifest in the concrete logic of Masaccio's "pittura-scienza." In this novel, it is more a question of "poesia-scienza."

As Sarah teaches Charles in Fowles's novel, to live is to create; to create is to be free. Science seems to Anteo the one way to make man alive and free (p. 84). Just as man has been created or constructed, his

fate too is to construct even better creatures. Anteo's desire to find the roots and evolution of man connect him to a basic narrative impulse of man — the impulse to myth. His treatise is indeed a mythic construct but one designed to explain the creativity as well as the existence of man.

Rewriting Darwin somewhat, Anteo sees the future of all life as inorganic (p. 48). The past is seen as "*il passato del naturale*" but the future is man's, and this means man's creativity: "*il futuro dell'artificiale*," that is, of all that can be made by man (p. 41, treatise italics). Man is a kind of *automa-autore* who creates another even greater than himself. Anteo writes in his treatise that in progressive civilizations which better living (mere "vivere") by developing existence, "esistenza" (from "esistere"), everything happens by a superimposition of new things. Therefore, he feels, evolution is the essence of the formation of the *automa-autore* (p. 171). Therefore he postulates a more powerful creator figure, not incompatible with the God of Christianity (pp. 54, 168, 194).

It is clear here that Volponi is attracted to the rural society of Italy and to the society too of rebels and misfits, because it is there that he can still find people who *invent*, who still have the courage to criticize their empirical reality and to dream and even construct a different one. According to his creator, Anteo's powerful fantasy lies in his search for a new reason behind engagement, human and political, and in his proving that man is not the slave of his surroundings, but the proud and potent animal who can modify both internal and external realities.[15]

For the understanding of this concept of freedom and creation, Anteo's theories must be examined more closely. As a boy, looking at the stars, he felt he perceived the mechanism, the unity of the universe, in such a way that he could use this knowledge to create other elements which would fit into this construct (pp. 32–33). He looked at his feet and saw that someone had made them. This concept of fabrication, as if by an author, led him to conceive of not one, but a whole race of primary, absent creators and from these he proceeded to an anatomy of the immense "macchina del creato" and of the infinite "tecnica della creazione" (pp. 10–11). In this vision of wholeness: "*Automa, Autore = Homo sapiens; Automa, non autore = regno minerale e vegetale*" (p. 10, treatise italics). The source of life is therefore the same (automated), but man is differentiated by his authorial or creative capacity. When Anteo first sees Massimina he feels at once that he must have designed and created her in all her beauty. He too is an author.

Anteo's theory of creativity is a mechanical version of Coleridge's organic metaphor for the imagination and its constructs. The creative moment is still eternal and god-like. Anteo's powerful socialist-scientific rhetoric is almost untranslatable:

15 Volponi in the interview with Camon in *Il mestiere di scrittore* (Milano: Garzanti, 1973), p. 141.

L'attimo creativo, concepito come integrità dinamica automatica, psicologico-scientifica, è l'origine della creazione, mossa dalla validità degli argomenti e dall'autorità degli strumenti degli automi-autori. Essi servono i bisogni perenni della creazione attraverso le capacità di provocare i quesiti e le possibilità di affrontare le questioni della civiltà progressiva, nella lotta serrata degli individui per le conquiste massicce delle generazioni [pp. 171–72, treatise italics].

What begins as a mechanical project aiming at perfection and happiness, ends as a recognition of the creative, poetic properties of that project that is Anteo's life; he equates poetic feeling and artistic vision and makes both instruments of science. He concludes that "la felicità delle macchine libere" is "una felicità artistica" (p. 274). And this happy, artistic, mechanical freedom is a social and moral one based on intention and result, as well as the very presence of fantasy.

Volponi too claims in an early autobiographical sketch that he writes with the idea of finding—through the novel form—another rational, poetic, and therefore historical possibility for reality. Just like the whole of Volponi's novel universe, Anteo's mechanical vision has its own moral code meant to relate to society or reality at large. It is because Anteo's machines have this moral dimension that physics becomes philosophy. Since the basis of his machine construction program was "profondamente morale," each move toward mechanical progress and perfection would be a move toward "un concetto superiore," as he claims, "in senso filosofico" (pp. 150–51).

This evolutionary creative meliorism leads to not a few questions regarding the ending of the novel. In a certain sense, Volponi is parodying the existential commonplace of the suicide. On the other hand, Anteo's death is also not a defeat. It is a rational, calculated act of freedom, not despair. It is a self-assassination for which the reader has been carefully prepared. Anteo makes a comment early in the novel that in telling all about his fate he risks abandoning the treatise and ending the journal just before he ends his own life, "soltanto il giorno prima di finire la mia vita" (p. 14). This is in part Tristram Shandy's problem of how to both live life and write about it, but it is also in part Anteo's intuition that the act of writing will lead him unavoidably to death, just as to reject the language of society because of all it represents can only lead to silence—or perhaps to new creation. "Adesso comincio"—"Now I begin"—are the final words of the novel.

Before this, however, Anteo begins preparations for his death coldly and carefully, as he always claimed he would when he began to feel he had reached that point at which he judged himself an inefficient machine, when his ideas became cumbersome and even compromised by "un meccanismo non controllabile" (p. 225)—that is, the point at which his scientific language became unclear, contaminated (by pain) with naturalistic artistic expressions (p. 263). Massimina's murder of their child, the antithesis of his human, aesthetic, and scientific hopes

for a more creative, free society, reveals to him the madness of society and makes his suicide decision firm—but never is it a defeat. It is an act of progress, "di andare avanti" (p. 273), even at the end.

Perhaps it is that Anteo gives up on the idea of reforming society by scientific treatise, realizing that *he* cannot change the world on a large scale, scientifically, but only on a limited one, through his journal-novel and through the reader to whom he addresses the words of his aesthetic vision. The reader, at least, will see the new referent of his language, the new way of viewing and creating things in his world. It is therefore fitting that his self-assassination weapon should be his amulet, both a work of art and a representative of the society he hates (that is, the religious statue he stole from the countess, which accompanied him on his travels and in his studies). His death is not a gesture of love for society, nor is it one of despair. It is the victory of the aesthetic poetic vision, a victory which Girolamo Aspri carries forward, living his fantasies as Joaquin Murieta beyond the last page of *Corporale*.

As this and the other linguistically narcissistic texts examined in the last chapter thematically reveal, there is a two-way pull of contradictory impulses in regarding the language of fiction—for both writer and reader. There is the impulse to communicate and so to treat language as a means (to order as well as to meaning), and there is also the impulse to make an artifact out of the linguistic materials and so to treat the medium as an end.[16] The reader of overtly self-conscious works learns that he is indeed in a paradoxical position: while the text demands that he acknowledge the fictive and linguistic artifact that is its universe, it also teaches and indeed compels him to respond "vitally," to attribute human significance to the process of creating imaginary worlds in words.

16 See William Gass's view of this paradox in *Fiction and the Figures of Life* (New York: Alfred A. Knopf, 1970), p. 94.

CHAPTER EIGHT

Generative Word Play: The Outer Limits of the Novel Genre

> Not surprisingly, some modern critics find the new kind of reading so difficult and so different from the old that they call it *writing*.
>
> Frank Kermode

In Donald Barthelme's *Snow White*, one character refers to "Klipschorn's" theories of "blanketing" in language: "That part, the 'filling' you might say, of which the expression 'you might say' is a good example."[1] The linguistic self-consciousness of this and other passages in the novel draws the reader's attention overtly to the fact that he is reading words, words with their different textures and meanings. In a more covert version of this narcissism, such thematization would give way to an implicit, actualized process which in effect would come most close to equating reading with writing as active, creative efforts with language. In order for this to be the case, however, the linguistic structures employed must be immanent and functional within the text. They must not be so subtle as to be invisible, nor should they be so obvious that the reader is not really made to work with language, but merely asked to appreciate the verbal cleverness (as in snippets of Nabokov's *Ada* such as the address to "young laymen and lemens—and not to grave men or gravemen," or the "bric-à-Bracques" or "Aujourd'hui [heute-toity]"). Yet to give but a brief example, one which many critics have developed in considerable detail, in Robbe-Grillet's *Le Voyeur* the language play actually serves to structure the plot: the *fillette* and her *ficelles*, her *corps* and the *cordelettes* (and *vaguelettes*), *Violette* and the *viol*, and so on. The act of reading words becomes one of structuring fictive worlds. As Ricardou explains: "lire, c'est explorer les relations spécifiques par lesquelles sont liés les éléments d'un texte.

1 (New York: Atheneum, 1967), p. 96.

Voilà pourquoi, à la limite, un livre qui ne résiste pas ne mérite guère lecture: avant même d'en avoir parcouru quelques pages, le lecteur sait qu'il l'a déjà lu en totalité."[2]

The linguistic self-reflectiveness or even self-generation of the text are forms of resistance to the act of reading, shifting attention to the semantic, syntactic, and often also phonetic texture of the words which actually serve to structure as well as constitute the work. This centripetal pull, however, does *not* cut the reader off from what has here been called "vital" or life experience. While it is true that the work becomes a self-contained artificial unit, nevertheless, the extramural link is made through the process of fiction-making in language, the creation of worlds in words.

While the early *nouveau roman* contented itself with delivering a challenge, primarily to fiction's diegetic identity, the more recent *nouveau nouveau roman* is more subversive in its linguistic orientation: a former division of diegetic unity becomes now a kind of unity of diegetic plurality,[3] of linguistic "plurisignification" that is generative of the "fiction" itself. Lest one think that this latest development constitutes a radical break, one ought to recall that there are precedents—the Grand Rhétoriqueurs, the Gongorists, and of course other fiction writers.[4] Saussure found anagrammatic play (whether ritualistic, mnemonic, or accidental, he did not know) in early Greek and Latin texts,[5] and certainly Raymond Roussel's work was in some ways as radical as Ricardou's. Linguistically generated "heterocosms" (and world visions) exist too outside the confines of the *nouveau nouveau roman*, in Nabokov's *Ada* (with its ardor in the arbors of Ardis) or in Volponi's *Corporale*.

As with the "auto, automa, autore, automatico" functional play examined earlier in *La macchina mondiale*, this latter novel offers structurally significant generative word play: Girolamo calms his nerves as a boy by reciting a list of Greek verbs (given to the reader in *Italian*) whose actions prefigure (generate?) all the major actions of the rest of the novel. He also makes anagrammatic and punning word associations throughout the novel, all of which are thematically or narratively functional. For instance: "Mussolini. Moschicida, moschettiere moschicida, uccidi le mosche."[6] To Girolamo, language is a means of

2 *Le Nouveau Roman*, p. 70.
3 Ibid., p. 139: "Le récit n'a donc pas disparu: au cours de son procès, il s'est multiplié et ce pluriel est entré en conflit avec lui-même."
4 See Bruce Morrissette, "Post-Modern Generative Fiction: Novel and Film," *Critical Inquiry* 2 no. 2 (Winter 1975), 253: and Jean Ricardou, in *Nouveau Roman: hier, aujourd'hui* 1 (Paris: Union Générale d'Editions, 10/18, 1972), 118-20.
5 See Jean Starobinski, *Les Mots sous les mots: les anagrammes de Ferdinand de Saussure* ([Paris]: Gallimard,1971).
6 (Torino: Einaudi, 1974), p. 161. See also pp. 27, 242. All further page references will be in parentheses in the text. Translations are more or less impossible on this verbal play level, and so will not appear.

ordering his life—a *mise en abyme* of Volponi's language viewed as a means of ordering the fiction:

Mi viene la voglia di definire qualcosa intorno a me che non vedo e che non conosco, ma che mi pressa e mi punzecchia con delle manazioni:
 1 microbo-radio
 1 radocobo
 1 coboradoc (c, c dolce).
 Ebbene, questo mi aiuta, mi dà la mia presenza allargando intorno a me la stretta, "il senso dello stato."
 Respirare in mezzo alle presse e intanto stabilire una mia codificazione [p. 142].

In Volponi's opinion, functional linguistic play has the capacity to revivify that part of reality that is structured and developed through language.

However, there is some truth in the statement that the practitioners of the *nouveau nouveau roman* use more frequent and more sustained linguistic play than any other writers, short of Joyce perhaps. They have also theorized upon their own practice at considerable length. This does not, by any means, however, signify communal agreement. In fact, at Cerisy in 1971, replying to Ricardou's earlier claims that *Projet pour une révolution à New York* was anagrammatically generated by the letters, syllables, sounds of "rouge,"[7] Robbe-Grillet felt the need to point out that it was rather the *colour* red (blood, torture, flames) that was the *authorial* generative key.[8] In this, it is no different from any other image that structures and thematically sustains a novel—the beam and shape of the lighthouse in Virginia Woolf's *To the Lighthouse*, for example. To Robbe-Grillet, words are signs; to Ricardou they are sounds, letters, syllables to be materially manipulated by writer and reader. This latter generative play would constitute the fourth type of narcissism mentioned in Chapter One—covert linguistic narcissism.

However, this mode proves to be hard to analyze even in terms of the devices or models employed. The pun and the anagram are the most frequently used, but others can exist. Ricardou's *Les Lieux-dits*, for example, is composed by means of an acrostic diagonal; more simply, *La Prise de Constantinople* contains repetitive play on the letters S and L, both overtly at the beginning of words (Lucky Strike, etc.) and in hidden form ("est-ce elle").

In *Ada*, Nabokov delights in interlanguage play (mostly Russian-English) which is both generative and self-reflective: "At the next turning, the *roman*tic mansion appeared on the gentle eminence of old *novels*."[9] One also finds the sequence: "half-dotty old doctor, doc, toc,

7 *Pour une théorie du nouveau roman* (Paris: Seuil, 1971), pp. 211-33.
8 *Nouveau Roman: hier, aujourd'hui* 2, 160.
9 (New York: McGraw-Hill, 1969), p. 38, italics mine. Other page references will be in parentheses in the text.

ditty, dotty, ballatetta, deboletta . . . tu, voce spigottita, spigotty e diavoletta . . . de lo cor dolente . . . con ballatetta va . . . va . . . della strutta, destruttamente . . . mente . . . mente" (p. 26). This bizarre linking reveals the actions of the novel to follow. A few of these are those involving *Doctor* Van, the theorist about time (*toc*), easing his broken heart (*cor dolente*) over Ada who has left him temporarily (*va*), and whose name in Russian, Adochka, is an anagram of *adova dochka*, Hell's daughter (*diavoletta*), and so on. (For Nabokov, interlanguage play is often linked to parody, as in the three blunders in the first paragraph of *Ada* which ridicule the mistranslations of the Russian classics.[10])

Still other devices are used. The steps of Slade's word-golf in Nabokov's *Pale Fire* function thematically in the novel: for example, "hate-love in three" or hate-late-lave-love. In the *nouveau roman* there is Simon's *La Bataille de Pharsale* in which *Duchemin* yields *de la rue* and *l'arrière-garde* produces *le dernier cavalier*.

The punning play of *Ulysses* and *Finnegans Wake* is perhaps the most blatant forerunner of the use of the pun as a structural linguistic model. Often, however, this device, while frequent enough and usually functional, seems difficult to sustain. In Barth's "Life-Story," one finds an isolated example that bears no extension: the writer sits in his "oak-wainscoted study" pondering morosely his fictive identity when "one of his mistresses whereof he had none entered his brown study."[11] It is the brevity and "occasional" quality of the pun that make it less structurally significant in fiction (and harder to discuss).

The anagram is perhaps more sustainable in a narrative, although even this has been challenged. Renato Barilli[12] claims that the anagram is a "microtrope" that is more poetic than novelistic. Ricardou's "epsilon-l'espion" play in *Les Lieux-dits* is therefore just a *pre*-textual stimulation, not a real textual generator. Given the confusion between pre-text genesis and in-text production even at that important Cerisy conference (usually the only distinction was an ideologically conditioned semantic one—genesis being bourgeois and romantic expressionism), the question of when and where the language play is conceived by the author had best be set temporarily aside. However, the objection of the limitation of scope that Barilli raises is more immediately significant. Does Ricardou's loose play on *rien* in *La prise de Constantinople* (*nier, rein, ire, renie, nerf, rang, dans, rire*) really work so as to order the entire novel? Likely not, for the *reader*. However this does not totally invalidate its structural function in the fiction, of course; it merely points to its limits of range.

10 The opening sentence is that of *Anna Karenina* turned inside out; her patronymic is given a masculine ending; and the title of Tolstoy's family chronicle is botched by the fictional translator.

11 *Lost in the Funhouse* (Garden City, New York: Doubleday, 1968), pp. 118 and 123.

12 *Nouveau Roman: hier, aujourd'hui* 1, 278-79.

In Sarraute's *Entre la vie et la mort*, a child, playing with the word "Hérault" (*héros, erre haut, R.O.*), is given ideas, stimulated by his discoveries. To Barilli, this would probably be a *mise en abyme* of the process of writing a *nouveau nouveau roman*. From the reader's point of view, a potential problem is suggested. In the Sarraute text, the puns and anagrams are thematized overtly; in other novels the structures might be covert but still remain perceivable by the reader and therefore thematically and structurally functional—as in Nabokov's play on insect-scient-incest in Ada's ardors in the arbors of Ardis, or his twins, Nodo (No, do) and Odon (Oh, don't), the traitor and helper in *Pale Fire*. This is true of the early works of Raymond Roussel as well. However, this is where the problem suggests itself more strongly. If linguistic play is going to activate the productive labour involved in reading, it presumably has to be textually immanent, and in some way evident: cryptograms are different from anagrams. While one would want to argue that the latter, by involving the reader in the same process as that of the writer, constitute a mode of narcissism which is still within the limits of the novel genre (as a process mimetic form), the former is another quite different case. And the use made of Roussel by the *nouveaux nouveaux romanciers* raises this issue very clearly.

Roussel's work seems to have inspired two separate kinds of novelistic narcissism. One, on a diegetic level, corresponds to Ricardou's "auto-représentation verticale, ascendante, productrice." It includes the *mises en abyme* of the novels (the plays, machines, and so on), of some of the "textes de grande jeunesse" ("Chiquenaude," "Nanon," "Une Page du folk-lore Breton," "Parmi les noirs"), and the stories within stories of "Documents pour servir de canevas." Similar diegetic constructions inspired by Roussel are evident in the works of Ollier, Ricardou, and Robbe-Grillet. However, the greater stress has been on the linguistic "procédé" of Roussel. This is what Ricardou refers to as "auto-représentation horizontale, littérale, productrice" in the *nouveau nouveau roman*. Or is it?

There were several stages in Roussel's discovery of the imaginative possibilities of language. Always a lover of children's games, especially word games (see "Parmi les noirs"), Roussel began toying with minute differences on the level of the signifier. In these "textes-genèse," he would select two almost identical words (*billard* and *pillard*), place them in two exact same sentences, then construct a logical, verisimilar plot for a story which would begin with one and end with the other. This linguistic play *precedes* the actual writing and the reader is only aware of the clever structure at the last sentence of the piece; it is not a case of the *nouveau nouveau roman*'s "production" in and by the text. This is even more evident in the amplified version of this process used in the novel, *Impressions d'Afrique*, where the mechanism is not *in* the text at all, not at all available to the reader. For example, he claims in the posthumously

published *Comment j'ai écrit certains des mes livres* ([Paris]: Pauvert, 1963) that the "queue de billard" yielded the "robe à traîne" of Talou, the "pillard."

The next stage of his language play is even more influential for modern French fiction—and even more problematic. Taking *any* phrase, Roussel proceeded to disintegrate it phonetically: "J'ai du bon tabac dans ma tabatière" gave him "jade tube onde aubade en mat a basse tièrce"—the key plot elements of "Le Poète et la Moresque." Unfortunately the process cannot be traced backwards; the play, from the reader's point of view, remains cryptogrammatic. Indeed, even Roussel could not recall the original words he used, beyond the few offered in *Comment j'ai écrit certains de mes livres*.

Surely the intention behind this dissimulation lies in the author's mystifying desire, and not in a desire to liberate the act of reading, as apparently is the case in the *nouveau nouveau roman*. But there are still other differences between the language play[13] of the new novelists and their forbear. The first of these has finally been acknowledged, after being long ignored (by Ricardou[14] in particular): Roussel's breakdown of words was done on the level of the phoneme—not the graphic letter, as is the case in Ricardou's *La Prise de Constantinople*. Secondly, as has already been pointed out, Roussel's play was a stimulus to his imagination, engendering the action and plot details. In other words, hidden to the reader, it *preceded* the actual textual composition. The *nouveau nouveau roman* on the other hand tries to make linguistic play into an immanent producer of the text, into a structural architecture. Roussel's texts do *not* point, however, to their linguistic pre-textual generators.

From what is known of Roussel, his language games were as much a defensive, infantile, protective shield against reality,[15] as an effort to offer a literary challenge to existing forms. Those games ultimately share the "gratuité pure" of the *nouveau nouveau roman*'s games, perhaps, but the conservative elitist Roussel certainly had no similar ideological end in view.[16] The *nouveau nouveau roman*'s linguistic work

13 The term *signifier* play has deliberately not been used here since the customary use of this is in fact only metaphoric. The Saussurian signifier or *signifiant* has no substance (phonic or graphic); it is only form—that is, those differentiating traits which have a function in the *langue* system.

14 See "Disparition élocutoire" in Leonardo Sciascia, *Actes relatifs à la mort de Raymond Roussel* (Paris: L'Herne, 1972), pp. 7-30.

15 See Michel Leiris, "Conception et réalité chez Raymond Roussel," *Critique* 10 no. 89 (octobre 1954), 829, and *Comment j'ai écrit certains de mes livres*, p. 132, a reprint of Pierre Janet's 1926 piece on Roussel in *De l'angoisse à l'extase* 1.

16 Ricardou, in "Disparition élocutoire," pp. 16-17, claims that "à mesure que s'accroissent le nombre et la rigueur des rapports entre les signifiants d'un texte . . . le langage tend à occuper toute la scène tandis que l'auteur, comme subjectivité propriétaire d'un sens, s'amenuise jusqu'à disparaître" and so farewell to the bourgeois Romantic ideology.

is intended to free both writer and reader,[17] but Roussel forgot to teach the rules of the liberation game to the reader. Ricardou seems to deny this difference in his writings on Roussel, claiming for him a modern textually (not pre-textually) challenging linguistic play. He points out that while *Comment j'ai écrit certains de mes livres* begins with the word "je,"[18] it ends with "livres," the important element that literally gets the last word.[19] At Cerisy (1971), however, the title of Butor's paper, "Comment se sont écrits certains de mes livres," points to what is really a difference, certainly of intent and even of result. The cryptogrammatic element already mentioned should also serve to separate Roussel's linguistic genesis from the modern "production" within the novel genre; if the word play of the former is not traceable, it is not functional within the text. It is not therefore *novelistic* narcissism. One has perhaps stepped into the Ovidian mythic pool and over to the other side.

This, then, raises the question of the limits of the genre. How linguistically self-reflective can the novel or short story be and still remain diegetic, that is, mimetic? In "Naissance d'une fiction,"[20] Ricardou revealed the linguistic mechanisms of *La Prise de Constantinople*. The question one is faced with now is this: how much of this play could a reader conceivably have discovered on his own? How much of it, in other words, is really textually immanent and functional, and how much is pre-textual genesis, inaccessible to the reader except in such statements of authorial intent as Ricardou is wont to make? That the word play somehow structures the work seems undeniable—once the author has pointed it out. But can the act of reading alone produce this knowledge?[21]

The fact that Ricardou was (though no longer is) an early member of the group centred around the journal, *Tel Quel*, might suggest that he has moved, despite his protestations to the contrary, beyond the limits of the *nouveau nouveau roman*. How far can auto-representation go before it becomes anti-representation? In order to answer this, one must look more closely at the reply given by *Tel Quel* itself and by the avant-garde of fiction writers in other countries, for there is no doubt that a formalized theoretical and creative move to supersede the genre has been in existence for at least a decade and a half. It must be decided if and where a line can be drawn at the outer confines of the novel as linguistically self-reflective metafiction.

One might logically begin this investigation, therefore, with the work of that early *Tel Quel* group. Aware of the dangers of reductionism for

17 See *Nouveau Roman: hier, aujourd'hui* 1, 128.
18 Ricardou chooses to ignore all the other Romantic references to "gloire," personal genius, and imagination in this same book.
19 "Disparition élocutoire," pp. 16-17.
20 *Nouveau Roman: hier, aujourd'hui* 2, 379-92. See also *Problèmes du nouveau roman* (Paris: Seuil, 1967), pp. 189-90.
21 See Ricardou's "La Population des miroirs," *Poétique* 22 (1975), 203.

which Sollers attacked Pingaud,[22] one must nevertheless attempt to outline the basic premises of the group. Unlike Pingaud's, however, the intention here is not to determine the value or validity of the group's theory or practice, but merely to examine their implication for a study of the limits of a genre. This purpose, of course, will also restrict the present discussion to the early writings of the group—critical and creative—since by the time ideas had coalesced into the *Théorie d'ensemble* (1968), the novel had been left behind. The more recent pronouncements—political, cultural, and critical—along with the latest texts of writers like Roche and Sollers, form yet another topic, too vast to be entered into at this point. The only concern here is with that fine line which is the outer limit of the novel in its most linguistic narcissistic form.

In its early years, then, *Tel Quel* sought, under the influence of Russian formalism, to break with the tradition of extra-literary justifications of literature. From its inception, however, the journal's adherents at least attempted—in theory and practice—to free literature from genre limitations, to help produce new formal "organisms," to "faire sortir la narration de son 'copiage' pseudo-réaliste ou imaginaire pour l'amener à une exploration en profondeur du fonctionnement et des permutations de la langue" (Sollers, *Théorie d'ensemble*, pp. 392–93). The break here implied was historically conditioned, for the newly articulated concepts of "écriture," "texte," and "intertextualité" could probably never have come into being without Lautréamont, Mallarmé, Marx, and Freud, as the *Tel Quel* articles which pay intellectual debts revealed. Derrida's first anti- or post-structuralist[23] statements and Kristeva's early semiological research joined with the early path-forging of Robbe-Grillet as the major contemporary forces at work in the beginning.

The linguistic orientation of *Tel Quel* was evident from the start, but soon an ideological (Marxist and then Maoist) dimension was added.

22 "Le Réflexe de réduction" in *Théorie d'ensemble: Tel Quel* (Paris: Seuil, 1968), pp. 391-98. All further page references to this volume will appear with *Théorie d'ensemble* in parentheses, with any necessary information regarding the title of the article and its author.

23 Umberto Eco, in "The Death of the Gruppo 63," *20th Century Studies* no. 5 (September 1971), 67-68, feels that the radical Italians of the same period used the open self-questioning structures of what Lévi-Strauss called "serial thought" while the co-generational French took structuralism as their more closed operational model (code-decoded message). This was only true, if ever, in the very beginning. Derrida's influence has proved stronger and his critique of structuralism's reductive spatial model has moved closer to Eco's "opera aperta" (as in the "jeu des pièces" concept). See Derrida's remarks in Richard Macksey and Eugenio Donato (eds.), *The Language of Criticism and the Sciences of Man: The Structuralist Controversy* (Baltimore: The Johns Hopkins Press, 1970), p. 268, and his earlier, more expanded version in "Force et signification," in *L'Ecriture et la différence* (Paris: Seuil, 1967), pp. 30 and 44. For more on Eco's distinction see his *La struttura assente* (Milano: Bompiani, 1968), p. 306.

"Écriture," the group's concern, was defined by Baudry as "une activité théorique qui a pour fonction de penser à la fois le système de langage, le relai d'informations par lequel cette société se parle et se vit et les nouveaux systèmes formels qui viennent à apparaître" ("Écriture, fiction, idéologie," *Théorie d'ensemble*, p. 127). What replaced mimesis and the novel in importance was the "écriture" and its manifestation, the "texte." With the maximal saturation of the signifier that this involved, came the increased difficulty in reading.

Michel Foucault ("Distance, aspect, origine," *Théorie d'ensemble*) found certain other common denominators in the works of the group, especially on the temporal and spatial levels. When the only given was language, literature became a network in which personal pronouns replaced proper names, fantastic elements were neutralized, and blanks appeared in the text—functioning as areas of muteness of articulation around which the language could pivot, in order to create "l'espace épais" in which experiences of dream, madness, repetition, doubling, and so on came into being.

The critics of the *Tel Quel* persuasion were not immune to a surprisingly naïve theoretical insularity. It is a critical truism that all fiction— not just "textes"—can only be judged by a criterion of literary validity, for "truth" has no meaning in literary theory. Yet the opening remarks of the *Théorie d'ensemble* attributed this constant to a new *Tel Quel* revelation. Pleynet's feeling (in "La Poésie doit avoir pour but...," *Théorie d'ensemble*, p. 94) that the novel had escaped naturalism, while poetry had yet to discover a new "realist articulation" revealed an odd refusal to acknowledge American New Criticism, then thirty years old. Is Kristeva's "intertextualité" really so far from the Russian formalist theory of parody? However, these problems remain minor in the light of the overall impact on fiction of *Tel Quel*, especially with regard to the functioning of the signifier and the political stance this entailed.

The linguistic theory was common to the early work of most members of the group, from Lacan's "chaîne signifiante" to Kristeva's "sémanalyse," which has been called a "réflexion sur le *signifiant se produisant en texte*."[24] The major problem posed by a deliberate destruction of the Saussurian sign by the idea of a signifier-generated text was that later raised by Fredric Jameson.[25] Was one not in danger of rejecting a transcendental signified in favour of an equally rigid transcendental signifier—a "prison-house of language"? And, in addition, given the very definition of the signifier, if one could separate it from the signified,[26] it would have no meaning, but would only be an object.

24 François Wahl in O. Ducrot and T. Todorov, *Dictionnaire encyclopédique des sciences du langage* (Paris: Seuil, 1972), p. 449, italics his.
25 *The Prison-House of Language* (Princeton: Princeton University Press, 1972), p. 185. See also Hélène Cixous, "Prédit," *Prénoms de personne* (Paris: Seuil, 1974), p. 9.
26 See Emile Benveniste, *Problèmes de linguistique générale* (Paris: Gallimard, 1967), p. 52 on "la consubstantialité du signifiant et du signifié."

While this was indeed the idea behind *Tel Quel*, is a system of signifiers in any way related to the genre one knows as the novel? And it is to this question alone that this chapter addresses itself.

Yes and no—was the reply of the early *Tel Quel*. The "texte" had simply replaced genre categories in its theorizing. In opposition to the idealism of a pre-existing meaning which was then concretized or expressed, the "texte" offered the materialism of an open play of the signifier. In that the "texte" made language into productive "travail," this could be seen as an extreme but still potentially novelistic version of the linguistic self-consciousness of much modern metafiction. The anagrammatic combinations, the "polysémie," the permutation of grammatical possibilities worked by and in the text, became the "travail" of the reader, labouring as he did from the "phéno-texte" to the "géno-texte," to use Kristeva's terms. This critic also specified that the text was "un appareil *trans-linguistique* qui redistribue l'ordre de la langue . . . donc une *productivité*" ("Problèmes de la structuration du texte," *Théorie d'ensemble*, p. 299). This redistribution function ultimately made mathematics and logic of more value than structuralist linguistics to the study of the "texte" as a self-generating mechanism.

The choice of this neutral term, "texte," was presumably intended to eliminate any suggestion of creation as the product of an individual personal effort. The "texte" was not to be consumed; it had no bourgeois market value; it was open, the property of all, a collective work of "productivité." This, of course, was where the ideological stand entered. Much of the theoretical work of *Tel Quel* was aimed at showing the close but subtle connection between radical literary practice (Lautréamont, Mallarmé, for example) and social or political revolution— usually interpreted in Marxist, Maoist, or even Freudian terms. Their practical literary efforts sought to bring about such a revolution of all value systems—linguistic, economic, psychoanalytic, and political. Imagination, creation, genius—all were considered bourgeois terms, individualistic and Romantic, and thus to be avoided.

The ideological stance of the journal was not naïve: unlike Sartre's *engagement* which ultimately acknowledged, in Sartre's own terms, that art could do nothing for a dying child, Ricardou's early idea of the "fonction critique"—the critical action of literature *as literature*— attempted to contest reality in operative terms only through the productive aspects of the "texte" as, in a now famous phrase, the "aventure d'une écriture" and not vice versa. Ricardou perceived this as the end result of a three-stage historical process.

From the "illusionisme représentatif" of Balzac, fiction moved to the narcissistic *mise en abyme* structures of the *nouveau roman* in which the only thing the novel represented was its own creation and functioning.[27] The next step he described—that taken by *Tel Quel* by 1968 at

27 Ricardou's more recent works seem to expand, but not substantially alter, his view of

least—is the problematic one here. From auto-representation, the form of fiction altered—to anti-representation—as literature became increasingly a challenge. Based on a principle of opposition, such "textes" aimed at disruption, at abolishing the representational categories (and so characters became mere grammatical entities— pronouns), at violently formalizing the narration itself in order to submit the signified to a permanent critique which would prevent it from coagulating and concealing the "travail" that formed it ("Fonc- tion critique," *Théorie d'ensemble*, p. 265).

Since representation was seen as the dominant mode of a society which the early *Tel Quel* condemned, the novel, and with it the tradi- tional mimetic and even structural methods of analysis, were at this point left behind. Saussure was replaced by generative grammar and semantics, as well as mathematics; Kristeva postulated a paragram- matic conception of literary language as the "seule infinité du code" which would make the text a double entity composed of "écriture- lecture": " 'Lire' dénote, donc, une participation agressive, une active appropriation de l'autre. 'Écrire' serait le 'lire' devenu production, industrie: l'écriture-lecture, l'écriture paragrammatique serait l'aspira- tion vers une agressivité et une participation totale."[28] The "texte" became a network of connections based on a non-linear tabular model, inspired by "grammes chinois," a potential Maoist exit from occidental discourse.

Although Sollers' *Drame* (Paris: Seuil, 1965) was said to be structured on the numerology of the Yi-King, this knowledge does not appear to be necessary to some comprehension at least of the chess-board struc- ture of the novel. *Drame*, from its opening—"D'abord (premier état, lignes, gravure—le jeu commence)"—to its closing—"On doit pouvoir considérer que le livre échoue ici—(brûle) (s'efface)"—invited the reader to doubt the closed nature of the novel without destroying the genre itself, although Sollers later claimed that a text "n'apparaît que pour s'effacer et réciter cette apparition qui s'efface" ("Ecriture et révolution," *Théorie d'ensemble*, p. 73). Like Sanguineti's *Il giuoco dell'oca*, *Drame* still narrated at least its own self-consuming narration; in that Aristotelian sense of mimesis (including diegesis), then, both could still be considered novels. However, the later works, such as *Nombres*, which aimed at making impossible what Sollers called novelistic exploitation, seemed to announce another genre, the "texte" or the "fiction," the manifestation of "écriture."

It would seem to be clear that the word "novel" on the title page or cover of a book would program the act of reading, ordering, and ultimately reducing complexity to a function of that reading. *Tel Quel*,

this process. See *Le Nouveau Roman*, pp. 53–57 especially, and "La Population des miroirs," pp. 196–226.

28 "Pour une sémiologie des paragrammes," *Tel Quel* 29 (Printemps 1967), 58.

in moving at this stage beyond the genre, sought to escape this closed structure. In its hands, semiology subversively destroyed not just genre distinctions, but literary/non-literary ones as well. "Literature" was seen as a concept which was historically and ideologically a product of a capitalist consumer society, as indeed was the notion of the sign itself. The destruction of the sign and of representation (even auto-representation) would seem to mean, then, that by 1968 at least, *Tel Quel* had passed beyond the novel genre, and so had passed beyond the scope of this discussion.

There appears, as well, to be a definite feeling that the anti-representation of even the early *Tel Quel is* indeed rather different from the *nouveau roman*'s auto-representation,[29] even in its more radical recent language-oriented form. In the latter, the inner linguistic mirrors are not destructive, but rather the doubling forms the "fiction" itself. The objective is more unification than disruption. Categories such as that of character are subverted without being destroyed, and the process of representation is not annulled but only turned in on itself, whether horizontally or vertically. The "fiction" in the latter case is invaded by the "narration," to return to Ricardou's basic terminology.

While an extreme form of this invasion—the actual devastation of the "fiction"—signals the moving beyond the novel, the early presence of the works of the later Joyce, of Gertrude Stein, and of the early Raymond Roussel suggests that there actually is room for a more productive, active notion of *novelistic* writing and reading. In the new new novel, the interest of fiction seems to be decentralized, drawn away from the story told toward the functioning of language or even broader diegetic processes shared by writer and reader. Language becomes a "matière langagière," the object of certain transforming operations which make it "matière signifiante,"[30] *not* because it might carry pre-existent meaning, but because of the multiple contextual significances given by the selection and organization processes.

Tel Quel, however, while sharing many of these same concepts, left the novel behind, and it was not alone in its rejection. At the 1966 Cerisy conference, Aldo Rossi tried to convince the critics that there was perfect synchrony between Italian and French avant-garde interests.[31] The fact that Sanguineti was published in *Tel Quel*, however, ought to be weighed against his somewhat antagonistic position at Cerisy in September of 1963. There were differences between the

29 As noted earlier, see *Nouveau Roman: hier, aujourd'hui* 2, 348 (Robbe-Grillet and Ricardou on Sollers) and Thibaudeau's remarks in Michel Foucault (directeur), "Débat sur le roman," *Tel Quel* 17 (Printemps 1964), 25-26.

30 Jean Ricardou, "Penser la littérature aujourd'hui," *Marche romane* 21 nos. 1–2 (1971), 12.

31 "Aspects de la critique en Italie," in Georges Poulet (ed.), *Les Chemins actuels de la critique* (Paris: Union Générale d'Editions, 10/18, 1968), pp. 41-42.

Italian radicals and their French colleagues—largely as a result of their working out of different literary, political, and social situations—but they shared a desire to push the novel form to its linguistic limits and, in theory at least, to surpass it.

Although we have been informed by a trustworthy source—Umberto Eco—that the *Gruppo 63* no longer exists,[32] it remains the closest non-French relative to those radical writers of *Tel Quel* in its early years. This family resemblance, however, must not be taken too literally, for there are significant differences between the two groups and their backgrounds. Italian literature, for instance, has been both very language-conscious and also very politically aware for some time, as it has struggled to overcome what it considered the bastardization and falsification of official language—first under fascism, then neo-capitalism. Unlike the contemporaneous literary situation in France, in Italy's essentially poetic literary tradition, it was understandably poetry that was the first genre to feel the linguistic effects of the protest against the neorealism and hermeticism of the first half of the twentieth century.

To the radical new poets and theoreticians of the fifties and sixties, poetry was opposition—to the dogma and conformity that was solidifying and immobilizing Italian culture. The reader was no longer to be a consumer of poetry, for the linguistic energy of these new poets would not allow such a passivity. Out of this fertile ground sprang the novelists of the neoavant-garde, bringing to the narrative genres a poetic inventiveness of form unknown to previous Italian fiction.

There was, however, at the start, no unified movement, no constant political or literary theory centred around a critical journal, as there was in France at the time. The yearly conventions of the mid-sixties revealed only a sort of general common intention to promote the fertile reciprocal influence of critical theory and literary practice, a working toward an end which included literary and social renovation through a critique of that super-structural dimension—language. The importance of the theoretical work of indigenous critics such as Umberto Eco is clearer than that of any imported structuralist influence, especially in the forming of the group's values, both positive (open, experimental) and negative (closed, traditional).

The *neo*avant-garde were so named in order to distinguish them from the earlier twentieth-century innovators—Proust, Joyce, Musil, Svevo, Pirandello. There seems little agreement, however, as to whether the new group shared or was in opposition to the concerns of that early avant-garde.[33] Robbe-Grillet was the single most important

32 "The Death of the Gruppo 63," pp. 60–71.
33 See Renato Barilli, *Il romanzo sperimentale* (Milano: Feltrinelli, 1966), p. 11; and "Le strutture del romanzo" in *Gruppo 63* (Milano: Feltrinelli, 1964), pp. 25-47; in opposition, see Angelo Guglielmi, *Il romanzo sperimentale*, pp. 32-33 and *Gruppo 63*, p. 16.

non-Italian liberating force, along with, of course, Beckett, the sur-realists, and a few Italian writers such as Gadda.[34]

In non-literary terms, though, it was the failure of the communists to gain control in the 1950s that likely provided the impetus for the birth and growth of the neoavant-garde. If politics proper had failed, perhaps literature as socio-linguistic contestation might succeed. A rejection of the vulgar Marxism of social realism in favour of a research-oriented Marxist perspective led the revolt against the tradi-tional "riformismo" of novelists such as Cassola, Tomasi, and Bassani. Journals sprang up (such as *Il Verri* in 1956) to give voice to the new linguistic experiments of the young poets who would constitute *I novissimi* by 1961. In 1962, *Il Menabò* shifted the weight of its emphasis from literature and industry to literature and language, and finally in 1963 at Palermo, the *Gruppo 63* met with seemingly only one common denominator—a rejection of traditional establishment means of ex-pression and the subsequent interest in linguistic renovation. Further meetings were to reveal a shift from poetry to fiction, and from revolt to reconstruction.

These poets-turned-novelists saw political implications in their de-nunciation of the traditional bourgeois normality which formed the optic of the "old" neorealistic novel. The imagination had to be liber-ated in order for it to become the only "altro regno possibile." The novelist's task became the declaiming of "fluent lies," not aiming at truth but exalting truth to the status of the lie.[35] Like other self-informing metafictions, their works were characterized by that same particular exhibition of their own arbitrary structures as valid, au-tonomous forms of experience which has been noted in Nabokov's *Ada* and Barth's *Lóst in the Funhouse*.

However, from this point on, there was little agreement among the members of the group. To one faction, literature had to be freed from ideology, voided, for it had no operative function. Novelistic language is autonomous; the novel is artificial verbal play with no ties to reality, or even to any communicative function. Another view held that lan-guage could never be void, naïve, innocent; it is always ideologically conditioned. But in this very fact resides the key to the de-structuring of society, through the anarchistic contesting of it by means of the historical and ideological entity called language. Yet another faction placed the neoavant-garde in a broader phenomenological perspective in order to situate its claims and contentions.

The first of these three groups, under Guglielmi's leadership, was set strongly against the operative function of literature for fear of risking a relapse into socialist realism. The problems that arise from the theoriz-

34 Angelo Guglielmi, *Vero e falso* (Milano: Feltrinelli, 1968), pp. 17-18, 100.
35 See remarks by Roberto De Marco and Giorgio Manganelli, *Il romanzo sperimentale*, pp. 158 and 174 respectively.

ing of this faction are rooted in a narrow provincialism that perhaps only the very early *Tel Quel* can rival. Guglielmi felt that all pre-*Gruppo 63* literature was extraneous and non-pertinent, because it worked, worked with objects, not words.[36] But the earlier universes of Svevo and even Verga are also decidedly direct products of self-informing linguistic effort: *La coscienza di Zeno* is as much a discourse on literature and language as is Giuliani's *Il giovane Max*. The lack of traditional novelistic qualities in this latter work once led Guglielmi to call it poetry, but the clue to its non-novelistic generic status lies more in the non-functional nature of the word play than in the presence of verbal exercise itself. It is not with the *Gruppo 63* that the concept of language as a mimetic medium is first called into question.[37] Readers of *Madame Bovary* know that this negation was thematized in fiction a hundred years earlier; and *Don Quijote* stands in the background, once again.

In contrast to the baroque but functional verbal energy of a Pynchon or, still in Italy, of the Volponi of *Corporale*, many of the writers of this faction tended to reduce language to a basic minimal form which was intended to intensify the literary experience almost to the point of a verbal equivalent of the Joycean epiphany. Grammatical and syntactical structures came under attack, as the "asemanticità" battlecry led the forces towards a de-structuring and de-functionalizing of the Italian language.

Within this faction, novelist Giorgio Manganelli asserted the autonomy of literature as a man-made creation. In *La letteratura come menzogna* (Milano: Feltrinelli, 1967), he offered the thesis that man has always feared literature, reducing it to lies, invention, mere game. Today, he felt, writers had to acknowledge this uselessness; their writing is never a social gesture but rather is giving testimony to language as the only stable and real condition in their existence—even in its very instability and unreality. The writer must understand what language demands of him. Like Roland Barthes, Manganelli opposed the monosignificance of a consumer view of literature: meaning is infinite and literature is artifice and artifact. Truth is a meaningless criterion, for art is not verifiable. In his own fiction—in *Agli dèi ulteriori* as in *Hilarotragoedia*—things exist only in and through language, peopling a proliferating linguistic universe structured and created self-consciously by the inventive power of verbal form. Like the signifier play in Massimo Ferretti's "Gazzarra" or the plotting of Arbasino's fictions around the operation of the author in organizing his verbal materials, Manganelli's texts do not touch or imitate any empirical reality; they remain autonomous linguistic entities which invent new realities, new fictive universes. And they remain novels.

36 *Vero e falso*, p. 43. See also his analysis of Giuliani's *Il giovane Max* in *La letteratura del risparmio* (Milano: Bompiani, 1973), p. 142.
37 As Guglielmi would have it in "Avanguardia e sperimentalismo," *Gruppo 63*, p. 19.

The second faction mentioned above accepted the autonomy of literature as a truism and proceeded to interpret it in ideological terms. Feeling strongly the political failure of neorealism, they too sought to contest the utilitarian functional concept of language and communication. Like *Tel Quel*, this group theoretically broke the bond between signifier and signified in an attempt to de-mystify and de-structure the reified communication systems. The next stage involved trying, again in theory, to separate the sign from its referent in order to negate the relation between language and reality—especially in the light of the mass media's reduction of language to a bourgeois product, pathologically deformed and aesthetically useless.

As early as 1963 the split between these two factions was evident. Guglielmi wanted to transform literature from within, gradually altering the public taste, but Sanguineti urged a terroristic break with the cultural establishment in order to effect social change. An operative emphasis had always been inherent in the desire of the entire group to change reading habits, to force the reader to question his ideological and literary concepts, not by confounding him with incomprehensible new codes, but by inner provocation (closer perhaps to the Russian formalist notion of "ostranienie").

All avant-garde writers, from Joyce to Sanguineti, seem to have shared a view of art as having a paradigmatic function in the opening and liberating of both the tradition of literature and the mind of the reader through self-conscious experimentation with language and the use of irony, parody, paradox, and so on. The Italian radicals, however, seemed to be more easily accepted—and tamed—by bourgeois society than their forbears. This potential neutralization had always been one of the greatest dangers to their political aspirations, for unlike their French brethren at *Tel Quel*, they had no common strong ideological base, as the disintegration of the journal *Quindici* later revealed.

Renato Barilli's phenomenological perspective formed what was almost a third viewpoint within the *Gruppo 63*, one that sought to link the new work with a vaster framework of contemporary cultural, scientific, and philosophical concerns. He presented, in *La barriera del naturalismo* (2nd ed., Milano: Mursia, 1970), a view of fiction which was based on his belief in the increasing modern suspension of judgment and pure projection of consciousness—free from ideology or the interference of the interpreting intellect. Because it was the least insular perspective of the three, Barilli's was perhaps less immediately relevant, but more interesting as an attempt to bridge the gap between French and Italian radical fiction: Barilli was present and active at that 1971 Cerisy conference on the *nouveau roman*.

These three views seriously divided the precarious unity of the *Gruppo 63* from the start, but two writers did eventually emerge as the

literary exemplars—Balestrini and Sanguineti. The former, since his major contribution has been in collage and computer poetry (although there do exist larger texts written prior to his post-1968 rejection of writing in favour of collecting documents on factory workers' movements), is of less interest to fiction theory than is the latter.

In an interview with Ferdinando Camon (reprinted, significantly, in *Tel Quel*[38]), Sanguineti outlined his views on language and ideology in fiction. Literary language is not a natural, neutral instrument; it is perfectly conditioned and ideologically characterized in order to create artificially a conventional product. Any use of language, by extension, is also a means of interpreting reality, an ideological filter. In many ways Sanguineti was the Ricardou or Sollers of Italy—the spokesman for radical views at conferences, academic defender, and explicator of his own creative work.

One of Sanguineti's most powerful means of literary challenge was the parody he deployed in his fiction—from *Capriccio italiano* to *Il giuoco del Satyricon: un'imitazione da Petronio*—in an attempt to achieve that greater availability of linguistic, literary, and intellectual materials that Eliot and Pound had brought to poetry earlier in the century. Carlo Salinari, a Marxist himself, attacked the political implications of this parody, or "mannerism," for he felt that the breaking of the language-thing link in favour of a language-literature one would never contribute to any social transformation.[39] Sanguineti disagreed; for him it was through the consciousness of its own fictiveness that the novel could and did achieve a genuine political function, as a challenge, a contesting.

The entire *Gruppo 63* was often accused, as was Sanguineti after the publication of *Il giuoco dell'oca*, of being too limited, of denying imagination, individuality, of overstressing trivial language concerns to the detriment of content implications, and ultimately of being unreadable. Their theoretical pronouncements were often greeted with nervous anger, yet also with some valid opposition to their evasion of certain issues, their insularity, vague terminology, and terrorist rhetoric. Their verbal play was accused of being gratuitous, deliberately nonfunctional in the texts. But that was not always the case in fact, if it often was in theory. And the writing of Manganelli, Arbasino, Sanguineti, and the others seems to have done more—through its avowedly fictive but ideologically significant nature—to liberate the Italian novel from the bonds of the "illusion" of neorealism and from a kind of vulgar Marxist degeneration of *engagement*, than has any other in recent memory.

This does not mean that there are not large problematic issues which were unearthed by the neoavant-garde. Did the critical awareness,

38 In *Il mestiere del poeta* (Milano: Lerici, 1965), reprinted as "Pour une avant-garde révolutionnaire," *Tel Quel* 29 (Printemps 1967), 76–95.
39 *Preludio e fine del realismo in Italia* (Napoli: Morano, 1967), p. 203.

experimentation, subversive intent, and so on really constitute anything so radically new? Is not *Don Quijote* equally contesting in literary and social terms? Perhaps one is dealing rather with a constant in the dialectical development of narrative: was Sanguineti to Cassola what Fielding was to Richardson?

The *Gruppo 63* has committed suicide, Eco has claimed. The events of May, 1968, the disintegration of *Quindici* (preceded by its more vigorous handling of political than literary matters), the hardening of the ideological arteries—all these had helped it decide not to become an ossified relic. Its success in the general cultural domain assisted in destroying the subversive value of the group, itself even more than ever a part of the cultural establishment of radio, television, publishing, and the universities.

On the other hand, the last few years have witnessed the resurrection of those writers the group fought to supersede—Cassola, Morante, and others. Perhaps the radical fiction failed even in its attempts to change the reading habits of a public whose tastes are rooted in the sentimental, realistic fiction of the past. Yet, the humour, the vitality, the novelty on a *literary* level have been positive additions to the range of Italian fiction—with one reservation. This energy tends to operate on the level of the page, not the book. The fascinating battle with language that had been intended, has perhaps ultimately led to an ignoring of the narrative battle with the reader.[40]

This suggests, however, that other possibility—that this kind of linguistic play could lead, or in some cases has already done so, to the formation of a new genre. The intended, if not always achieved, de-functionalizing and de-structuring of traditionally novelistic language in, for example, Balestrini's text *Tristano* obviously implies a passing beyond the boundaries of an already elastic genre. The more radical work of the Italian neoavant-garde seemed to share with that of *Tel Quel* at least an *intent* to go beyond mimesis—even a diegetic or linguistically self-reflecting version of it. In the words of Enrico Filippini: "il romanzo sperimentale avrà finalmente prodotto, tramite il salutare olocausto di un genere, la fine oggettiva di un linguaggio indiretto e avrà aperto canali non irrilevanti ad altre prassi."[41]

The less political *nouveaux nouveaux romanciers* turned to Roussel, among others, for linguistic inspiration. The roots of the differences between their fiction and the creative work of *Tel Quel* can be seen in Julia Kristeva's response to Roussel's *Impressions d'Afrique*.[42] She perceived a duality here. There are two meanings of the "impressions" of the title: the product which has been imprinted and an active process.

40 See Guido Almansi, "The Aging Vanguard of Italy," *Times Literary Supplement* 11 (October 1974), 1141.

41 *Il romanzo sperimentale*, p. 165.

42 "La Productivité dite texte," *Communications* no. 11 (1968), 59-83.

The former she condemned as auto-representation (and therefore still novelistic, mimetic) which gave in to the reader conditioned to look for "vraisemblance" (warning him that if he was not accustomed to the author's technique, then he had best read Part Two of the novel first). All Roussel did here, claimed Kristeva, was reverse the usual order of literary consuming by putting the "travail" after the "texte." To her mind, Roussel was not part of that radical break in the conception of the linguistic sign that has culminated in *Tel Quel*'s productivity of the "trans-signe"; he represents only a transition. The un-novelistic cryptogrammatic play alone, which tends (because of its lack of self-sufficiency and its need for extratextual intention for comprehension) to go beyond the narrative genre, was the only area in which she would grant him a semblance of textual "productivité," for it was based on a resemblance of signifiers and a difference of signifieds (a system hidden to the reader, however). She ultimately could accept as valid only the poetic and parenthetic *Nouvelles Impressions d'Afrique* because of its auto-destructive, anti-representational verbal structure. The new new novelists, on the other hand, drew from *all* of Roussel's various language games.

It would appear, then, that some sort of political-literary dividing line between narrative or novels and "textes" or "fictions" has been drawn by *Tel Quel* itself which one ought to take into account, for a similar distinction has appeared, in the theory at any rate, of the Italian neoavant-garde. In the latter case, however, the superseding of the traditional genre depended mostly upon a theoretical de-functionalizing, de-structuring ("asemanticità") which often did not, in fact, take place. *Tel Quel*, on the other hand, almost over-functionalized on the level of the anti-representational "texte" by transferring critical and ideological attention to the linguistic process of the signifier within the "texte" itself, the manifestation of that "écriture" which was their primary concern.

This is not exactly the case with the *nouveau nouveau roman*. Its often extreme linguistic self-reflectiveness is usually still auto-*representational*, still part of the elastic mimetic genre one calls the novel. This is the feeling that one has in reading the extended analyses of this covert linguistic mode of textual narcissism that appear in the proceedings of that Cerisy conference (*Nouveau Roman: hier, aujourd'hui* 1 and 2). Many critics, plus authors such as Pinget, Ricardou, and Robbe-Grillet, provide interpretations or descriptions of linguistic play in the *nouveau nouveau roman* that are fuller and more informed than any that could be offered here. Instead the focus of this chapter has been the investigation of the issue of the very serious implications of this particular mode of metafiction for the novel genre itself. And it would appear that it is not so much a matter of intense textual self-consciousness being self-destructive, or leading to the death of the novel; it is rather a case

of its *suggesting* a further but different stage—anti-representation—
which, usually for ideological reasons, would deny mimesis and even
diegesis. When this stage is reached, one requires the extra-textual aid
of the author—from *Comment j'ai écrit certains de mes livres* to those
crucially important back-cover comments of the *Tel Quel* literary
collection—in order to understand the functioning of the "textes."
There are obviously limits to the novel's elasticity. It seems evident that
a new genre—in theory and perhaps even in practice—has been born
of the novel, but it would be more than premature to suggest that
consequently the novel itself has died in childbirth—or expired, self-
obsessed, by Narcissus' pool.

Composite Identity: The Reader, the Writer, the Critic

> Being literature, it can never escape
> from itself. But it can approach the door.
> It can communicate its own communica-
> tive nature. It knows that it is not only
> written but also read.
>
> David Caute

All of the four types of narcissistic narrative have appeared to turn in on the reader, forcing him to face his responsibility for the text he is reading, the dynamic "heterocosm" he is creating through the fictive referents of literary language. For complicated philosophical and sociological reasons, many a modern novelist seems to feel akin to the founders of the novel genre. He may reject a nineteenth-century relationship with his reader, one based on the convention of omnis-cient presentation of a mirror of empirical "reality," as if that were an absolute objective entity. He may even reject the twentieth-century narrowed first-person perspective on any "reality." What he is now willing to offer his reader seems, to some people, minimal: a relation-ship based on a mirroring of the actual process in which he is engaged at that moment as he puts pen to paper—the process of bringing to life the fictive worlds of his imagination in and through language. The reader once again is engaged in an analogous creation but in the opposite order, from those same words to the worlds of *his* imagina-tion.

Throughout this discussion the term "reader" has been employed in a general sense. But in self-conscious fiction, especially of the overt variety, the "reader" is close to what Gerald Prince calls a "narratee," and Gérard Cenette, a "narrataire."[1] Following Todorov's[2] lead, this

1 "On Readers and Listeners in Narrative," *Neophilologus* 55 (1971), 117-22 and "Notes toward a Categorization of Fictional 'Narratees'," *Genre* 4 no. 1 (March 1971), 100-106; and Gérard Genette, *Figures* 3 (Paris: Seuil, 1972), 265-67.
2 *Introduction à la littérature fantastique* (Paris: Seuil, 1970), pp. 24, 35-36.

chapter will nevertheless continue with the term "reader," meaning by it the receiver of the text at the level of the *énonciation*. The reader is, then, a function implicit in the text, an element of the narrative situation. No specific real person is meant; the reader has only a diegetic identity and an active diegetic role to play. As Cortazar wrote in *Rayuela (Hopscotch)*: "Let us say that the world is a figure, it has to be read. By read let us understand generated."[3]

When a person opens any novel, this very act suddenly plunges him into a narrative situation in which he must take part. Certain expectations of a novelistic code are immediately established, and he becomes a reader in the above-mentioned sense of the word. Overtly narcissistic texts make this act a self-conscious one, integrating the reader in the text, teaching him, one might say, how to play the literary music. Like the musician deciphering the symbolic code of musical notation, the reader is here involved in a creative, interpretative process from which he will learn how the book is read.[4] In covertly narcissistic texts the teaching is done by disruption and discontinuity, by disturbing the comfortable habits of the actual act of reading. That some texts pander to the reader and indeed satisfy him, while others — especially modern ones — disturb him, has been pointed out already.[5] The unsettled reader is forced to scrutinize his concepts of art as well as his life values. Often he must revise his understanding of what he reads so frequently that he comes to question the very possibility of understanding. In doing so he might be freed from enslavement not only to the empirical, but also to his own set patterns of thought and imagination.

In self-conscious parodic literature, the reader-character identification circuit is often broken. It is sacrificed in order to engage the reader in an active dialogue with the generic models of his time, an exercise that is usually only the writer's.[6] By reminding the reader of the book's identity as artifice, the text parodies his expectations, his desire for verisimilitude, and forces him to an awareness of his own role in creating the universe of fiction. Reading and writing share those two significantly human paradigmatic functions. The first is the making of

3 *Hopscotch,* trans. Gregory Rabassa (New York: Random House, 1966), p. 379.

4 See novelist Kurt Vonnegut's remarks on this learning process, as published in Jerome Klinkowitz, *Literary Disruptions* (Urbana: University of Illinois Press, 1975), p. 62.

5 Two most eloquent and systematic statements of this view are those of Roland Barthes in "Bords" of *Le Plaisir du texte* (Paris: Seuil,1973), and Stanley E. Fish's work on seventeenth-century literature, *Surprised by Sin: The Reader in* Paradise Lost (London: Macmillan, and New York: St. Martin's Press, 1967) and *Self-Consuming Artifacts* (Berkeley: University of California Press, 1972), especially p. xiii. See also Walter J. Slatoff, "The Discomforts of Reading," in *With Respect to Readers* (Ithaca: Cornell University Press, 1970), pp. 137-59, and the already-mentioned book by Jerome Klinkowitz, *Literary Disruptions.*

6 This is what Claudio Guillén calls genre versus countergenre, in *Literature as System* (Princeton: Princeton University Press, 1971), pp. 154–55.

ordered fictions, which is not unlike the myth-making impulse in its imaginative freedom that paradoxically creates order and meaning. And the second is the use of language to create those fictional worlds. In the face of a growing lack of faith in the ability of language to reproduce reality, linguistically and diegetically self-conscious fiction asserts both the autonomy and validity of these creations of language, and the important "vital" function of that creative action itself — for author and reader. The novel is experientially or "vitally" significant *because* it insists on its own reality, confronting the reader, constructing and comprising his experience, operating upon his consciousness. In the beginning *is* the word, as William Gass too has remarked,[7] and the word creates a world through the co-operative activity of the sender and the receiver of the text.

As the reader progresses through any novel, the effect of the author's guiding rhetoric, of the narrator's mediation, and of the accumulation of fictive referents, is to force him to bridge the gap between his own world and the potential fictional universe. When he begins to read, because language is public, he can only read by relating the words to his knowledge of linguistic, objective, or subjective realities. However, the cumulative effect of reading is to transform this transparency of language into an increasingly dense set of aesthetic entities, into the fictive heterocosm. All this has already been examined in Chapter Six. All novels manage to interrelate what appear at first to be outwardly referential signs in order to create a self-sufficient, mutually supportive system. The narcissistic work, however, appropriates the reader's consciousness in a more deliberate and paradoxical manner, for here he must live within an *acknowledgedly* fictional universe as he reads. Yet the work constantly demands responses comparable in scope and perhaps even in intensity to those of his life experience — thanks to the reader's active participation in the very formation of that fiction.

The paradoxical demand — for both intra- and extra-mural validity — constitutes a challenge for the modern novelist, faced as he is with an empirical reality more readily communicated and more sensational in content than anything he could probably create. He must forge new connections between his art and his reader's life by forcing the reader to re-examine and re-evaluate his relationship to the text and to the world outside it.[8] The language of the text itself becomes what Murray Krieger, in a somewhat different context,[9] has described

7 *Fiction and the Figures of Life* (New York: Alfred Knopf, 1970), p. 18.

8 In his essay, "Su Lombardi e Arbasino," in *Il Verri* no. 13 (1964), 79-80, Angelo Guglielmi claims that in *La controra,* Arbasino offers his reader both a certain content and its de-mystification, and that this is brought about purely by a linguistic act, with no declarative, narrational help. In this way, claims Guglielmi, a purely linguistic operation becomes an operation conducted on reality itself.

9 *A Window to Criticism: Shakespeare's* Sonnets *and Modern Poetics* (Princeton: Princeton University Press, 1964), p. 3.

as an enclosed set of endlessly faceted mirrors, closed in on itself, which becomes, "magically," a window to the world. The reader is both trapped *in* the looking glass and led *through* it.

This same paradox has been described in ideological terms by David Caute as that of a "dialectical"[10] literature which recognizes its own nature, is self-conscious, and self-critical. It is a process as well as a product; both transitive and intransitive, it is itself the paradox facing the reader. It attempts representation while discarding the myth of representation. It tries to transcend its own textual limitations while never forgetting that this is impossible. It "makes a primary virtue of honesty and yet proves its virtue by means of cunning tricks." Such fiction is narcissistic in that it encourages an active personal response to itself *and* creates a space for that response within itself. Again, it is Cervantes and Sterne who stand as the forbears of the modern form of this art for Caute as well. However, he rejects texts that are explicitly about writing and novels as too elitist, too introverted, and thus too divorced from his wider social, moral, and political concerns. This would only be true if one ignored the equation of reading and writing, the pulling of the reader into and through the looking glass. Narcissistic texts merely make explicit the two directions—centripetal and centrifugal—in which the reader's attention moves in reading *all* literature, as Northrop Frye has pointed out. It is not only the early *nouveaux romanciers* who sought "de nouvelles formes romanesques capables d'exprimer (ou de créer) de nouvelles relations entre l'homme et le monde," and who decided "à inventer le roman, c'est-à-dire, à inventer l'homme."[11]

The reader of fiction is *always* an actively[12] mediating presence; the text's reality is established by his response and reconstituted by his active participation. The writers of narcissistic fiction merely make the reader conscious of this fact of his experience.[13] All texts are to some extent "scriptible,"[14] that is, produced rather than consumed by the reader. In the serialized novel, for example, the reader works to

10 *The Illusion* (New York: Harper and Row, 1972), p. 265: "The dialectical novel must inevitably de-mystify fiction by recognizing its fictitious nature and by using it as an operating principle within literature, within the Book and within the general field of linguistic communication." The subsequent discussion in the text is derived from pp. 177, 178 of Caute's book.

11 Alain Robbe-Grillet, *Pour un nouveau roman* (Paris: Gallimard, 1963), p. 9.

12 Critics still assign overly passive roles to readers, however. For example, Walter J. Ong, S.J., "The Writer's Audience Is Always a Fiction," *PMLA* 90 (1975), 12: "A reader has to play the role in which the author has cast him." And Lianne Norman, "Risk and Redundancy," *PMLA* 90 (1975), 285: "He gives himself up, in other words, to imaginative experience."

13 See, for instance, Nabokov's realization of this in the interview with Paul Sufrin for *Swiss Broadcast* (September 8, 1971), reprinted in *Strong Opinions* (New York: McGraw-Hill, 1973), p. 183; and Donald Barthelme's in "After Joyce," *Location* 1 (Summer 1964), 14.

14 The term is that of Roland Barthes in *S/Z* (Paris: Seuil, 1970), p. 17.

imagine what happens next, since suspense determines the cut. Dickens, for this reason, saw his reader as a co-author.[15] The sense of a journey with which so many of Hardy's novels open is the storyteller's way of getting his reader on the road as well. In *Emma*, Jane Austen creates, in the Box Hill episode, the illusion of understanding in both the reader and her characters (Mr. Knightly, Frank, Jane), so that the *reading* of the novel from this point on will *enact* the puzzle of misunderstandings that the author wants to illustrate. Like Emma, the reader is made to feel his fallibility; he is made aware of how fiction works and of what happens to him as he reads.[16] Tales such as Stendhal's *Armance*, which have ordering and constructing as a theme, can become paradigms of reading.[17]

In fact, as has already been pointed out, other earlier texts such as *Don Quijote* and *Madame Bovary* overtly thematize the imaginative power of reading. The epistolary (and sometimes the journal) novel actually makes the act of reading diegetically functional. Yet some sort of historical progression does seem to be visible. Fielding tells his reader, as consumer of his wares, how to read; he prescribes his imaginative participation. Sterne parodies this in *Tristram Shandy* in order to show his respect for his reader's imagination — leaving blanks, for instance, in the text in order to promote active reader involvement. The meaning of texts such as Ford's *The Good Soldier* is co-extensive with the reading process, and not its product. The reader is an active interpreter here.[18] Again Sterne had anticipated this role in a self-conscious manner. It is not in the conventional direct addresses to the reader that Tristram's narrative is narcissistic in a modern way. It is so rather through the characters who act as surrogates for the reader, anticipating his various interpretative responses. Part of both the novel's theme and its method involves watching the responder at work.[19] The protagonists of Part Two of *Don Quijote* become the readers of Part One, the creators of themselves.

This same thematization (and allegorization) of the role and activity of the reader is characteristic of overtly narcissistic texts.[20] Borges' Pierre

15 See Kathleen Tillotson, *Novels of the Eighteen-Forties* (New York: Oxford University Press, 1962), pp. 25ff.

16 See Ian Gregor, "Criticism as an Individual Activity: The Approach through Reading," in Malcolm Bradbury and David Palmer (eds.), *Contemporary Criticism*, Stratford-upon-Avon Studies 12 (London: Edward Arnold, 1970), 208-209.

17 See Tzvetan Todorov, "La Lecture comme construction," *Poétique* 24 (1975), 423-24.

18 See Frank Kermode, "Novels: Recognition and Deception," *Critical Inquiry* 1 no. 1 (September 1974), 106-11.

19 See J. Paul Hunter, "Response as Reformation: *Tristram Shandy* and the Art of Interruption," *Novel* 4 no. 2 (Winter 1971), 132-46. For a similar argument, with the use of the "observer" as reader surrogate in Manzoni, see S. B. Chandler, "Point of View in the Descriptions of *I Promessi Sposi*," *Italica* 43 no. 4 (1966), 396-98.

20 As a matter of policy, to avoid disrupting the text, no page numbers will be given for brief references to novels mentioned or quoted in this section.

Menard is the perfect reader, enriching a "halting and rudimentary" art by *writing* the *Quijote*. We are not surprised to hear that Cervantes' text and Menard's are verbally identical, but that the second is almost infinitely richer. John Barth's *Lost in the Funhouse* is a set of meditations on the act of reading (and listening) as life-granting ("You who listen give me life in a manner of speaking") and life-creating. In "Title," the reader is constantly asked to fill in the blanks (for example: "Just as people would do if adverbial clause of obvious analogical nature."). He is requested by the narrator to acknowledge his complicity in both the fictional creation *and* the self-consciousness about it: "You tell me it's self-defeating to talk about it instead of just up and doing it; but to acknowledge what I'm doing while I'm doing it is exactly the point." The writer is a reader too and must face this knowledge, as does the narrator of "Life-Story": "don't you think he knows who gives his creatures their lives and deaths? Do they exist except as he or others read their words?" In "Petition," this power of granting death as well as life is explicitly delegated to the "intradiegetic" reader, that is, the reader included within the narrative.

That the reader's desires and expectations ought to be met is the spring-board for the frustration of these very demands (as in the opening of Steve Katz's *The Exagggerations* [sic] *of Peter Prince*) in an attempt to raise the reader's consciousness of his act. Part One of Barthelme's *Snow White* ends in a questionnaire to the reader querying his interest—"Do you like the story so far? Yes () No ()"; his understanding of plot and symbols; his requests for the continuation of the book. He is also asked to rate the novel on a scale of 1 to 10. But more interestingly, the reader is brought back at the very end to his concrete nondiegetic identity outside the text: "14) Do you stand up when you read? () Lie down? () Sit? ()." Nabokov's novels also mock the reader's notions of both reality and fiction, while making explicit demands on the reader for the novelistic worlds' imaginative existence. Humbert Humbert tells the reader of his manuscript and the reader of *Lolita* both: "do not skip these essential pages! Imagine me; I shall not exist if you do not imagine me." Lolita too, of course, is only the product of his own erotic imagination.

Such overt challenges to the reader's conventional responses are matched by more covert subtle ones in texts by the *nouveaux romanciers*, by their Anglicizers (such as Giles Gordon), by the Italian neoavant-garde and also by American writers such as Sukenick, Federman, and Sorrentino (from whose work many of the chapter epigraphs of this study have been taken). Here the process of ordering, interpreting, and imaginatively "concretizing" is the same as that overtly taught by Barth and Nabokov, but reading is either allegorized as a creative process shared with the author (see the last paragraph of Pinget's *Passacaille* or the back-cover comment of Sanguineti's *Il giuoco dell'oca*),

or it is actually made so disruptive and challenging as to force the reader, if he is to read at all, to do that ordering, interpreting, and imagining for himself.[21] Pinget has stated that the reader ought not to be given any clarity or facile order as he reads, since the author had no such thing as he wrote.[22] Ricardou added: "pas de préface, ni postface: les règles du texte sont dans le texte. C'est en lisant qu'on apprend à lire: on ne peut pas faire le travail de lecture à la place du lecteur."[23] The reader must work to decipher the text as hard as the writer did to cipher it, with the result that the stress of the work is displaced from the communicating of a message to the inciting to produce meaning, as well as order. This demand for action, claims Ricardou, "suscite chez le lecteur un mouvement de production tel qu'il doit logiquement aboutir à l'écriture."[24] Pinget too claims that his reader "participe lui-même au travail d'élucidation, de décortication que je m'impose page après page, prendre conscience que le livre se fait sous ses yeux avec tous les doutes de l'auteur, ses hésitations, ses passions, ses reculs, ses élans."[25]

The act of reading becomes a creative, interpretative one that partakes of the experience of writing itself. These fictions are about their own processes, as experienced and created by the reader's responses. They also contain, however, in their self-consciousness, their own self-criticism. "When consciousness of its own form," writes Ronald Sukenick, "is incorporated in the dynamic structure of the text—its composition, as the painters say—theory can once again become part of the story rather than about it. One of the tasks of modern fiction, therefore, is to displace, energize, and re-embody its criticism—to literally reunite it with our experience of the text."[26] It is not accidental that Sukenick, like Barth, Federman, and many other metafictionists, is himself an academic. The critical and the creative meet in their fiction as they do in all narcissistic texts. *The reader, like the writer, becomes the critic*; without sacrificing his I-Thou amateur relation to the text, the reader also establishes an I-It distanced rapport. He is both drawn intramurally and pulled extramurally, into and through the looking glass. Reading is sequential and open to memory and association; criticism is usually systematic and reasoned discourse. But, the reading of these texts—especially covertly narcissistic ones—is often a rereading, a necessary constructing of meaning and system in the mind of the reader. The work is both an object and a performance.

21 See Jean Ricardou on Simon's *Corps conducteurs* in *Le Nouveau Roman* ([Paris]: Seuil, 1973), p. 65.
22 "Pseudo-principes d'esthétique," *Nouveau Roman: hier, aujourd'hui* 2 (Paris: Union Générale d'Editions, 10/18, 1972), 317.
23 Ibid., p. 407 (in the discussion).
24 Ibid., p. 154 (in the discussion).
25 "Pseudo-principes d'esthétique," p. 317.
26 "Twelve Digressions Toward a Study of Composition," *New Literary History* 6 (Winter 1975), 430. See also David Caute, *The Illusion*, pp. 22-23.

Page by page, the reader creates the meaning of the text, reshaping and reordering former unities into new ones as he proceeds. This is true of any text. The reader's progress is conditioned by many factors. Formalistic, structuralist, stylistic, and linguistic analyses all tend to ignore the importance of pace, for example, to the reader's understanding. Critics such as Ian Gregor and Stanley Fish have attempted to return to the dynamics of the reading experience as a key to theorizing about and teaching the novel. It is the developing responses of the reader, in relation to the words as presented in a linear consecutive fashion, that condition meaning, as metafiction teaches and illustrates so well.

Because the novels that have been discussed here make these demands upon the reader and constitute their own critical framework (in part), the existing theories of "reader aesthetics" are of only partial use to the critic/reader. Of course, no one critical model is ever complete; the subject and the model are never the same thing, although in a sense one might want to claim that the model distorts and so creates its own subject. When the model is the *text itself*, however, this problem is undercut. Yet there are approaches to the dynamics of reading which do cast useful light on this topic. Bateson's concept of the historical reader and Richards' psychological balancing of reader tensions are not at issue here, though. Nor shall this study be based in any way on the reader's desires, as was Virginia Woolf's in her "Phases of Fiction." There are other approaches, however—in particular, the Freudian, the phenomenological, and the rhetorical—which *can* account for part, but rarely all, of that paradoxical position in which the reader finds himself, as he is forced to remain within the world of fiction and yet see the act of reading as an experiential phenomenon analogous to the act of writing, and so related to both public language and private imagination.

Freud believed that the writer aimed at awakening in the reader the same emotions and "mental constellation" that produced in him the impetus to create.[27] While this is not far from what has been suggested here as being true of metafictional texts themselves, Freud's perspective was more general, his concern being the unconscious and not just the literary. In *The Dynamics of Literary Response* (New York: Oxford University Press, 1968), Norman Holland tried, by a critical method which relied specifically on his *own* reading response to a text's stimulus, to reach the "core of fantasy" of that text and so develop a general model for the interaction of literary works with the human mind. Yet another Freudian, Frederick Crews, disagreed with this endeavour to present, as the basis of literature, a disguised infantile

27 See in *On Creativity and the Unconscious* (New York: Harper and Row, 1958), "The Moses of Michelangelo," p. 12 and "The Relation of the Poet to Day-dreaming," p. 54.

fantasy that had somehow acquired significance. The real value of literary psychoanalysis for the reader is, he feels, that it can "embolden us to be alone with books, to recognize our own image in them, and from that recognition to begin comprehending their hold over us."[28] However close to what self-informing narrative suggests about the reading and writing processes as extramural, "vital" functions of art, this view denies the other half of the paradox of literary response — that the reader can "lose himself" within the fictive world he has created.

Another critical perspective offers more suggestive assistance to the critic/reader of metafiction. Literary phenomenology is a general term for many related but differing theories. For instance, much of the recent German investigation into an aesthetics of reception and impact seems more an effort to rejuvenate literary history seen as a dialogue of the present and the past, than a concentration on the experience of reading (although Hans Robert Jauss[29] does rightly bring to attention the fact that both the reader's response and his judging of a work are based on his past experience of *literary* data).

One does come very close to another kind of phenomenological approach, however, when the statement is made that self-conscious fiction teaches that a novel only becomes a living aesthetic reality when actualized by the act of being read. Mikel Dufrenne defines the aesthetic object (the work of art as executed by the reader's perception) as the "en-soi-pour-nous": "cet être est suspendu à la perception et s'achève en elle. Cet être est un apparaître."[30] This object cannot be reduced to mere representation; it has its own ontological reality. Yet this perspective tends to deny the outwardly directed paradigmatic half of the reading paradox. If the reader sets the work off in its intentionality by defining it in its perceptual characteristics alone, he must try to "bracket out" as irrelevant all his beliefs, prejudices, and preferences as reader. If he attends only to how art looks or sounds, he ignores one very important aspect for literature: the public, shared nature of language that does indeed carry meaning beyond the surface texture. The cutting off of the practical context by the phenomenological *epoche* endangers just that response which narcissistic fiction demands.

The lack of concern for the whole of the reader's paradoxical position here is also a problem in the consideration of Georges Poulet's views on the "Phenomenology of Reading."[31] Poulet does accept as premises both the heterocosmic nature of the fictional world of literature, and its absorption of the consciousness of the reader during the act

28 "Anaesthetic Criticism," *Psychoanalysis and Literary Process* (Cambridge, Massachusetts: Winthrop Publishers, 1970), p. 20.

29 "Literary History as a Challenge to Literary Theory," *New Literary History* 2 (Autumn 1970), 9-10.

30 *Phénoménologie de l'expérience esthétique* 1 (Paris: Presses Universitaires de France, 1953), 287.

31 *New Literary History* 1 (Autumn 1969) 53-68.

of reading. The text, for him, contains "a mental activity profoundly engaged in objective forms"—originally the author's—which the reader discovers "exposed in its ineffability and its fundamental indeterminacy." But, since it is this "transcendence of the mind" and not the text itself or even the reader as such that interests Poulet, his approach is not of much value in actually explaining the paradox of reader-oriented but self-informing fiction.

This same objection, that only half of the problem can be considered, could also be raised against the Geneva phenomenological group as a whole. One must agree with Jean Rousset when he claims: "Il n'y a de lecture complète que celle qui transforme le livre en un réseau simultané de relations réciproques."[32] The reader is a participant, not a spectator; thus, writes Rousset, he must reserve all judgment. Yet if this critical distance, this ability to judge, is forbidden, how can Rousset claim, as he does a few pages earlier, that: "la contemplation de l'oeuvre implique une mise en question de notre mode d'existence et un déplacement de toutes nos perspectives"? Narcissistic narrative demands just this sort of involvement, *yet* also a detachment and ability to judge, to face certain implications for both art and life.

The theories of Roman Ingarden, however, seem to come closer to the needs of metafictional criticism, and confirm from a different critical and philosophical vantage point many of the observations offered in this study as a whole regarding the heuristic value and paradigmatic nature of the teachings of self-reflective fiction. The Ingarden view of the "heteronomy," the stratified tissue that creates a "*habitus* of reality" (different from "real space")[33] in literature is essentially the concept presented earlier as the fictive referent and the heterocosm. And for Ingarden as well, it is the reader who concretizes the work of art: "Concretizations constitute, as it were, the connecting link between the reader and the work and emerge when the reader approaches it cognitively and aesthetically" (p. 352). Ingarden's stratum of represented objects (and their aspects) is equivalent to what have here been called the text's fictive referents, and like them, is both outside the strictly linguistic sign system and cannot be judged in terms of truth (see pp. 167–69): "the directional factors of the nominal meanings do not point beyond the purely intentional objects to any determinate real objectivities" (p. 170).

However, even Ingarden's phenomenological perspective would seem to conflict at several points with the findings presented regarding narcissistic fiction in particular. Ingarden distinguished, as Dufrenne

32 *Forme et signification* (Paris: José Corti, 1964), p. xiii.
33 *The Literary Work of Art: An Investigation on the Borderlines of Ontology, Logic, and Theory of Literature*, 3rd ed., trans. George G. Grabowicz (1965; Evanston, Illinois: Northwestern University Press, 1973), p. 221. All other page references will be in the text in parentheses.

would later, between the *work of art* itself and the work as an *aesthetic object* concretized through the various intentional acts involved in reading it. Yet the overtly narcissistic fiction that has been examined thematizes and makes conscious, within the *work of art*, the fact that it is an *aesthetic object* thanks to reader involvement. Little is left, in fact, of Ingarden's distinction. A second reservation is related to this. Ingarden feels that titles, narrative shifts, quotation marks, and so on, distance the reader (as would, in other art forms, a stage or a picture frame), and necessitate a conscious, intersubjective bracketing of experience. Yet, it appears that narcissistic works use these very same techniques to bring about the *closeness* of the reader to the text, through the activating of the imaginative processes.

Ingarden also claims that the reader abandons his own centre of orientation and distances himself from his own world in order to enter the world of art. On this basis, he decides that the objects of this world cannot, therefore, be "imaginational" because they "would then have to be perceived by internal perception, where in each case the center of orientation would necessarily have to be [the reader's] own" (p. 231). Yet narcissistic narrative, in breaking the traditional realistic illusion, constantly jolts the reader back to his own orientation, reminding him that he is reading a novel or short-story. Perhaps, then, the heterocosms of self-conscious fiction *are* "imaginational" in this sense.

Working from certain of Ingarden's premises, Wolfgang Iser[34] has outlined a view which is of more direct relevance to this discussion, for it deals specifically with the active involvement of the reader in what he is producing as the epitome of how all experience is acquired—that is, through the forming of *Gestalten*, the recognition of their inadequacies and the subsequent re-forming of information into new consistencies. Iser has examined in detail the mechanism behind what has here been called the creation of the fictive heterocosm by the reader's accumulation of fictive referents. But he has done so in terms of the text's repertoire, consistency-building and breaking, the filling of textual gaps and non-textual vacancies, and the reader's structuring of a field which finally brings the imaginary object into being.

Modern art, Iser feels, induces the reader to a more self-conscious participation in the text, causing him to reflect on the various operations he is asked to carry out. While Iser's perspective allows him to

34 The most detailed presentation of these theories was first made to a seminar in the Graduate Programme in Comparative Literature at the University of Toronto, September 19-November 7, 1974. Subsequently these ideas appeared in *The Act of Reading* (Baltimore: Johns Hopkins Press, 1978). See *The Implied Reader* (Baltimore: The Johns Hopkins Press, 1974) as well, which includes the important article "The Reading Process: A Phenomenological Approach" from *New Literary History* 3 (Winter 1972), 279-99. Also see his "Indeterminacy and the Reader's Response in Prose Fiction" in J. Hillis Miller (ed.), *Aspects of Narrative* (New York: Columbia University Press, 1971), pp. 1-45.

speculate on the effects of such reading upon the individual (heightening his perceptions, educating his sensibility), the concern in this chapter is more with the simple fact that all fiction does have an effect on the reader at a "vital" level and that narcissistic texts tend to relocate that effect. In other words, it is no longer a matter of the reader's having to identify with a character in order to be involved in the work; the act of reading itself is the real, dynamic function to which the text draws his attention. Like writing, reading is bound by a consciousness of generic tradition: one has to learn what stories are, as a child, in order to enjoy them. Similarly one has to learn to read—actively, imaginatively—in order to enjoy the demanding fiction of today.

The only problem with Iser's theories in relation to such texts arises when he agrees that the autonomous world of fiction is created by the reader, but that this is accomplished by the reader's temporarily leaving his personality and experience behind in order to select, order, anticipate, and remember—in order to make the text into a living event. However, self-conscious fiction tries actively to *prevent* even a temporary abandoning of human experiential responses, while also trying, it is true, simultaneously to lure the reader into an overtly fictive universe.

These last points suggest a third critical perspective which has a certain relevance in the discussion of metafiction—that of the rhetorical tradition. Wayne Booth's *The Rhetoric of Fiction* (Chicago: University of Chicago Press, 1961) was the first large-scale examination of the novel as an art of communication, of the rhetorical resources available to an author intent on making his reader create a valid fictional universe. Every author has a rhetoric, whether or not he writes with his reader specifically in mind; his only choice is in what kind he will use. Every word he writes, according to Booth, will guide his reader's response in some degree to certain values and beliefs upon which the work depends. Every sentence will contribute to making the reader see what he has never seen before, to moving him into a new order of perception and experience—imaginative, presumably, as well as more directly "vital." The rhetorical-objectivist tradition here includes both a technical interest and a concern for the reader's response.[35]

Plato had felt the danger of art because of its power over man's emotions. Aristotle had seen the positive purgative potential of this power. The Romantic poets felt that art refined the emotions. M. H. Abrams claimed that a "pragmatic" art theory which grew out of the rhetorical tradition (aided by explicit Horatian theories of art as teaching through pleasure) has been the dominant theory since the eighteenth century. This evolution through the years may have pre-

35 See Wayne C. Booth, "*The Rhetoric of Fiction* and the Poetics of Fictions," *Novel* 1 (Winter 1968), 113: "Though an effect on audiences was implied by its form, the critic pursued the internal nature of the poem by analyzing its parts in relation to the whole work."

pared the way for the increase today in what has here been named process mimesis; the artist developed from the straightforward mimetic poet, assigned the minimal rôle of holding a mirror up to nature, through to the pragmatic poet who is ultimately measured by his ability to come to terms with his reader.[36] This pragmatic-rhetorical point of view could combine the recognition of the independent ontological status of the novelistic world with a regard for the life-art link— through the reader—that mimesis demands (even mimesis of process).

From the rhetoric of Sterne to that of John Fowles, self-conscious novels have asserted their fictiveness while refusing to allow the reader the particular kind of distance that comes of passivity or lack of involvement. In his study, *Balzac to Beckett* (New York: Oxford University Press, 1970), Leo Bersani has shown the validity of regarding the changing relationship between the reader and the novelistic language as the point of reference for theories of realism. If the reader's relation to the novel is felt to be purely in terms of his own experience, that is, if language is thought to be only referential to empirical reality, then it is a case of a Balzacian situation in which the fictional world seems to reflect confidently some external reality (in other words, product mimesis). With Flaubert's realism, the reader's relation is primarily to language itself and this language, the reader is made to feel, can never correspond to reality. This is, in fact, according to Bersani, Emma Bovary's tragedy and what makes that novel an interrogation of the value of art. With more modern metafiction, the reader has yet another role. He is left to make his own meaning, to fill the void, to activate the work. He is assaulted, frustrated in his normal novelistic expectations. The author seems to want to change the nature of literature by altering the nature of the reader's participation in it.

As creator, the writer has always had only limited control over the particular responses of his reader. Phenomenological awareness has perhaps increased authorial consciousness of the fact that the work of art has no existence in and of itself; only through the imagination and understanding of the reader is it made to live. While acknowledging the reality of the reader's power, often overtly, the writer must also combat the implicit refusal of many critical theories—from phenomenological to formalist—to consider that aesthetic connection with the reader's own experience that is implied in any act of making fictions and in any creative and rhetorical use of language. In narcissistic fiction, the problems and joys in the act of shaping language and experience are part of the content. The reader can somehow participate in the novelistic heterocosm and still share in the personal struggle of its creation. There is always a certain tension between involvement and self-awareness in the act of reading, and self-conscious fiction only dramatizes this tension within the work itself.

36 *The Mirror and the Lamp* (1953; reprinted, New York: W. W. Norton, 1958), p. 26.

The metafictionist, by this mirroring of process, may intend to upset his reader, as did Gide in the past. Reading is not always the pleasant, controlled, harmonious experience that the Classical and Romantic traditions both suggest. It can be disrupting, challenging, not to say threatening. Narrators such as that of John Barth's "Life-Story" (in *Lost in the Funhouse*) are on the attack: "The reader! You, dogged, uninsultable, print-oriented bastard, it's you I'm addressing, who else, from inside this monstrous fiction. You've read me this far, then? Even this far? . . . Can nothing surfeit, saturate you, turn you off?" *Novelists* know of their relationship to their readers. Likewise the idea of the reader as participant — as a perhaps disturbed, but unavoidably active, reagent or crypto-creator — is not particularly a novelty to *critical* theory. In 1921, Percy Lubbock wrote that the reader was a kind of novelist, "the maker of a book which may or may not please his taste when it is finished, but of a book for which he must take his own share of the responsibility."[37] The reader has always been a collaborator, an accomplice. Metafiction explicitly adds the dimension of reading as a process parallel to writing as an imaginative creative act. The result is that the reader's degree of participation appears to increase. He must do his share of the work, be it bridging Iserian gaps of "indeterminacy" or coping with what Kermode calls "hermeneutic confusion and problematic closure."[38]

Umberto Eco has dubbed this kind of art a form of "opera aperta" and offers as a critical framework, "serial" rather than structuralist thought. The latter, of course, has obvious limitations for the study of narcissistic texts since it refuses — in theory — to deal with the subject and with elements outside the closed structure it investigates.[39] It also concentrates on the shared code-decoded message relationship while, in "serial" thought, the message itself self-consciously puts the code into question. Here each message establishes its own code; each work appears to be its own linguistic foundation, its own poetics. Each work is therefore the key to its own reading.[40] Where structuralism aims at discovering, by the use of the linguistic model, serial thought aims at

37 *The Craft of Fiction* (1921; reprinted, New York: Viking, Compass, 1957), p. 17. See also Lowry Nelson, Jr., "The Fictive Reader and Literary Self-Reflexiveness," in Peter Demetz, Thomas Greene and Lowry Nelson, Jr. (eds.), *The Disciplines of Criticism* (New Haven: Yale University Press, 1968), pp. 173-91.

38 Iser's theory is best seen in the above-mentioned, "Indeterminacy and the Reader's Response in Prose Fiction," pp. 42ff.; Kermode's is expounded in "Novels: Recognition and Deception," p. 117.

39 Gérard Genette has suggested that structuralism could be used as a complement to a hermeneutic approach which *would* consider the intersubjective interiorizing contact of reader and text which structuralism must ignore. See "Structuralisme et critique littéraire" in *Figures* 1 (Paris: Seuil, 1966), p. 161.

40 See Eco's *La Struttura assente: introduzione alla ricerca semiologica* (Milano: Bompiani, 1968), p. 306. See also his *Opera aperta: forma e indeterminazione nelle poetiche contemporanee*, 2nd ed. (Milano: Bompiani, 1967).

producing. Series, then, are self-doubting structures which cannot but see themselves as historical. The value of such a theoretical framework for self-conscious fiction is evident, although it offers little actual concrete aid to the critic, short of directing him back to his own reading of the text. Then again, fiction which establishes, indeed constitutes, its own frame of critical reference can likely not be approached in any other manner. The critic, freed from the need for any external props for his analysis, need only revel in the text and in his own liberation. He is now reader, writer, and critic.

The reader of narcissistic fiction is indeed left with more than his usual share of freedom to create order, to build unities and relationships between parts. The author lets the reader complete the "open" work but he still, obviously, retains some control. It is "open" but in a field of relations (created by the novelist) which imply some sort of inner coherence. The reader never really creates literary meaning freely; there are codes and rules and conventions that underlie its production. Selection and isolation procedures are inevitably restricting, but they are also necessary. The paradigmatic nature of metafiction—its imaginative and linguistic analogues of process with the reader's experience—adds another dimension, that of freedom, to this situation. Like the writer, the reader can evade the mundane and the empirical; he can enter a world of his own making, a world constructed through language. In *Imaginary Qualities of Actual Things*, Sorrentino's narrator refuses to give the reader traditional character details (hair colour, etc.), preferring to root his meaning in language, not in fake real people. If the reader needs (as he well might) more concrete details to form his imaginative impression of the characters, he is free, according to the narrator, "to write the book that I have no interest in writing."

The book is a material object; it can be opened and closed at will. It can be read in bits, violating its temporality; it can be *re*read in part or whole, violating its linearity. It moves with the reader and is still when he abandons it. This material freedom has its analogue in the imaginative realm. The paradoxically "induced" liberation as taught by Fowles's heroine and surrogate in *The French Lieutenant's Woman*, is felt by the reader, as by the author. The critic too is freed from the restrictions of any single methodology by the fact, emphasized throughout this study, that metafiction embodies within itself its own critical frame of reference as part of its theme and often its form. Freudian, rhetorical, and phenomenological theories are suggestive, but in no way definitive in their contributions to the understanding of narcissistic narrative. Self-interpreting texts imply the amalgamation of the functions of reader, writer, and critic in the single and demanding experience of reading.

Conclusion and Speculations

Theory is a sign of ignorance. It becomes important when we are no longer sure what we are doing. We are passing through a time when all the "paradigms" of fiction are called into question and in consequence we begin to see the development of a poetics of fiction. Preferably the theory should be implicit in the novel, the poetics part of the poem.

Ronald Sukenick

At the end of his exhaustive examination of the *mise en abyme*, one of the major techniques of literary narcissism, Lucien Dällenbach is forced to concede that the "textes" of some contemporary French writers constitute a distinct rupture with what he calls "la pensée représentative," or what has been referred to here as (process and product) mimesis.[1] But to reason from this rupture to an assertion that "the novel is dead" would be faulty logic. While such a statement is conveniently dismissive, it is inaccurate. That the novel has changed is undeniable, but then again, it never was static: no art form ever is. The self-reflective metafiction of today is not the product of a break or an eclipse in any novelistic tradition. It is rather a continuation of an already existing narcissistic trend in the novel as it began parodically in *Don Quijote* and was handed on, through eighteenth-century critical self-awareness to nineteenth-century self-mirroring. Within Romanticism lie the seeds of the challenge to the almost contemporaneous concept of novelistic "realism." Early in this century Virginia Woolf, Proust, Unamuno, and others began reminding their readers that, as Aristotle too had suggested, mimesis includes diegesis.

1 *Le Recit spéculaire* (Paris: Seuil, 1977), pp.205-206: "Or, éclairés par la logique propre de leur travail et l'avancée théorique qui s'est opérée partout entre 1960 et 1970, certains nouveaux romanciers ont pris conscience qu'ils ne quitteraient pas le terrain du réalisme tant qu'ils ne souscriraient pas à une pratique de l'*écriture* conçue comme expérience radicale du langage. Cette conviction portait à conséquence: faire sienne la notion d'*écriture* ainsi que celles, tout aussi fondamentales, de *texte* et de *production*, n'était-ce pas congédier, du même coup, l'ancienne mise en abyme fictionnelle?"

Although the roots of modern metafiction are obviously in such a realization, the primary distinction between the self-consciousness of the novels of Gide or of Huxley, and the modern auto-awareness of the novels of Fowles or of Ricardou, lies in the newly expanded scope of the "vital" mimetic contact between "art" and "life." In the earlier texts, the main interest is in the *writing* process and its product. The focus today broadens to include a parallel process of equal importance to the "concretization" of the text—that of reading. This equating of the two acts has been a recurring point in the analyses of metafiction in this study. This is so because it is this fact that sets modern metafiction apart from previous novelistic self-consciousness. In overtly or covertly baring its fictional and linguistic systems, narcissistic narrative transforms the authorial process of shaping, of making, into part of the pleasure and challenge of reading as a co-operative, interpretative experience.

That this textual self-awareness can lead to another *form* of literature has not been denied. Just as metafiction grew out of a tradition, it continues to develop and in its most extreme forms—that is, in what has here been called the covert linguistic mode—the challenge to the novel's identity as a representational genre is evident. This diachronic context can perhaps most succinctly be recalled and summarized in a visual manner:

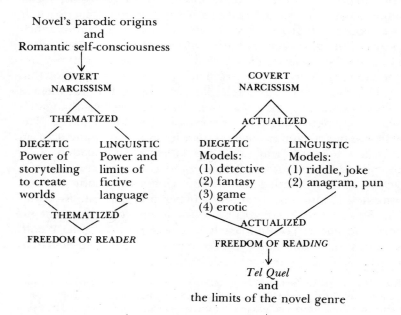

The synchronic pattern here implied, while less symbolically decorative than Ricardou's auto-representational cross, is not intended as restrictive or normative in any way. Rather it is an attempt to make

room for as wide a range as possible of distinctive types of narrative self-consciousness. There is obviously still considerable room to move, even within the confines of a mimetic genre.

What this pattern does not reveal clearly, of course, except by implication, is the second major focus of this study. While its first intention was to investigate the modes, forms, and techniques of narrative narcissism—a task as yet not undertaken by critics of metafiction—its other aim was to study the implications of these formal observations both for the theory of the novel as a representational genre and also for the theory of the interpretative and creative functions of the act of reading. This investigation was conducted by means of metafictional texts themselves, particularly those overt forms which thematized these very theoretical issues. The problems raised by these works were then brought to bear on existing theories (both of the novel and of reading), not to provide a survey of modern criticism, but to investigate the changes in *theory* which the *practice* of fiction itself suggests, if not demands. There can be no "theory" of metafiction, only "implications" for theory; each self-informing work internalizes its own critical context. To ignore that is to falsify the text itself.

Since this two-directional investigation has been guided by continual reference to these central points about the inner structures and theoretical repercussions of auto-referential texts, an alternative to a concluding summary of these arguments seems both possible and indeed desirable. Hugh Kenner recounts that Ezra Pound's advice to writers was always to finish their books by "opening out" and not by "closing in." One way of heeding this counsel is suggested by John Fowles's reminder that the novel is the most free and freeing literary form. In Chapter Four, *The French Lieutenant's Woman* was seen as allegorically presenting the theme of liberation through fiction-making. This new involvement of the reader in a freedom-inducing act offers another potentially ideological implication of the paradox of intramurally and extramurally directed metafiction. If self-reflecting texts can actually lure the reader into participating in the creation of a novelistic universe, perhaps he can also be seduced into action—even direct political action. Two metafictional novels written in the mid-1960s by two Montreal writers imply that there might indeed be such a possibility; the narcissistic novel as incitement to revolutionary activity would be the ultimate defence of self-conscious fiction against claims of self-preening introversion.

One of the former leaders of the Québec Rassemblement pour l'Indépendance Nationale, Hubert Aquin, wrote his first novel, *Prochain Épisode* (Montréal: Le Cercle du livre de France, 1965), while under arrest for carrying arms. The equally subversive narrator of that first work, in a similar situation, also writes a novel and seems to sense by the end of it that the truly revolutionary act for him is that of

writing—writing the work the reader has just finished. Nevertheless, the title of the novel negates this and points explicitly to the *next* episode, the episode of guns, the real revolution to come after the writing and reading of the novel is over. In Aquin's second novel, *Trou de mémoire* (Montréal: Le Cercle du livre de France, 1968), however, the major writer and revolutionary figure, Pierre X. Magnant, appears willing to accept the fact that the act of writing itself is a truly revolutionary one. For the author, this insight involves no crude *engagement* on the level of political content; it is, in fact, through metafictional *form* that Aquin hopes to liberate his country and his literature. In an article the year after *Trou de mémoire* was written, he urged the modern writer to abandon any expressivity, any sig-nification—that is, any message—or run the risk of finding himself "domestiqué et fonctionnalisé par la société."[2] Narrative conventions are changing, argued Aquin, and the essential artifice of the genre must now be acknowledged, made manifest, and then gloried in—by both author and reader.

In 1974 he further theorized upon this latter conjunction: "la littérature existe pleinement non pas quand l'oeuvre est écrite, mais quand un lecteur remonte le cours des phrases et des mots pour devenir, par ce moyen, cocréateur de l'oeuvre."[3] Yet this same insight, *politicized,* was used earlier, both thematically and structurally, in *Trou de mémoire.* Both overtly and covertly, the author of that novel aims at transforming the way his reader reads and thinks—as the first step to transforming the political reality he lives in. The act of reading, as well as that of writing, is part of the very action of the plot, as the editor reads and comments upon the manuscript of the revolutionary, Pierre X. Magnant, and as the mysterious RR reads and comments upon the texts of both Magnant and the editor.

Just as Aquin employs the structures of the journal and the episto-lary novel—both forms which again make self-conscious the acts of writing and reading—so does another Canadian novelist, writing at almost the same time, about almost the same things. Leonard Cohen's novel, *Beautiful Losers* (Toronto: McClelland & Stewart, 1966), also consists in part of a journal (of sorts) of a nameless narrator, and of a letter read by this same character, and written by a French-Canadian revolutionary.

The motives for this self-conscious writing, in both novels, seem paradoxical. On the one hand Cohen's nameless narrator and Aquin's murderer-revolutionary claim to write to come to terms with—that is, almost to forget—a dead woman, a lover. Magnant writes: "Je me vois écrire ce que j'écris, conscient à l'extrême de recouvrir le corps de Joan

2 "Littérature et aliénation" (1968), in *Blocs erratiques: textes (1948–1977)* (Montréal: Edition Quinze, 1977), p. 129.
3 "'La Disparition élocutoire du poète' (Mallarmé)," in *Blocs erratiques*, p. 266.

d'une grande pièce de toile damassée d'hyperboles et de syncopes: j'improvise un véritable tissu d'art, mot à mot, afin d'en vêtir celle qui est nue, mais morte."[4] In an attempt to *cover* over Joan's death with words, Pierre X. Magnant, like the narrator of Book One of Cohen's novel, manages to *un*cover details for the reader, to reveal the "facts" of the past. This second direction, this revelatory unveiling for the reader (the reader both as a character in the novel and as an external agent) is explicitly the motive for writing for both the editor in Aquin's novel and for F., the revolutionary-magician-madman of *Beautiful Losers*.

There seems to be yet another reason for writing, however. When the third-person narrator of the epilogue of Cohen's novel calls out: "Welcome to you who read me today," he is inviting the reader into the work, inviting him to participate, rather than to sit back and watch — the recent fate of those initially active in the now dissipated Revolution of the "second chancers." In *Trou de mémoire*, the reader finally realizes that Pierre X. Magnant's pseudo-suicide has allowed him to return incognito to work for the revolution — by being the editor of his own manuscript. Is the reader to believe RR when she then claims that the "editor" has also committed suicide, by a strange coincidence, using the same method Magnant was supposed to have employed? Or has the revolutionary been secretly resurrected once again? After all, Aquin did write a note on January 19, 1967, to the effect that "P.X. Magnant est l'auteur et l'éditeur de ce *Trou de mémoire*."[5] Note that he does not write that Magnant is the author and editor of Magnant's manuscript, but of the published novel, *Trou de mémoire*.

In both of these novels the reader is left literally to "make sense" of the willed ambiguities, the paradoxes, even contradictions, of the text. The details cannot be ordered by using traditional novelistic assumptions. To use Cohen's metaphor, the reader must learn to exercise "a kind of balance in the chaos," for "there is something arrogant and warlike in the notion of a man setting the universe in order."[6] Both novelists work to frustrate the reader's attempts to systematize, his efforts to order the texts by conventional literary means. For instance, there are no single, individual, psychologically motivated characters in either novel. By the end of *Beautiful Losers*, a seventeenth-century Iroquois virgin, Catherine Tekakwitha, has merged with Edith, a twentieth-century Indian sexual virtuoso. Both come together in a central Isis figure whose final manifestation is a semi-naked, moccasin-wearing blonde who is — or rather who drives — the vehicle that takes the hero to his destiny. This hero, himself an amalgam of the

4 *Trou de mémoire* (Montréal: Le Cercle du livre de France, 1968), p. 55. All subsequent page references will be in parentheses in the text.
5 Published in "Un Drôle de souvenir . . . ," in *Point de fuite* (Montréal: Le Cercle du livre de France, 1971), p. 95.
6 *Beautiful Losers* (Toronto: McClelland and Stewart, 1966), p. 95. Subsequent page references will be in parentheses in the text.

nameless narrator, his friend, F., and Catherine's aged uncle, proceeds to metamorphose into a Ray Charles movie. However, the reader of Aquin's novel has no easier task, as P. X. Magnant, revolutionary pharmacist, and the editor of his manuscript are revealed to be one and the same person. The Black African revolutionary and pharmacist, Olympe Ghezzo-Quénum, then turns out to be his double. The Ruskin sisters, Joan and Rachel, are more than just sisters in the novel. In one version of RR's tale, they are lesbian lovers; in another, they too are doubles, as Rachel continues her dead sister's destiny beyond the last pages of the novel, as Anne-Lise Jamieson.

Should the reader try to cling to conventional notions of narrative time, there too he will be frustrated. The "long letter from F." which forms the second part of *Beautiful Losers* logically precedes the first part by several years, for it was to be given to the narrator five years after F.'s death. But just as Book One ends with the narrator fleeing to the treehouse F. left him in his will, so Book Two also ends with F.'s escape from the asylum-prison to that same treehouse outside Montreal. When, then, does the third part of the novel take place? It opens with a man in a treehouse. Who is he? He has burnt fingers, like the narrator, but he also has a missing thumb, like F. He is identified both with a local pervert and with a terrorist leader who escaped *"yesterday."* It is not only characters that merge, then, but also time sequences. This is also true in Aquin's novel, but the use of time is even more complex. The narrative clock and calendar work *backwards,* against even all plot logic, from Olympe's letter dated September 28, 1966 to his journal which begins May 14, 1966. This symbolic reversal serves to fill in the *trou de mémoire,* the traumatic rape that RR must face and which she only faces, she tells us, by reading the texts the reader too has read. However, the editor also claims that the events narrated by the otherwise very precise Olympe actually took place, not in 1966 as Olympe had obsessively written, but in 1967. And in a sense, the reader realizes, they did, since Aquin wrote them in 1967.

The frustrated and bewildered reader is not even allowed a linear plot for comfort. The hermeneutic difficulties multiply when he realizes that both novels operate on two distinct but simultaneous levels of discourse. On the one hand there is a private story—in both cases, a story of love, death, and sexual triangles, the familiar narrative staples. But on the other hand, both novels present a parallel public or political level. While seeking his own identity, Cohen's narrator stumbles across what he calls "the horrible truth about Canada." The cast of symbolic orphans in this novel includes one nameless English-Canadian historian, his Indian wife, Edith (and her historical surrogate, Catherine Tekakwitha), and their bisexual lover, F., the Québécois revolutionary Member of Parliament who, after his parliamentary disgrace, is incarcerated in an asylum for the criminally insane. He claims that this is an

English plot to silence him. This trio plays out the history and destiny of Canada, of her successive conquests (the deaths of the Indian, Edith, and the French, F.), and perhaps of her future fate (turning into an American movie). In Aquin's novel, the Québécois revolutionary strangles his stereotypical English-Canadian lover, who claims she wants to become a French-Canadian, a feat she actually does perform in death; Magnant, haunted by her corpse, writes: "Notre pays est un cadavre encombrant" (p.48). Her murder is both an attempt to destroy a dominating force and a sign of the impotence of the dominated.

The reader, it would seem, might have a better chance at "making sense" of these two levels of discourse if he were to adopt certain metaphoric unities, such as that provided in both novels by the theme of the sexualization of politics. Both Cohen and Aquin overtly present Québec political rally scenes and both do so in similar erotic terms. *In the crowd* at one rally, Cohen's narrator is literally and symbolically caressed and seduced, by an unknown, unseen female; similarly, the once promiscuous, and later sexually impotent Pierre X. Magnant, as revolutionary *speaker,* regards his audience as victims waiting to be raped: "Mon comportement sexuel est l'image d'un comportement national frappé d'impuissance: plus ça va, plus je sens bien que je veux violer" (p. 112). It is important that Aquin too claimed that he wanted to seduce, embrace, even rape his reader in *Trou de mémoire.*[7]

In both novels as well, there is a narrative rape that is part of the past, part of history, both public and private. As Cohen's Indian girl, Edith, is raped with pens, pipes, twigs, and fingers by the impotent Frenchmen in her village (pp. 58-61), so Pierre X. Magnant goes back in time to reverse the traumatic rape that is the symbol of the conquest of French Canada, by murdering his English lover, Joan, and raping her sister. The futility of this act of impotence for himself is counteracted by that hope for the future—Rachel's child of rape, "qui s'appellera Magnant . . . sans avoir peur de son nom" (p.204).

What Cohen sees as a Canadian historical chain of victimizers turned victims (the Indians defeated by the French who in turn are defeated by the English who are likely to be defeated by the Americans), Aquin perceives in terms of the colonizers and the colonized. Both the narrator of *Beautiful Losers* and Pierre X. Magnant claim to be specialists in the study of failure. Cohen's own contribution to the investigation of the psychology of the victim leads him to posit an ultimate "beautiful loser," Ray Charles, whose sung words, "Somebody said lift that bale," significantly form the novel's epigraph, but whose

7 "Aquin par Aquin," in *Le Québec littéraire* no. 2 (1976), 134: "j'admets qu'il y a une 'danse de séduction' [avec le lecteur] . . . qu'il y a des procédés de mystification, j'admets que j'essaie d'étreindre le lecteur littéralement dans *Trou de mémoire,* ou de le violer même, à la limite, et de l'agresser pour ensuite le relâcher et le reprendre indéfiniment. Malgré tout, c'est une opération dirigée vers le lecteur étant donné que c'est lui qui crée le livre."

final movie image quells the revolution. He is both a victim (a Black, a blind entertainer) and a symbol of American victimization of Canadian culture. Aquin too uses a Black—Olympe—but an African Black, and he too uses him as a symbol, but this time of a colonized mentality. Aquin's own fascination with the collective psychology of dominated peoples is seen in his interest in the theories of Frantz Fanon, Albert Memmi, and especially Jacques Berque.[8] There is frequent mention made in the novel to "les Patriotes," whose defeat in the 1837 Rebellion in Canada Aquin sees as having "l'air d'un échec longuement prémédité, d'un chef-d'oeuvre de noirceur et d'inconscience."[9] That Magnant too sees himself as a Patriot is significant. That Olympe, Black revolutionary, identifies with Magnant is significant as well.

The African nations mentioned in the novel are almost all former parts of *French* West Africa. The issue Aquin raises here places the Canadian historical fact of the defeat and colonization of the French into an international context in which the French themselves were once colonizers. Olympe's schizoid alienated responses to both Europe and to his own culture and race—his pride and his scorn—echo Magnant's hatred and love for the English Joan. Olympe's flight from Africa to Europe echoes Magnant's earlier one from Montreal to London, where he finds the psychology of success in Sherlock Holmes and the perfect crime. But Montreal is the final scene of the death of both men, and also of the future birth of the child of Magnant's all too easy rape of Olympe's lover, Rachel. Aquin is careful, despite this similarity of fate, to point to the essential difference of race between his two characters. Like Cohen's Ray Charles, Olympe is doubly colonized—by an enslaving nation and by the white race.

This same politicization of the interpretative act works on the reader not only in this thematic and structural way, forcing him to understand and extend certain key narrative metaphors, but also in forcing his awareness, on a formal, literal level, of the artifice, the artifacts that self-consciously constitute both of these novels. The *trompe-l'oeil* of Holbein's painting of the "Two Ambassadors" is given an allegorical reading by the editor within Aquin's novel: the two ambassadors are Joan and Magnant, linked only by this written fabric of words, like the oriental cloth the two men touch in the painting. The anamorphosis of the skull is, to his thinking, Joan's murder. The editor goes so far as to claim: "Je ne crains pas d'affirmer que Pierre X. Magnant s'est inspiré de la composition de Holbein, non seulement dans son style, mais aussi dans la forme même du récit" (p.145). The reader, however, might see another possible interpretation of the painting, one suggested by this last notion. The Holbein work could be seen as a *mise en abyme*, a

8 See Patricia Smart, *Hubert Aquin: agent double* (Montréal: Les Presses de l'Université de Montréal, 1973), pp. 72ff.

9 "L'Art de la défaite" (1965), *Blocs erratiques*, p. 118.

mirroring microcosm, of the politics as well as the aesthetics of the novel. The two *French* ambassadors are painted in *England;* two colonizing nations meet, in the august presence of European art (the lute in the painting), religion (the hymnbook), and science (the globe, sundial, and quadrant). Some of these same objects of culture and power later fascinate the colonized African, Olympe, on a trip to a European museum. Given this perspective, the projected anamorphosis in the centre might represent the traumatic conquest, the act of colonization whose memory is erased by the cultural amnesia, the *trou de mémoire*. It too, like the skull, can only be perceived from a certain angle and from a certain distance, and it is Aquin's revolutionary aim to manoeuvre the reader into that position. For Cohen, the political/aesthetic *mise en abyme* is the Ray Charles movie, escaped from the System Theatre and projected this time against the sky. But in the text, the revolution is extinguished by the film. Everyone stops and sits back to watch: "Thank God it's only a movie" (p.242). Only the reader who does *not* turn passive can "make meaning" out of this final image.

Both Aquin and Cohen seem to want to force their texts, and by extension their readers, out of what Aquin calls the coherence of domination: "Faire la révolution, c'est sortir du dialogue dominé-dominateur."[10] His subsequent description of the revolutionary's act is one which aptly fits both novels here: "[il] s'engage inconsidérément dans un monologue interrompu à chaque parole, nourri d'autant d'hésitations qu'il comporte de distance avec la raison dominante." At the end of *Beautiful Losers*, Cohen pulls his reader into his text and he enters or else risks missing him "forever" in his "trip to the end" (p. 243). Perhaps he must become a beautiful loser, balancing the chaos of meaning. Aquin asks him to go a step further, to become a real co-creator, as real as the editor and RR who literally co-create Magnant's text. In both novels the reader's position is a paradoxical one. On the one hand, as in the viewing of the Holbein painting, a certain distance is required of him. He must recognize and acknowledge the artifice, the self-conscious auto-referentiality of both texts. On the other hand, this very artificiality is revelled in, actually made sacred, "sacralisé." The equation of reading and writing, the "échange entre le lecteur et l'écrivain"[11] that Aquin sees as the essence of the text, is what allows for a total breaking out of the limits of introverted self-informing narcissism in both novels. As Magnant writes: "Par l'action matricielle de la parole, l'action passe à l'action" (p.57).

To read is to act; to act is both to interpret and to create anew—to be revolutionary, perhaps in political as well as in literary terms. There is much freedom-inducing potential in metafiction generally, not when seen as a degenerate version of a moribund genre, but when recog-

10 "Profession: Ecrivain" (1963), *Point de fuite*, p. 53.
11 "La Mort de l'écrivain maudit" (1969), *Blocs erratiques*, p. 147.

nized as a significant "vital" mimetic form of literature. In Aquin's words: "La parole est une forme de vie et, par ce biais magnifique, un mode d'action. Chose certaine, il n'y a pas plus de vanité à écrire qu'à agir, autant que ce qui relève de l'action émane d'un ordre créé par la pensée."[12] To "Ovidian" critics, Narcissus may die by the mirroring pool; but the fact remains that, in another sense, he also lives on, still self-regarding, *received* into the next world with open arms.

12 "Comprendre dangereusement" (1962), *Blocs erratiques*, p. 46.

Index of Subjects and Names

ABRAMS, M. H.: 41, 149-50

ACTUALIZATION: 6, 23, 30-35, 45, 71-86, 101, 118-37, 154

ALLEGORY: 7, 8, 21, 23, 28, 29, 53, 56, 58, 70, 83, 84, 88, 106, 142, 143

ALTER, ROBERT: 3, 4-5, 20

AMBLER, ERIC; *A Coffin for Dimitrios*: 72

ANAGRAM: 34, 101, 119-20, 121-24

ANTI-REPRESENTATION: 14, 31, 34-35, 124, 128, 129, 136-37

APPEL, ALFRED JR.: 49, 50, 76n, 101n

AQUIN, HUBERT: 155-62; *Prochain Episode*: 155-56; *Trou de mémoire*: 56, 156-62

ARISTOTLE: 8, 40-41, 42, 43, 44, 63, 90, 128, 149, 153

ARNOLD, MATTHEW: 59, 70

AUERBACH, ERICH: 5, 9, 37n, 44

AUSTEN, JANE: 59, 68; *Emma*: 142

AUTO-REFERENTIALITY: see NARCIS-SISM; REFERENT

AUTO-REPRESENTATION: 6, 14, 21-23, 26-27, 28, 31, 34, 35, 39, 46, 122, 124, 128, 129, 136

BALESTRINI, NINO: 134; *Tristano*: 135

BALZAC, HONORÉ DE: 9, 44, 81, 91, 127, 150

BARILLI, RENATO: 84n, 121-22, 130n, 133

BARTH, JOHN: 2, 3, 18, 19, 20, 21, 35, 37, 48, 50, 52-53, 56, 71, 121, 143, 144; *Chimera*: 22, 33, 47, 85; *The End of the Road*: 53, 89-90, 102; *The Floating Opera*: 28; *Giles Goat-Boy*: 24, 52; *Lost in the Funhouse*: 48, 52-53, 55, 56, 99-101, 121, 131, 143, 151; *The Sot-Weed Factor*: 24

BARTHELME, DONALD: 21, 29n, 104, 141n; *Snow White*: 118, 143

BARTHES, ROLAND: 9, 15, 23, 29, 33, 42, 46, 59, 77n, 94, 96, 132, 139n, 141n

BAUMGARTEN, MURRAY: 27n, 37n

BECKETT, SAMUEL: 14, 33, 91, 130

BEEBE, MAURICE: 18n

BELLEMIN-NOËL, JEAN: 81

BENVENISTE, EMILE: 126n

BERSANI, LEO: 38n, 150

BERTO, GIUSEPPE; *Il male oscuro*: 51-52

BIASIN, GIAN-PAOLO: 79n

BIERCE, AMBROSE; "The Damned Thing": 92

BILDUNGSROMAN (ENTWICKLUNGSRO-MAN): 11, 60

BLANCHOT, MAURICE: 10, 18, 93, 94, 95, 97, 98

BOOTH, WAYNE C.: 149

BORGES, JORGE LUIS: 18, 19, 20, 25, 32, 37, 41, 47, 50n, 54, 72, 76, 78, 88,

98, 100, 142-43; *Labyrinths*: 52, 53, 55, 74, 99; *Seis Problemas Para Don Isidro Parodi*: 74; *A Universal History of Infamy*: 20n
BRECHT, BERTOLT: 49, 59
BRUNER, JEROME S.: 43n
BUTOR, MICHEL: 81, 91n; *L'Emploi du temps*: 52

CALVINO, ITALO; *Città invisibili*: 78, 83; *Cosmicomiche*: 79; *Ti con zero*: 53, 79-80
CARPENTIER, ALEJO; *El Camino de Santiago*: 34; *Guerra del Tiempo*: 80-81
CARY, JOYCE: 43
CASEY, JOHN: 43n, 97n
CAUTE, DAVID: 17, 138, 141
CERVANTES, MIGUEL DE: 12, 30, 38, 39, 47, 52, 59, 141, 143; *Don Quijote*: 3, 4, 5, 8, 9, 18, 23, 24, 37, 40, 94, 99, 113, 134, 135, 142, 153
CHESS (GAME MODEL): 33, 83, 128
CHESTERTON, G. K.: 53, 73, 76
CHINESE-BOX STRUCTURE: 57-58, 64, 101, 105
CHRISTIE, AGATHA: 73; *And Then There Were None*: 72; *Nemesis*: 32; *The Pale Horse*: 31
CIXOUS, HÉLÈNE: 126n; *Tombe*: 33
COHEN, LEONARD: 37, 156-61; *Beautiful Losers*: 33, 156-61
CONAN DOYLE, SIR ARTHUR: 31, 73, 76, 83
CONCRETIZATION: 6, 34, 39, 76, 127, 143, 147, 154
CONNOTATION: see DENOTATION/CONNOTATION
CONRAD, JOSEPH: 59
COOVER, ROBERT: 21, 37; *Pricksongs and Descants*: 28, 38, 85; *The Universal Baseball Association, J. Henry Waugh, Prop.*: 33, 83-84
CORTAZAR, JULIO: 37; *Rayuela*: 30, 139
COVERT: see DIEGETIC and LINGUISTIC NARCISSISM
CREWS, FREDERICK: 145-46
CULLER, JONATHAN: 25, 30n, 95n

DÄLLENBACH, LUCIEN: 4, 21, 55-56, 153
DEFOE, DANIEL: 9, 38, 47, 60, 78
DENOTATION/CONNOTATION: 94
DERRIDA, JACQUES: 6, 44, 125, 125n

DETECTIVE PLOT: 31-32, 71-76, 83, 86, 91
DIDEROT, DENIS: 9, 18, 27, 39, 45, 101; *Jacques le Fataliste*: 9, 44
DIEGESIS: 5, 40-41, 43, 44, 47, 48, 51, 128, 137, 139
DIEGETIC NARCISSISM; DEFINITION: 5, 7, 22-23, 28, 41, 71, 154; OVERT FORM: 7, 23, 28-29, 48-56, 57-70, 122; COVERT FORM: 7, 23, 30-34, 71-86
DOLEŽEL, LUBOMÍR: 97n
DUFRENNE, MIKEL: 146, 147-48
DURRELL, LAWRENCE; *The Alexandria Quartet*: 12

ECO, UMBERTO: 15n, 79, 125n, 130, 135, 151
ÉCRITURE: 74, 125-29, 153n
ELIOT, T. S.: 25, 44, 134
ÉNONCÉ/ÉNONCIATION: 56, 139
ENTWICKLUNGSROMAN: see *BILDUNGSROMAN*
EROTIC (MODEL): 33, 71, 85-86
EXISTENTIALISM: 19-20, 21, 30, 57, 61-62, 70, 89, 116

FABULATORS: 19, 20
FANTASY: 32, 47, 64, 71, 76-82, 86, 92, 97, 98, 115, 116
FEDERMAN, RAYMOND: xi, 143, 144; *Double or Nothing*: 53
FIELDING, HENRY: 38, 135, 142; *Tom Jones*: 27, 44
FILIPPINI, ENRICO: 135
FISH, STANLEY: 37n, 139n, 145
FLAUBERT, GUSTAVE: 15, 45, 59, 60, 91, 150; *Madame Bovary*: 38, 85, 94, 99, 132, 142, 150
FORD, FORD MADOX: 59; *The Good Soldier*: 142
FOUCAULT, MICHEL: 12, 13, 19, 35n, 38n, 126
FOWLES, JOHN: 18, 19, 37, 41, 57-70, 105, 150, 154; *The Aristos*: 61; *The Collector*: 33, 60; *The Ebony Tower*: 31, 60; *The French Lieutenant's Woman*: 24, 28, 32, 50, 57-70, 76, 85, 89, 97, 99, 114, 152, 155; *The Magus*: 60, 64
FREGE, GOTTLOB: 42n
FREUD, SIGMUND: 1, 8, 48n, 51, 125, 127, 145-46, 152
FRYE, NORTHROP: 8, 81n, 82, 141

GADDA, CARLO EMILIO: 131
GAME (MODEL): 32-33, 71, 82-85, 86, 123
GARCÍA MÁRQUEZ, GABRIEL; *Cien Años de Soledad*: 32, 92
GARDNER, JOHN: 20
GASS, WILLIAM: 21, 117n, 140; *Willie Masters' Lonesome Wife*: 33, 85-86
GENERATIVE WORD PLAY: see WORD PLAY: ACTUALIZED
GENETTE, GÉRARD: 40n, 46, 138, 151n
GENEVA SCHOOL: see PHENOMENOLOGY
GIDE, ANDRÉ: 5, 9, 15, 23, 25, 26, 45, 55, 58, 60, 151, 154; *Les Faux-monnayeurs*: 18, 26, 27; *Le Journal des faux-monnayeurs*: 26; *La Symphonie pastorale*: 27
GRAFF, GERALD: 3
GREGOR, IAN: 142n, 145
GRUPPO 63: 37, 110, 130-36
GUGLIELMI, ANGELO: 131-32, 140n
GUILLÉN, CLAUDIO: 26n, 36, 39, 45n, 47, 82, 139n

HARDY, BARBARA: 47n, 48
HARDY, THOMAS: 59, 66, 142
HASSAN, IHAB: 3
HAWKES, JOHN: 57; *Lunar Landscapes*: 29
HERMENEUTIC GAPS: 72, 151
HERMENEUTICS: see PHENOMENOLOGY
HETEROCOSM: 6, 39, 42, 58, 64, 87-103, 111, 119, 138, 140, 150
HOLLAND, NORMAN: 145
HOMER: 32, 40, 80
HUGO, VICTOR: 34
HUXLEY, ALDOUS: 15, 45, 154; *Point Counter Point*: 12

IL MENABÒ: 131
IL VERRI: 131
INGARDEN, ROMAN: 6, 39, 42, 147-48
INTERTEXTUALITY: 24, 53, 59, 125, 126; see also PARODY
INTROSPECTIVE: see NARCISSISM
INTROVERTED: see NARCISSISM
ISER, WOLFGANG: 6, 37, 148-49, 151

JAKOBSON, ROMAN: 44n
JAMES, HENRY: 15, 42, 43, 59, 96
JAMES, WILLIAM: 26
JAMESON, FREDRIC: 14, 15, 50n, 126
JAUSS, HANS ROBERT: 146

JOURNAL NOVEL FORM: 12, 52, 106, 111, 117, 142, 156
JOYCE, JAMES: 14, 15, 25, 44, 45, 91, 120, 129, 130, 132, 133, 141n; *Ulysses*: 99, 121; *Finnegans Wake*: 34, 121

KAFKA, FRANZ: 96; *Die Verwandlung*: 91
KATZ, STEVE; *The Exagggerations* [sic] *of Peter Prince*: 143
KERMODE, FRANK: 40, 72n, 88-89, 118, 142n, 151
KLINKOWITZ, JEROME: 139n
KRIEGER, MURRAY: 105n, 140-41
KRISTEVA, JULIA: 24n, 125, 126, 127, 128, 135-36
KUNDERA, MILAN: 27
KÜNSTLERROMAN: 11-12, 13, 18, 26, 44

LACAN, JACQUES: 126
LANGUE/PAROLE: 93-95
LAUTRÉAMONT: 125, 127
LAVIS, GEORGES: 42n, 93-94, 95-96
LAWRENCE, D. H.: 60
LEVIN, HARRY: 9
LINDSAY, DAVID; *A Voyage to Arcturus*: 92
LINGUISTIC NARCISSISM; DEFINITION: 7, 22-23, 28-29, 35, 41, 46, 87-103, 154; OVERT: 7, 23, 29, 99-103, 104-117, 118; COVERT: 7, 23, 34-35, 99, 118-37
LODGE, DAVID: 91
LUBBOCK, PERCY: 151
LUKÁCS, GEORGES: 9, 91n

MAILER, NORMAN; *Armies of the Night*: 29, 94
MALLARMÉ, STÉPHANE: 15, 125, 127
MANGANELLI, GIORGIO: 131, 132, 134; *Agli dèi ulteriori*: 32, 132; *Hilaro-tragoedia*: 132
MANN, THOMAS: 15
MANZONI, ALESSANDRO: 15, 27, 51
MASACCIO: 106, 111, 114
MAURIAC, CLAUDE: 24
MARX, KARL and MARXISM: 17, 61, 65, 68, 125, 127, 130, 134
METAFICTION: see NARCISSISM
MIMESIS: 18, 25, 36-47, 63, 87, 90, 92, 126, 135-37, 150; PROCESS MIMESIS: 5, 6, 8, 11, 17, 24, 25, 29,

39-47, 51, 56, 87, 113, 122, 138, 150, 153; PRODUCT MIMESIS: 5, 8, 25, 30, 38-47, 59, 113, 153
MIRRORING: see MISE EN ABYME and NARCISSISM
MISE EN ABYME: 9, 22, 28, 40, 42, 53-56, 58, 59, 70, 72, 83-84, 97, 101, 105, 111, 120, 122, 127, 153, 160-61
MODERNISM: 2, 3, 41
MOORE, G. E.: 26
MORAWSKI, STEFAN: 43
MURDOCH, IRIS; The Black Prince: 101-102; The Word Child: 29, 102
MUSIL, ROBERT: 51, 130; Der Mann ohne Eigenschaften: 88

NABOKOV, VLADIMIR: 50n, 50, 55, 73, 76, 78, 83, 91, 141n, 143; Ada: 49, 78, 99, 100, 101, 118, 120-21, 122, 131; Bend Sinister: 78; The Defense: 83; Lolita: 73, 85, 99, 101, 143; Pale Fire: 52, 73, 78, 121, 122; The Real Life of Sebastian Knight: 49, 52, 53, 54-55, 73
NARCISSISM, TEXTUAL; DEFINITION (GENERAL): 1, 6, 7, 12, 13, 20; HISTORY AND LIMITS: 8-16, 17-19, 23, 34-35, 51, 124-37, 153-54; TYPES: see DIEGETIC NARCISSISM AND LINGUISTIC NARCISSISM
NARCISSUS MYTH: 1, 8-16, 30-31, 34, 56, 86, 137, 162
NARRATAIRE/NARRATEE: see READER
NEOAVANT-GARDE: 104, 105, 110-111, 130-36
NEOREALISM (ITALY): 104, 105, 130, 131, 133, 134
NEW CRITICISM: 87-88, 102, 126
NON-FICTIONAL NOVEL: 16
NOUVEAU NOUVEAU ROMAN: 7, 14, 34, 35, 46, 47, 119-20, 122-24, 135, 136, 143
NOUVEAU ROMAN: 4, 7, 14, 18, 32, 37, 46, 47, 54, 58, 59, 64, 77, 82, 105, 119, 121, 127, 128, 133, 141

O'BRIEN, FLANN: 26, 45; At Swim-Two-Birds: 18
ORTEGA Y GASSET: 20
OVERT: see DIEGETIC and LINGUISTIC NARCISSISM
OVID: 8-16, 18, 30, 124, 162

PARODY: 9, 10, 18, 20, 23-25, 28, 31, 32, 33-34, 38, 49-53, 57, 59-61, 70, 73, 83, 84, 99, 101n, 104, 105, 106, 110, 111, 116, 121, 126, 133, 134, 139, 153, 154
PHENOMENOLOGY: 145, 146-49, 150, 152
PINGET, ROBERT: 136, 144; Passacaille: 143
PIRANDELLO, LUIGI: 25, 26, 46, 58, 89, 130; Il fu Mattia Pascal: 18, 46n; Serafino Gubbio, operatore: 18; Uno, nessuno, e centomila: 27
PLATO: 40, 44, 90, 149
POE, EDGAR ALLAN: 76, 82, 100
POIESIS: 20, 41, 88
POIRIER, RICHARD: 50n
POSTMODERNISM: 2-4, 5, 8
POULET, GEORGES: 95, 129n, 146-47
PRE-RAPHAELITES: 68-69
PROCESS: see PROCESS MIMESIS
PRODUCT: see PROCESS MIMESIS
PRODUCTION: 6, 76, 86, 122, 124, 128, 144, 153n
PROUST, MARCEL: 5, 12, 15, 25, 26, 46, 59, 130, 153; A la recherche du temps perdu: 46n
PSYCHOANALYTIC CRITICISM: 145-46; see also FREUD, SIGMUND
PSYCHOLOGICAL REALISM: see REALISM, PSYCHOLOGICAL
PUN: see ANAGRAM
PYNCHON, THOMAS: 132; The Crying of Lot 49: 20, 33; V: 31n, 33

QUEEN, ELLERY; The Finishing Stroke: 73, 83; The Roman Hat Mystery: 73
QUINDICI: 133, 135

RABELAIS, FRANÇOIS: 24
READER: 138-52; AS ACTIVE PARTICIPANT: 3, 9, 14, 25-26, 39, 41, 49, 53, 60, 72-73, 114, 130, 133, 138-52, 154; EXPECTATION: 92, 95-96, 102, 139; FREEDOM: 19-20, 27, 30, 36, 49, 63, 66-67, 69-70, 71, 77, 79, 82, 91, 97, 124, 139, 140, 152, 155, 156-62; PARADOXICAL ROLE: 5, 7, 30, 36, 117, 119, 140, 141, 146, 147, 150, 161; RESPONSIBILITY: 20, 27, 30, 36, 39
READING PROCESS: 5, 20, 27, 28, 29-35, 37, 39, 71-86, 89, 98, 99, 106, 138, 139-52, 154, 156-62

REALISM (NATURALISM): 4, 5, 9, 11, 12, 13, 14, 16, 17, 18, 19, 25, 27, 35, 36-47, 52, 59, 78, 81, 94, 95, 98, 102, 125, 138, 148, 150, 153

REALISM, PSYCHOLOGICAL (SUBJECTIVE): 5, 12, 25-26, 46, 138, 153

RECEPTION THEORY: see PHENOMENOLOGY

REFERENT; FICTIVE: 10, 27, 29, 32, 76, 79, 87, 88, 91, 92-103, 112-13, 140, 147; REAL: 79, 88, 90, 92-96, 112-13

REFERENTIALITY and REFERENCE: 6, 47, 94, 98, 102-103, 112

REVOLUTION: 3, 38, 68, 131, 155-61

RHETORICAL TRADITION: 39, 145, 149-50, 152

RICARDOU, JEAN: xi, 4, 14, 21-23, 28, 31, 34, 35, 35n, 43, 45, 46, 54, 75, 93, 95n, 96, 100, 118-19, 119n, 120, 122, 123n, 124, 127, 129n, 134, 136, 144, 154; Les Lieux-dits: 100, 120, 121; La Prise de Constantinople: 120, 121, 124

RICHARDSON, SAMUEL: 9, 38, 44, 135; Pamela: 23, 93

RICOEUR, PAUL: 42n, 95

ROBBE-GRILLET, ALAIN: 15, 32, 35n, 43, 44, 47, 72, 82, 96, 122, 125, 130, 136, 141n; Dans le labyrinthe: 54; Les Gommes: 74-76; Projet pour une révolution à New York: 120; Le Voyeur: 74, 118

ROMANTICISM: 3, 11, 15, 18, 23, 25, 26, 39, 44, 58, 115, 123n, 124n, 127, 149, 151, 153, 154

ROSENBAUM, S. P.: 26n

ROSENBERG, HAROLD: 41

ROUSSEL, RAYMOND: 14, 22, 34, 100, 119, 122-24, 135-36; Comment j'ai écrit certains de mes livres: 122-24, 137; Impressions d'Afrique: 122, 135-36; Nouvelles Impressions d'Afrique: 136

ROUSSET, JEAN: 147

ROVANI, GIUSEPPE: 27

RUSSIAN FORMALISM: 10n, 23-24, 50, 50n, 59, 125, 126, 133

SALINARI, CARLO: 134

SANGUINETI, EDOARDO: 14, 18, 129, 133, 134; Capriccio italiano: 134; Il giuoco dell'oca: 30, 33, 84-85, 128, 134, 143; Il giuoco del Satyricon: un'imitazione da Petronio: 134

SAPORTA, MARC; Composition N⁰ 1: 84

SARDUY, SEVERO: 2

SAROYAN, WILLIAM: 26-27

SARRAUTE, NATHALIE; Entre la vie et la mort: 122; Portrait d'un inconnu: 12

SARTRE, JEAN-PAUL: 42, 50, 88n, 127; La Nausée: 52, 91

SAUSSURE, FERDINAND DE: 6, 34, 42, 93, 94, 119, 126, 128

SAYERS, DOROTHY: 31; Have His Carcase: 72

SCHOLES, ROBERT: 4, 19-20, 21, 37n, 85

SCIENCE FICTION: 24, 77, 79n, 81n

SCOTT, WALTER: 59, 63, 68, 81

SELF-CONSCIOUS; SELF-INFORMING; SELF-REFLECTIVE; SELF-REFLEXIVE: see NARCISSISM

SHAKESPEARE, WILLIAM: 52; Hamlet: 101-102; The Tempest: 33, 60

SIGNIFIED (SIGNIFIÉ): 6, 42, 94, 95, 96n, 126, 133, 136

SIGNIFIER (SIGNIFIANT): 6, 42, 122, 123n, 126-27, 133, 136

SIMENON, GEORGES; The Methods of Maigret: 73

SIMON, CLAUDE: 144n; La Bataille de Pharsale: 121; La Route des Flandres: 96

SOLLERS, PHILIPPE: 18, 23, 35n, 125, 134; Drame: 33, 128; Nombres: 128

SORRENTINO, GILBERT: 36, 87, 143; Imaginary Qualities of Actual Things: 152

SPENDER, STEPHEN: 44n

STAROBINSKI, JEAN: 34n, 119n

STENDHAL (HENRI BEYLE): 44, 47, 63, 81; Armance: 142

STERNE, LAURENCE: 13, 18, 30, 38, 39, 47, 52, 101, 141, 150; Tristram Shandy: 8, 9, 18, 27, 37, 40, 44, 52, 91, 116, 142

STREAM OF CONSCIOUSNESS: 26

STRUCTURALISM: 6, 12, 14-15, 19-20, 30, 42, 87, 97, 102, 125n, 130, 145, 151-52

SUKENICK, RONALD: 143, 144, 153

SVEVO, ITALO: 5, 15, 25, 26, 130; La coscienza di Zeno: 51, 90, 132; "Il Vecchione": 90

TEL QUEL: 14, 34-35, 46n, 124-29, 130, 132, 133, 134, 135-37, 154

TEXTE: 34-35, 125-29

THACKERAY, WILLIAM MAKEPEACE: 51, 59; *Vanity Fair*: 44

THEMATIZATION: 7, 23, 27, 28-29, 30, 45, 53, 57-70, 71, 88, 92, 97, 99, 101, 102, 104-17, 132, 142, 154-55

THÉORIE D'ENSEMBLE: TEL QUEL: 125-28

TODOROV, TZVETAN: 10n, 12, 32, 44n, 46, 98, 138-39, 142n

TOLKIEN, J. R.: 32, 77, 77n, 78, 92

TRUTH: see VALIDITY

UNAMUNO, MIGUEL DE: 58, 64, 153

VALÉRY, PAUL: 11

VALIDITY: 42, 91, 94-95, 97, 103, 126, 140

VERBAL PLAY: see WORD PLAY

VERNE, JULES: 34, 83

VERRIER, JEAN: 12, 45n

VICTORIAN NOVEL: 24, 57, 59-60, 69-70

VOLPONI, PAOLO: 104-17; *Corporale*: 105n, 106-107, 108, 117, 119-20, 132; *La macchina mondiale*: 29, 104-17; *Memoriale*: 105n, 107

VONNEGUT, KURT: 139n

WATT, IAN: 5, 9, 16, 38, 43, 88n

WELLEK, RENÉ: 17, 18, 43, 44n

WITTGENSTEIN, LUDWIG: 91, 97, 109, 111

WOLFE, TOM: 16n, 43n

WOOLF, VIRGINIA: 5, 23, 25, 26, 43, 46, 145, 153; *Jacob's Room*: 26, 52; *To the Lighthouse*: 120.

WORD PLAY; THEMATIZED: 101, 105, 107-10; ACTUALIZED: 118-37

ZOLA, ÉMILE: 78